▷ ◁▷ ◁▷ ◁▷ ◁▷ ◁▷ ◁▷ ◁▷ ◁▷ ◁▷ ◁▷ ◁▷ ◁▷ ◁▷ ◁▷ ◁▷ ◁▷ ◁▷ ◁▷ ◁

THE AEGEAN CRUCIBLE

▷ ◁▷ ◁▷ ◁▷ ◁▷ ◁▷ ◁▷ ◁▷ ◁▷ ◁▷ ◁▷ ◁▷ ◁▷ ◁▷ ◁▷ ◁▷ ◁▷ ◁▷ ◁▷ ◁

▷ ◁

THE AEGEAN CRUCIBLE

▷ ◁

Tracing Vernacular Architecture in Post-Byzantine Centuries

Constantine E. Michaelides, FAIA

To Cole Thomson
Enjoy your trip to
Greece and the
Islands Dinos

July 5 2004

Delos Press
Saint Louis, Missouri

Published by Delos Press, 735 Radcliffe Avenue
St. Louis MO 63130. First Edition. All rights reserved, including the right of repro-
duction in whole or in part in any form.

Cataloging Data:

Michaelides, Constantine E., 1930-
The Aegean Crucible: Tracing Vernacular Architecture in Post-Byzantine Centuries
/ Constantine E. Michaelides
p.   cm.
Includes bibliographical references, index, and gazetteer.
Contents: 1. The Mediterranean Sea. 2. Franks, Turks, Pirates, and Grand Tourists.
3. The Aegean Archipelago. 4. Collective Fortification: Kastro.
5. Aegean Towns: Typology and Materials. 6. Hydra Revisited. 7. Santorini
Observed. 8.The Urban Fabric.
ISBN : 0-9729723-0-7
1.Vernacular architecture -- Aegean Islands (Greece and Turkey). 2. Aegean Islands
(Greece and Turkey) – History. 3. Architecture, Modern – 18th century – Aegean
Islands (Greece and Turkey). 4. Cities and towns – Aegean Islands (Greece and
Turkey). 5. Mediterranean Region – Civilization. 6. Aegean Islands (Greece and
Turkey) – Description and travel.
I. Title.
NA1091 .M53 2003

This book has been composed in Garamond BE and Optima.

Printed in China.

October 2003

For

Constantine Alexander
Matthew Evangelos
Athena Justine
Sofia Demetra

To remind them of their heritage

▷◁

CONTENTS

▷◁

Acknowledgments

Upon entering the National Technical University of Athens in the fall of 1947, the first-year architecture class anticipated that its rigorous and demanding studies would be rewarded with a prestigious diploma and a license to practice architecture in a country ravaged by World War II and very much in need of formally educated young professionals. Probably none of them had given serious thought to the existence of a national vernacular architecture tradition. Soon, however, they encountered Professor Dimitris Pikionis, a great teacher who, in his eloquent and convincing way, impressed and surprised them with examples of work by thousands of unschooled and unlicensed builders who had produced a great volume of accomplished, meaningful, and beautiful *laiki*, or popular, vernacular architecture in the immediate Greek past. These buildings offered thought-provoking messages to young architecture students who wanted to search for a "Greek character" in their work. This book traces its origin to that formative encounter with Pikionis and his inspiring teaching.

I am also indebted to Professor Eduard F. Sekler of Harvard University, who in the 1950s encouraged his young teaching assistant to present his first-ever lecture on the vernacular architecture of the Aegean archipelago with black-and-white transparencies. This presentation confirmed personal and broader   interests and enhanced the possibility of further study of the subject on this side of the Atlantic. A lifelong academic appointment at the School of Architecture of Washington University in St. Louis provided the milieu and the time for the research, travel, observation, data accumulation, lectures, and seminars that eventually led to the book at hand.

Hydra, a Greek Island Town, which I published in the late 1960s, drew from a very scant list of existing background material and bibliography. More than thirty years later, the situation has dramatically improved, and a substantial volume of work on vernacular architecture has been published in both Greek and English. This book has benefited from that work and especially from that of my colleagues and friends in Greece -- Professors Anastasia Tzakou on Sifnos, Maro Philippa-Apostolou on Antiparos and Sifnos, and Dimitri Philippides on Greek traditional architecture. The work of Professors Wolfram Hoepfner and Hartwig Schmidt, of Berlin and Karlsruhe, respectively, has also been very helpful in writing the section on Kimolos.

Dr Fani-Maria Tsigakou, Curator of the Department of Painting, Prints and Drawings at the Benaki Museum in Athens, has been very generous with her assistance, and I am particularly thankful to her for introducing me to the work of Thomas Hope. Jessica Morgan, a very talented graduate student in the School of Architecture, helped me greatly in digitizing and coordinating the images to produce a convincing manuscript. The enthusiasm of my editor Jill Levin, the dedication of my book designer John Niederschmidt, and the professionalism of both turned this manuscript into a book.

Finally, *The Aegean Crucible* has resulted from the creative environment of Givens Hall, the home of the School of Architecture. To the countless undergraduate and graduate students who have listened to my lectures and participated in my seminars over the years, to my colleagues on the faculty, and particularly to my former student and successor Dean Cynthia Weese, I am deeply grateful for their attentiveness, encouragement, and support.

CM St. Louis May, 2003

▷ ◁ ▷ ◁

PROLOGUE

▷ ◁ ▷ ◁

This is a book about architecture written by an architect and addressed to the general public. Its subject is the vernacular architecture of the Aegean islands, whose forms represent an inspiring marriage between the man-made and the natural and between remarkable buildings and an equally remarkable archipelagic landscape and seascape. Observations and "notes" in the form of an extensive collection of color slides I accumulated during many visits over a span of forty years form the foundation of this book.

The text and images combined examine the mutually informing, frequently cohabiting, and often ambivalent relationship between formal and vernacular architecture. Typically, architects begin the design process with the available programmatic and contextual information and proceed to create the final, full-scale form of the planned edifice. By observing and recording the current forms of the Aegean island towns in text and illustrations, I reverse the typical architectural design process to trace and uncover the programmatic and contextual conditions, the geopolitical and cultural forces that underlay the creation and survival of the island towns into the present. Architects and architectural historians argue that architecture expresses the life and culture of the society it serves. As this book illustrates, the reverse argument holds true as well, for life and culture can also be understood through an examination of architectural form.

Sponsorship and delivery provide criteria by which to describe architecture as either formal or vernacular. Formal architecture is sponsored by ruling groups, be they royal, democratic, religious, entrepreneurial, or non-governmental. Royals, elected leaders, princes of the Church, mayors, city councils, boards of trustees, and others have sponsored the Pyramids, the Acropolis of Athens, the French cathedrals, the Eiffel Tower, the Seagram building, the St. Louis Gateway Arch, the Bilbao Guggenheim Museum, and many other buildings of distinction. The formal architecture of monuments is the subject of most, if not all, courses on the history of architecture taught at academic institutions. Formal architecture in most instances is eponymous; that is, the architect's name is affixed to the building, an association that in today's highly commercial world produces "signature" architecture, architecture inseparable from the celebrity status of the architect.

Vernacular architecture, by contrast, has no prestigious sponsors. Rarely is vernacular architecture mentioned in academic courses on the history of architecture. Its architects remain by and large anonymous. Vernacular architecture is perhaps better described as "architecture without architects," the term coined for an exhibition assembled by Bernard Rudofsky in the 1960s. More precisely, vernacular architecture can be seen as architecture created without the participation of formally educated, degreed, and licensed architects. More often than not, in the myriad examples of vernacular architecture the world over, the sponsor and the architect are the same person. More importantly, formal and vernacular architecture often evolve within the same space, mutually informing rather than antagonizing one another as the following examples illustrate.

The aerial photograph of Arles (Fig. PRO-1.01) provides an example of a clear distinction between formal architecture, as expressed in such large public-scale buildings as the Roman amphitheater and the antique theater in the illustration, and vernacular architecture, as exemplified by the red-tiled roofs of private-scale dwellings, a contemporary distinction not unlike that which prevailed in Roman times. As the Roman Empire collapsed, Arles lost its importance as a commercial center and the gateway to Roman Gaul. During the impoverished Middle Ages, Arles was in effect reduced to a one-building town, its size determined by the periphery of the Roman amphitheater (Fig. PRO-1.02). Squatters turned the spaces under the arches into urban dwellings and used material quarried from the top tier and other parts of the amphitheater to build defense towers on the perimeter and houses and other public buildings to fill the arena. This process merged the remnants of formal architecture with the improvisations of vernacular architecture into one building, and the result provides a splendid example of cohabitation and the mutually supportive architectural relationship between the formal and the vernacular.

Fig. PRO-1.01 Arles, city	Fig. PRO-1.02 Arles, amphitheater, Middle Ages

The "View of the Propylaea" (Fig. PRO-1.03), a watercolor painted by Hugh William Williams in 1819 just before the Greek war of independence, records another instance of the merging of formal architecture with vernacular architecture, the formal in this case being represented by the Propylaea, the Erechtheion, and the Parthenon and the vernacular by the barracks and houses of the Turkish garrison at the Acropolis fortress. Writing about his travels, Williams melancholically describes how "the pillars of the Propylaea shoot through the crumbling ruins of successive ages," nostalgically roman-

Fig. PRO-1.03 Hugh William Williams, "View of the Propylaea," 1819

ticizing formal architecture and implicitly dismissing the vernacular. It is important to note that in both cases, the amphitheater of Arles and the Acropolis of Athens, nineteenth-century ideology, with its deep admiration of antiquity, shattered the cohabiting and intimate relationship between the vernacular and the formal by demolishing the former to privilege the latter (Fig. PRO-1.04, -1.05 -1.06).

A number of less-than-exact terms currently in use for discussing architecture without architects need clarification. For example, "indigenous" alludes to an autochthonous form emerging from a specific place and climate and expresses a concept appropriate to an architecture with such an intimate relationship to its immediate site. Indigenous animals or plants and the term "an indigenous school of poetry" suggest a range of meanings for the word. "Traditional" identifies a building form handed down through the generations by practice and oral communication rather than by written record. Furniture and jewelry design, embroidered work, costume making, and other arts and crafts on a scale smaller than but related to that of architecture all enrich the meaning of the term. "Anonymous" refers to building forms of unknown authorship that lack acknowledged names for their builders and is thus a term particularly pertinent to the discussion at hand, since it relates the anonymity of Greek Orthodox Church iconographers to that of Aegean island town builders. "Vernacular," which means "belonging to a particular place or characteristic locality," is the only term discussed here that dictionaries define with reference to the architectural materials and building techniques of a geographic region, historic period, or group of people. Each of these terms illuminates the theme of this book in part, but none describes it adequately. However, given its contemporary currency, "vernacular" emerges as the best word to convey the idea and substance of the manmade physical environment of the Aegean island towns. As a result, "vernacular" forms part of the title of this book and will have a strong presence in the pages that follow.

Architects will be attracted to this book. However, it is written for the general public in the United States, and more specifically, for those interested in other cultures, the natural and man-made environments, and architecture itself. Although the text and illustrations are organized to be enjoyed at a distance from the Aegean archipelago, a reading of the book in situ will yield additional rewards. I discovered vernacular architecture during my early student days in Greece in the late 1940s. Visiting islands like Aegina (1948), Hydra (1949), Paros (1949), Santorini (1951), and others with fellow students who shared a spirit of inquiry gave me an early visual exposure to and an elementary understanding of the vernacular architecture of the

Fig. PRO-1.04 Acropolis, Athens, 1991

Fig. PRO-1.05 Arles, amphitheater, 1981

Fig. PRO-1.06 Arles, amphitheater, 1981

Aegean islands from close proximity. Since then, intermittent visits to the islands from the United States, where I have lived since 1960, have produced the observations and data that inspired this book. Written at a considerable distance from the actual site and freed from the limitations of proximity, I attempt in this book to offer a broad perspective on how the architectural forms of the Aegean island towns we observe today came into being over the last several centuries. This perspective is informed by the belief shared by most, if not all, architects that architecture, both vernacular and formal, reveals the everyday life and aspirations of the people who produce and inhabit it.

A brief profile of the Mediterranean Sea is presented in Chapter ONE. The physical outline, geographic divisions, and size of the Mediterranean are noted, along with its substantial salinity, high evaporation rate, abundance of sun and wind, limited rainfall, and frequent volcanic eruptions and earthquakes, all of which must be considered to produce a useful sketch of this large and environmentally dominant geographic container for the smaller Aegean archipelago.

The geopolitics of the Aegean Sea after the early thirteenth century Fourth Crusade is the subject of Chapter TWO. Between the early-thirteenth and the mid-sixteenth centuries, the Duchy of the Archipelago and the Knights Hospitaller of Saint John in Rhodes emerged as the political powers whose presence, resources, and activities, commercial and military, contributed most to the development of both the formal and the vernacular architecture of the archipelago. Their histories are the subjects of sections one and two. The Ottoman Turkish conquest of the area in the sixteenth century established Turkish rule, or *Tourkokratia*, and unified the region politically. The third part of the chapter examines Tourkokratia with particular attention to the *millet* system and the special tax on the Aegean islands that provided crews for the Ottoman fleet, and then turns to the *Koinotis*, the self-governing institution common to the island towns during the later years of Turkish rule. During these post-Byzantine centuries, piracy, both Christian and Moslem, emerged as the most potent force dictating the forms of the Aegean island towns. Chapter TWO discusses piracy as a profession and a Mediterranean institution; the collective fortifications built as defenses against piracy are examined in detail in Chapter FOUR. The rediscovery of Greece, a long process that returned the Acropolis of Athens and the Parthenon to the intellectual and artistic traditions of Western Europe, is discussed next. European rivalries as they affected the rush to acquire Greek antiquities; the ideology of the new Greek state of the 1830s as expressed in its architectural neoclassicism; and the beginning of a sympathetic interest in vernacular architecture in the early twentieth century conclude Chapter TWO.

The Aegean archipelago as the larger territory of the island towns and its unique interplay of landscape and seascape is the theme of Chapter THREE. History and geology define the Aegean Sea as, respectively, the oldest and the youngest region of the globe. Mythology, submerged mountain chains, an extensive shoreline, island proximity, the sun and the wind, a calendar for sailing ships, and other factors discussed in this chapter attempt to explain the distinctive physical character of the archipelago. An extended quotation from the historian William H. McNeill elucidates the ecology of the region and adds immensely to our understanding of the life and culture of the islands. An account of a hike to a summit in Sifnos at the end of this chapter describes the breathtaking views of the island landscape and shoreline from there; a diagram that divides the topography of a typical island into four zones of flora and fauna concludes the chapter.

In order for an Aegean island town to survive in the age of piracy, defensible site selection and collective fortification were absolute necessities. Built on a two-hundred-meter-high hill, the town of Serifos exemplifies the use of site features to enhance the defense of an Aegean town and introduces Chapter FOUR. Seven fortified towns, or *Kastra* (the plural of *Kastro*), have been selected from the many existing possibilities to illustrate the collective fortification principle and its variable but consistent application. Three of the seven discussed are still inhabited. Among them, the Sifnos Kastro, the second oldest, remains in excellent condition and forms the subject of part three. The Antiparos Kastro (part two) is doing well, but the Kimolos Kastro (part five) is mostly in ruins, with few of its dwelling units still occupied. All three underscore the point that the Aegean Kastra are living organisms that have adjusted themselves to the needs of successive generations of inhabitants rather than museums that enshrine an untouchable past. The building and ownership of the Kimolos Kastro at the end of the sixteenth century also confirm a dramatic shift in Aegean geopolitics that is discussed in detail in this chapter. Sitting on a massive rock formation, the enclosing walls of the Astypalaia Kastro still exist and form the subject of part four. Save for two meticulously maintained churches, the old, enclosed *monochoro* ("single space") dwelling units gradually collapsed and disappeared as the last occupants of the Kastro moved at the end of World War II into the now-thriving town of Chora below. The eradication of piracy from the Mediterranean and Aegean Seas after the 1830s resulted in the gradual disappearance of the collective fortifications of Skaros in Santorini and Kastro in Skiathos (part six). Chapter FOUR discusses the dramatic aspects of their respective sites, which can still be seen. A 1795 drawing of Skaros by Thomas Hope together with the late-nineteenth century story *Ftochos Ayios* by Alexandros Papadiamantis about folk traditions in Skiathos provide insights into the vanished vernacular architecture forms of these two towns. The last fortification to be discussed in the chapter, the Monastery of Saint John the Theologian in Patmos built in the eleventh century, is the oldest of the seven fortified settlements examined. Despite its provenance in formal architecture, the Monastery and the Chora that came to surround it have developed within the larger Aegean vernacular architecture milieu. For purposes of comparison, plans of the five extant collective fortifications– Patmos, Sifnos, Astypalaia, Antiparos, and Kimolos–drawn to the same architectural scale are shown on a single page in figure FOUR-7.34. Based on assumptions about its original parts and taking more recent alterations into account, a digital extrapolation from a 1985 illustration of Sifnos Kastro suggests its possible appearance in the middle of the eighteenth century and concludes the chapter.

Crucial to the visual unity of the towns of the Aegean archipelago is their limited number of building types. Chapter FIVE first traces the typology of dwellings, churches, and chapels. The monochoro dwelling unit is tied indissolubly to the principle of collective fortification mentioned above. Indeed, a collective fortification is in effect an assembly of *monochora* related vertically and horizontally as they adjust to a particular site. The courtyard house dating from antiquity reappeared as the Aegean towns grew beyond their tight defensive enclosures and is examined next. Each island counts amongst its buildings hundreds of churches and chapels (part two). Their multitude and diminutive scale in both urban and freestanding settings give a special character to the vernacular architecture of the islands, and they are discussed next, in section two. An extensive account of the important Panayia Paraportiani chapels in Mykonos and the Panayia Katapoliani church in Paros concludes this segment of the chapter.

Windmills, dovecotes, and monasteries, fewer in number than dwellings and chapels, nevertheless significantly enrich the limited building typology of the islands and are the subjects of parts three through five. The existence of significant wind power in the Aegean allowed the windmill to become an integral part of its island communities in form and function. In addition, social and economic conditions allowed large numbers of dovecotes to be built on Tenos, the only Aegean island to remain in Venetian hands as late as 1715. A simple building not intended for human occupancy, the dovecote provides instances of extraordinary and delightful architecture in the hands of gifted builders. Monasteries (part five), much larger than windmills or dovecotes, confirm the continuity between the Byzantine and post-Byzantine culture and architecture of the archipelago just as churches and chapels do. The plan of a typical monastery concludes the typologies discussed in the chapter. The second half of Chapter FIVE, "Wall Thicknesses, Structural Spans," deals with the building materials and methods traditionally employed throughout the Aegean archipelago. Two-foot-thick stone masonry walls, flat roofs that act as ramparts and rainwater catchments, and multiple layers of whitewash give the settlements their distinctive vernacular character. Specific features like gates and windows and the recent introduction of modern building techniques are discussed in this concluding segment of Chapter FIVE.

Chapter SIX concerns the town of Hydra, the form and development of which was the subject of my earlier study, summarized in the first three parts of the chapter. The fourth segment, "Continuity and Change, 1963-1998," focuses on one of the specific neighborhood components of the town; twelve pairs of color slides dating, respectively, from 1963 and 1998 measure the changes in building density, color, utility wiring, vegetation, and other architectural elements that have occurred over thirty-five years, a useful microcosmic examination in a book devoted to chronicling similar changes over a much longer period and under more complicated conditions.

From sea level, Fira, Merovigli and Oia, present-day settlements on the island of Santorini, seem to form white eyebrows framing the polychrome face of the caldera cliffs below. Chapter SEVEN observes and reflects on the physical relationship of these settlements, which are outstanding examples of Aegean vernacular architecture, to the awe-inspiring site of Santorini, the product of a violent volcanic eruption that occurred thirty-six hundred years ago.

Earlier chapters of this book deal, metaphorically, with the forest. Chapter EIGHT focuses on the trees. The figure on the first page of this chapter (Fig.EIGHT-1.01) represents an appropriate visual summary of the chapter's intent. The unwritten principles that have guided the building of the archipelago towns are confirmed by these randomly selected illustrations of such architectural elements as bell towers, portals, and steps and such building techniques as recycling and whitewashing.

There are more than six hundred illustrations in this book. More than seventy-five percent have been culled from the author's collection. Covering the forty years from 1960 to 2000, these illustrations constitute the backbone of the book: the text was written using these illustrations as notes, and then specific illustrations were selected to illuminate the text. The intimate relationship thus created between text and illustrations will, I hope, make reading this book easy and enjoyable and will enhance the public understanding of architecture.

Bernard Maybeck, a California architect (1862-1957), once said, "Architecture is the handwriting of man." This book attempts to decipher the handwriting of the builders of the vernacular architecture of the Aegean archipelago, and, in turn, to illuminate a remarkable cultural and architectural heritage that technology and globalization have now made accessible to all.

ONE

▷◁

THE MEDITERRANEAN SEA

▷◁

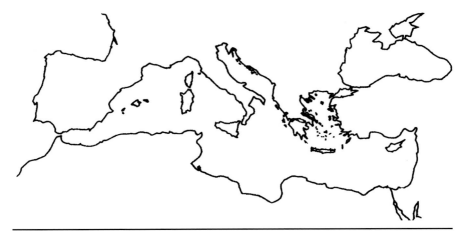

Fig. ONE-1.01 Mediterranean Sea, outline

Separating Europe from Africa, the Mediterranean Sea together with the Black Sea, which touches the shores of Asia, delimits the large physical arena within which the Aegean island towns developed.

The name "Mediterranean," from the Latin by the way of the Greek *Mesogeios*, means "middle of the earth" or "surrounded by land"–both appropriate names for a sea that has mediated the geological and historical conflicts that have arisen from the interrelationships among the Old World continents of Africa, Asia, and Europe.

The familiar visual outline of the Mediterranean coastline (Fig. ONE-1.01), easily recognizable from maps, globes, and satellite images, derives from the Tethys Sea that existed several million years ago. From this ancient and substantial body of water, the Mediterranean evolved as a much smaller sea.

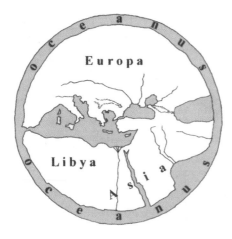

Fig. ONE-1.02 Hecataeus Map of the World

The outline of today's Mediterranean is already recognizable in the Hecataeus Map of the World (Fig. ONE-1.02). Hecataeus of Miletus (sixth-fifth centuries B.C.) produced the first known book of geography. Surviving fragments of this book make it possible to reconstruct the author's conception of the earth as surrounded by a continuous ocean. The Mediterranean Sea occupies a central position on this map, further confirming the etymology of both "Mesogeios" and "Mediterranean."

The Mediterranean and Black Seas lie comfortably between 30 and 50 degrees north latitude. Extended eastward from 110 to 150 degrees east latitude, these parallels also enclose the northern shores of China, Korea, and Japan. Extended westward between 60 and 130 degrees west longitude, they contain the majority of the landmass of the continental United States (Fig. ONE-1.03).

Fig. ONE-1.03

The straits of Gibraltar allow the Mediterranean to serve as an eastern extension of the Atlantic Ocean. Linking the Mediterranean to the Black Sea in the northeast are the Dardanelles, the Sea of Marmara, and the Bosporus Strait. The Suez Canal, a man-made connection between the Red Sea and the Mediterranean that was built in the second half of the nineteenth century, underscores the Mediterranean's importance as an international waterway for the last one hundred fifty years.

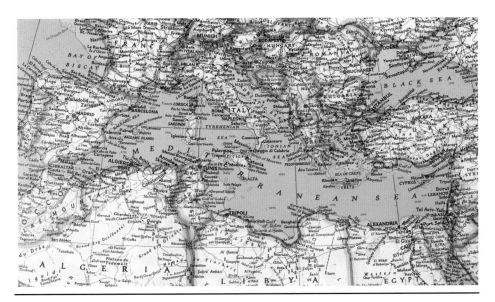

Fig. ONE-1.04 Mediterranean Sea, political map

The world's largest inland sea, comparable in length to the distance between San Francisco and Baltimore, the Mediterranean covers nearly 3,000,000 square kilometers or 1,150,000 square miles, equal in area to about one-fifth of the landmass of the twenty countries that border it. These countries are, moving clockwise around the map: Spain, France, Monaco, Italy, Slovenia, Croatia, Yugoslavia, Albania, Greece, Turkey, Syria, Lebanon, Israel, Egypt, Libya, Tunisia, Algeria, and Morocco. Cyprus and Malta are island states within the Mediterranean (Fig. ONE-1.04).

An underwater ridge between Sicily and the African coast divides the Mediterranean into western and eastern basins. The two basins differ in size, shape, and characteristics. The eastern basin, which comprises more than sixty percent of the whole, lies, by and large, farther south than the western one. Cyprus and Crete, the two southernmost major islands in the eastern basin, are located farther south than the Algerian coast of the western basin.

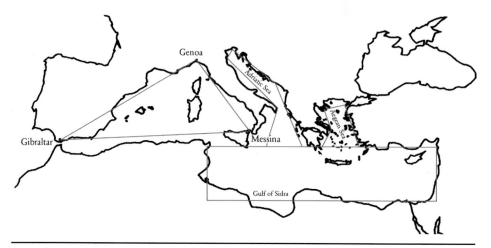

The two basins also differ substantially in shape. The western basin can be seen as a right triangle whose hypotenuse extends from Gibraltar to Messina and whose peak touches Genoa. By contrast, the eastern basin resembles a rectangle with a central axis defined by the 34 degree north parallel and includes such irregular attachments as the Adriatic and Aegean Seas in the north and the Gulf of Sidra in the south (Fig. ONE-1.05).

The African seaboard of the Mediterranean presents a relatively smooth and continuous outline. Two large continental promontories—Tunisia and Cyrenaica—divide the coast into three nearly equal parts. The northern seaboard is, by comparison, irregular. It includes the Gulfe du Lion and the Ligurian Sea, the long and shallow Adriatic Sea, and the Aegean Sea, the last serving as an anteroom to the Black Sea (Fig. ONE-1.06).

Mountain ranges overlook the entire northern coast of each basin and form a ring around the western one. The flat lands of Libya and Egypt, however, allow the Sahara desert—with its high temperatures, aridity, and hot winds—to play an important role in the ecology and life of the eastern Mediterranean basin.

The eastern basin is about six degrees farther south than the western one, which accounts for its higher surface water temperature. More extreme surface water temperatures can be found in the north Adriatic, where mean temperatures fall to about forty-one degrees Fahrenheit or five degrees Celsius in February, and in the gulf of Sidra, where temperatures rise to about eighty-eight degrees Fahrenheit or thirty-one degrees Celsius in August.

Fig. ONE-1.06 Mediterranean Sea, physical map

The most common sea depth in the western Mediterranean basin is a little less than three thousand meters. The exception is the Tyrrhenian Sea, which has areas as deep as thirty-five hundred meters. In the eastern basin, the waters deepen in the Ionian Sea between southern Italy and Greece. The deepest point in the Mediterranean lies off the southwestern tip of the Peloponnesos, where the depth is nearly five thousand meters.

Thousands of islands of varying sizes are scattered throughout the Mediterranean. In descending order, the five largest are Sicily, Sardinia, Corsica, Cyprus, and Crete. Medium-sized and small islands include the Balearic Islands off the Iberian coast; the Aeolian Islands north of Sicily; the Dalmatian Islands off the coast of Croatia and Yugoslavia; and the Ionian Islands off western Greece. Malta, despite its small size and population, is one of the two independent island republics of the Mediterranean. Cyprus is the other. Finally, the thousands of islands of the Aegean archipelago—small islands in a self-contained sea within the larger Mediterranean—provide a distinctive sense of the geographic character, size, and scale of the Mediterranean seascape by their size and proximity to one another.

Direct exposure to the sun and to the hot Sahara desert winds causes the Mediterranean to evaporate at the remarkably high rate of four million cubic feet or one hundred and fifteen thousand cubic meters per second. This evaporation is counterbalanced by a continuous inflow of surface water from the Atlantic Ocean, which compensates for about seventy percent of the water removed by evaporation. A much smaller amount of water, about three percent of the evaporation, enters the Mediterranean as a surface current from the Black Sea in the northeast.

After passing through the Straits of Gibraltar, the incoming Atlantic Ocean surface current flows eastward along the north coast of the African continent. This current, most powerful during the summer months when evaporation is at its height, is the most crucial contributor to water circulation in the Mediterranean. The flow is recognizable as a surface current in the Sicilian channel and even on the coast of Lebanon.

Evaporation makes the Mediterranean's water unusually saline. This high salinity and the buoyancy it imparts are easily noticed by bathers used to freshwater lakes or swimming pools and can lead to an unpleasant surprise should the unwary swallow a mouthful.

Water dense with salt sinks deeper than fresh water. Excess water returns to the Atlantic Ocean through the Straits of Gibraltar as a west-going current below the incoming one. Extending from the surface down to 250 feet, these currents make the Mediterranean a breathing organism, inhaling surface water from the Atlantic Ocean and exhaling water heavier with salt back into it. A rather sinister use of this breathing movement occurred during World War II. To minimize the chances of detection from listening equipment installed in British Gibraltar, German and Italian submarines moving through the straits in either direction placed themselves at the appropriate depth, cut off their engines, and allowed the flow of the current to lead them to their destination.

In addition to the Atlantic Ocean and Black Sea inflow currents, rivers and rainfall replenish the rest of the evaporated water. These rivers include the Nile, the longest river on earth, and the Rhone, much shorter but historically important as the gateway to France from the Mediterranean. Many other smaller rivers in Spain, Italy, Greece, and Asia Minor play a role as well in replenishing the Mediterranean. Historically, seasonal variations in the discharge of the Nile affected the salinity as well as the productivity of the waters of the southeastern segment of the Mediterranean, but thousands of years of repetition of this annual phenomenon came to an end when the Aswan High Dam was completed in the early 1970s. The Rhone flows into the northwestern Mediterranean at a location nearly symmetrical to the Nile's. Glacial in origin, the Rhone is fed in the spring by the melting snows of the Alps and in the fall and winter by tributaries originating in the Massif Central of southwestern France. These two complementary feeding systems keep the Rhone's flow into the Mediterranean fairly constant throughout the year.

It is difficult to generalize about the distribution and amount of rainfall in the Mediterranean. Suffice it to say that the differences are greatest in the center of the region. Annual rainfall of more than ten inches or twenty-five centimeters along the Libyan coast is rare, while more than one hundred inches or two hundred fifty centimeters is normal for the coast of Dalmatia.

Most visitors, inspired by travel posters of blue waters and tranquil sun-drenched fishing villages, think of the Mediterranean as an inviting, perennially calm, and untroubled sea. But this is not always the case. Beneath its frequently placid appearance, the Mediterranean can be as unpredictable as any other sea. Storms can be tempestuous, and winds, violent. After all, it was in the Mediterranean that an angry Poseidon prevented Odysseus from sailing back to his home in Ithaca for ten years.

As the Mediterranean Sea physically divides Europe and Africa, its

Fig. ONE-1.07 Santorini, *meltemi*, 1992   Santorini, calm sea, 1992

weather emanates from air masses that form over each of the two continents. When moisture-charged polar winds originating over the northeast Atlantic come into contact with warm air from the south, they create heavy rainfall in Italy and Greece. Cold, dry continental polar air flowing south across the Russian steppes interacts with the warm, comparatively moist air of the Aegean archipelago to determine much of the weather from the Adriatic to Cyprus. As these polar air masses meet the reservoir of intensely dry air from the Sahara, they produce local winds—each with a name and particular character.

These winds, including the *mistral* in southern France, the *meltemi* in the Aegean (Fig. ONE-1.07), and the *khamsin* in North Africa, color Mediterranean life by their intensity and persistence.

The Mediterranean region is also tectonically active, which has profoundly affected human life and activity in the area. The great Bronze Age volcanic eruption of Thera (or Santorini) provides physical evidence of these effects at its awe-inspiring site (Fig. ONE-1.08), even though the date of the eruption and its historic consequences are still debated. And the catastrophic eruption of Vesuvius that engulfed Pompeii in 79 A.D. continues to provide archaeological evidence that expands our understanding of life during the first century after Christ (Fig. ONE-1.09). The island of Stromboli, in the southeast corner of the Tyrrhenian Sea, suffers mini-eruptions at almost regular intervals. These blasts, which can be observed from the deck of a cruise ship (Fig. ONE-1.10), provide vivid evidence of continuous volcanic activity under the surface of the Mediterranean even today.

In addition to volcanic eruptions, earthquakes also frequently shake the region. Instrument-detectable minor tremors occur daily. Disastrous earthquakes have struck practically every country on the shores of the Mediterranean, including Morocco, Italy, and more recently, Turkey and Greece.

The usual description of the Mediterranean climate as relatively calm with hot, dry summers and mild, wet winters is in truth not very revealing. This summary sketch of the physical features of the Mediterranean is an attempt to go a step farther and offer a sense of the geography of the area as the context for an examination of the life lived amid this set of unique land formations.

Richard Carrington, who traveled, lived, and wrote about the region in

Fig. ONE-1.08 Santorini, Akrotiri, 1982

Fig. ONE-1.09 Pompeii, 1992   Fig. ONE-1.10 Stromboli, 1981

the decades following World War II and whose observations have provided useful insights for thinking about this chapter, offers an interpretation of the Mediterranean region as:

> the land lying within the olive line. This olive zone, which extends along the sea's shores to varying depths everywhere except to the north of the Libyan and Western Deserts may be likened to a vast botanical garden enclosing a salt-water lake. Not only do such typical Mediterranean trees as olives, pines, and holm oaks grow there, but [so does] a rich flora, wild and cultivated, native and exotic, utilitarian and ornamental, which exceeds in variety, interest, and sheer voluptuousness any to be found in a similarly limited and well-defined area in any other part of the world. (Carrington 197 and Fig.ONE-1.11)

Carrington's is an evocative and revealing description of the broader physical arena that has shaped, over centuries, the vernacular architecture forms of the Aegean island towns.

Fig. ONE-1.11
Olive trees,
Troizinia, 1998,
1985, 1998

TWO

FRANKS, TURKS, PIRATES, AND GRAND TOURISTS

The islands of the Aegean archipelago share a culture with origins traceable to Minoan times and before. However, the present-day vernacular architecture forms of the island towns are best understood in the context of geopolitical developments dating from the beginning of the thirteenth century, with the diversion of the Fourth Crusade from Egypt, its original destination, to the sacking of Constantinople. These events began the inevitable decline and disappearance of Byzantine imperial and political power from the Aegean Sea, a decline hastened by the creation of the Venetian Duchy of the Archipelago in the Cyclades Islands and the establishment of the Knights Hospitaller of Saint John on Rhodes and in the Dodecanese Islands. The Turkish conquest of the sixteenth century replaced Latin rule and ushered in the long period of Tourkokratia, or Turkish rule, in the Aegean. Politically reunifying the Aegean Sea with both the Greek peninsula and the Asia Minor littorals, Tourkokratia eventually led to the emergence of the Greek state in the 1830s. Latin rule, Tourkokratia, and national independence together provide the immediate political and cultural context within which the towns of the archipelago acquired their distinctive present-day forms. This chapter will present a brief account of this historical context, with special attention to piracy, an institution that threatened the very existence of the island settlements, and to the slow rediscovery of Greece by Western Europeans in the seventeenth and eighteenth centuries. The Europeans came to see the sites of classical antiquity and to aquire its riches. In the process, they came face to face with contemporary Greece, its people, and its vernacular culture and architecture. The testimony of these European visitors will be cited throughout the later parts of this chapter.

2.1 The Duchy of the Archipelago

Fig. TWO-1.01 Vittore Carpaccio, "The Lion of Saint Mark," 1516

Venice emerged from the fall of Rome as a lagoon-based city-state with political authority over the countryside surrounding it. A city of merchants well equipped with war galleys, Venice eventually formed an ever-shifting overseas empire of coastal settlements and islands. The Venetian empire extended beyond the Adriatic and into the eastern Mediterranean Sea and was organized to protect and facilitate the Republic's commercial interests.

Never big, Venice attained its power and riches by securing trading rights in many of the cities of the Levant and transporting the products of the East back to Venice (Fig. TWO-1.01). In this way, Venice became a locus for distributing products from the Orient throughout Western Europe. The ports of Constantinople, the Black Sea, Alexandria, and the coast of Syria determined the trading routes of the *Serenissima Repubblica*, the Most Serene Republic, as Venice called itself. Venice was a true mercantile empire, and her possessions, ports, and fortifications dotted her trading routes. In her glory days during the fifteenth century, "a Venetian ship need put in at no foreign harbour all the way from its owner's quay to the warehouses of the

Fig. TWO-1.02 Venetian possessions in the eastern Mediterranean

Levant" (Morris 9), as the Dalmatian Islands and Ionian Islands taken together "provided a stopping route from Venice to Crete...[as such] islands running along the axis of her power, were Venice's stationary fleet" (Braudel 149 and Fig. TWO-1.02).

In the summer of 1198, Pope Innocent III declared the Fourth Crusade with Egypt as its destination. Egypt was the power base of Saladin, a Kurd from what is now Iraq, who had recently reclaimed from the crusader kingdoms most of Palestine for the Moslem world. Only Venice had the knowledge and the naval resources to transport the crusader army to its destination. Agreement was soon reached between the crusaders and the Venetians on the substantial sum of 80,000 silver marks. Yet no money was available when the crusader force assembled in Venice in October 1202. At this critical moment, the octogenarian Doge Enrico Dandolo took over. Using a dynastic crisis in the Byzantine Empire as a Machiavellian pretext, the Doge shamelessly suggested a new destination for this predominantly French crusade --Constantinople -- to replace the agreed-on silver marks the crusaders had failed to raise. Venetian commercial interests rather than the crusaders' religious commitments were to be served by the new destination and task, Constantinople and its pillage. Accordingly, in the spring of 1204, the crusaders stormed and looted the city, the capital of the Greek-speaking, Orthodox Christian eastern half of the Roman Empire. The sack of the great city of Constantinople established Venice as the undisputed mistress of the eastern Mediterranean sea lanes.

Dandolo, as the strategist of the crusade, led it to Constantinople. He presided over the division of the Byzantine Empire into many petty feudal kingdoms, the continuous rivalries amongst whom brought about a state of anarchy that lasted until the sixteenth century, when the Ottoman Turks ruthlessly imposed their rule on the region. Long-term policy, statecraft, and the art of governing an empire were beyond the crusader nobility's expertise. But the Venetians had a political experience and sophistication that matched the Byzantines'. To the Venetians, the crusaders were innocent children to be manipulated, and Venice benefited from their naiveté, gaining the most and retaining it the longest. Indeed, Dandolo's political intuition led him to recognize that the resources of the Venetian Republic were limited compared with the burden of managing the captured territories, so he parceled them out to Venetian citizens to run as personal fiefs, saving Venice the administrative and defense costs of direct rule. Falling into the hands of Venetian overlords was the fate of the Aegean islands for the next three centuries (Fig. TWO-1.03). The rape of Constantinople was also the consequence of a religious rift and of an atmosphere of mistrust and enmity that had been escalating for centuries between the western and eastern halves of the Roman Empire. This enmity, increased by the events of 1204, influenced the relationship between overlord and subject when parts of the Byzantine Empire -- such as the Aegean islands -- came under the rule of "the accursed Latins."

In 1205, the year after the capture of Constantinople, Enrico Dandolo died. His successor, Doge Pietro Ziani, offered the Cyclades Islands to "qualified" individuals: enterprising young Venetians prepared to risk life and fortune and able to amass enough men and ships were encouraged to take an island or two to hold as fiefs. Such entrepreneurs were not required to acknowledge Venetian sovereignty. They were expected, however, to remain loyal to the mother city and to her commercial ventures. Marco Sanudo, who had served his uncle, the Doge Dandolo, in the expedition against Constantinople, possessed just such qualifications and was the first to muster a company of like-minded adventurers and to equip a flotilla of galleys. He crossed the Dardanelles and captured a number of the Cyclades Islands, declaring himself the Duke of the Archipelago. The Greek population of the undefended islands offered no resistance. Indeed, fighting occurred only at Naxos, which in 1207 had to be captured from a Genoese band that had previously laid claim to it. Naxos, the largest and most fertile of the Cyclades, provided the seat for the capital of the new duchy. In a shrewd political move, Sanudo offered his homage to Henri, the Latin Emperor of Constantinople. As a reward Henri confirmed Sanudo's title

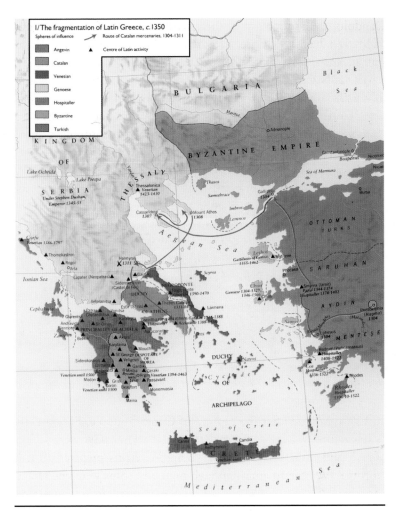

Fig. TWO-1.03 The fragmentation of Latin Greece c.1350

and the implicit abandonment of his duchy's formal allegiance to Venice.

In addition to Naxos (Fig.TWO-1.04 -1.05 –1.06), Sanudo kept for himself the islands of Paros, Antiparos, Melos, and Santorini. As recent scholarship reveals (Kallivretakis), the many skirmishes and feudal disputes that took place over several decades eventually allowed Sanudo and his heirs to turn other Aegean islands into subfiefs of the Duchy of the Archipelago, conquests that associated some of the most celebrated Venetian family names with the Cyclades: a Dandolo received Andros; a Querini, Astypalaia; Santorini went to a Barozzi; Anafi to a Foscolo; and Serifos to a Gustiniani. The Ghizi brothers took Tenos and Mykonos from the Cyclades and

Skyros, Skiathos, and Skopelos in the northern Aegean. Beyond the Cyclades, Kythera, one of the mythological birthplaces of Aphrodite, went to Marco Venier, who, as his family name indicated ("Venier" from Venus, the Latin name for Aphrodite), claimed descent from the goddess.

Given the thirteenth-century conditions from which the Duchy of the Archipelago emerged, the principal town and seat of the feudal ruler of each island had to be fortified. Kastro in Sifnos, one of the earliest such examples of fortification that survives reasonably intact and is still inhabited today, is examined in detail in Chapter FOUR, as are such fortifications of later provenance as Antiparos, Astypalaia, and Kimolos.

Fig. TWO-1.04 Naxos, 1988

The adventurous, seafaring lifestyle of Marco Sanudo and his comrades was determined by the geography of the Cycladic Islands and the limited resources and relatively small size of the duchy. Sanudo and his Venetian aristocrats straddled the thin line separating legal behavior from piracy, promoting their stature and expanding their holdings at any opportunity. Such an occasion for aggrandizement presented itself in 1212 when the Venetian governor of newly acquired Crete faced a powerful native Greek insurrection. Sanudo sailed to his aid, allying himself with both sides and hoping to acquire the island as a reward for his willingness to take risks in the power struggle within the Venetian nobility. At first he seemed to be succeeding, but when reinforcements arrived from Venice, it became apparent that he had bitten off more than he could chew. A truce was arranged which allowed Sanudo to withdraw to his duchy without penalty for his disloyalty to the mother city. The Venetian magnanimity towards Sanudo in this instance illustrates the willingness of the *Serenissima* to tolerate a measure of misbehavior from the Duke of the Archipelago, the "prime duke of Christendom" as he was otherwise known, so that the mother city could continue her strategy of avoiding the absorption of the Aegean islands into her already overextended insular empire.

Failure in Crete did not discourage Sanudo from another try. The following year, with only eight ships under his command, he seized the port city of Smyrna on the coast of Asia Minor, part of the realm of Theodore Laskaris, the emperor of Nicaea. The strategy behind this aggressive act is not very clear, but again, it misfired. The much stronger Nicaean forces counterattacked, recaptured Smyrna, and took Sanudo prisoner, although he could hardly be said to have been mistreated:

> From his predicament he was saved by his luck and charm, for Theodore found his personal qualities so attractive that he set him free and gave him his sister in marriage, an outcome which enhanced his prestige with his Greek islanders and even with his Latin overlord.... Marco was the first of the great Latin magnates of Greece to take a Greek bride. (Cheetham 226)

By taking a Greek bride, Sanudo set a pattern of intermarriage between Latins and Greeks that over the centuries led the Venetian overlord families to become Hellenized and assimilated into the much larger Greek population of the islands; indeed, family names of Venetian origin can easily be found today in the telephone directory of the Aegean islands. Allied by marriage with an Orthodox imperial family, Sanudo also bought peace with his Greek subjects by allowing the Greek Orthodox Church to function undisturbed. However, he also brought the Roman Catholic Church into the duchy to attend to the religious needs of the increasing numbers of Venetians gravitating to the Aegean in search of a promising future. The existence of these parallel institutions may explain the numerous double-nave, single-chapel buildings seen on many of the islands, an issue which will be discussed in Chapter FIVE under "Churches and Chapels."

From the fragments of the Byzantine Empire, Sanudo created a new, insular state that would outlive its competitors, surviving continuous internal and external conflict for a remarkable 359 years, until the sixteenth-century imposition of Ottoman rule. The annals of the Duchy of the Archipelago are filled with the continuous struggle of its nobility for land and power.

Islands passed from one family to another by marriage, inheritance, dynastic intrigue, oft-disputed succession, and, occasionally, war. Fortified against pirates, the island citadels were often besieged by the minuscule army of a neighboring island. Competition between island lords was so fierce that open warfare could erupt over even minor incidents. In 1286 corsairs carried off a valuable donkey belonging to a Ghizi of Tenos and sold it to a member of the Sanudo family of Syros. Marked with its owner's initials, the prized donkey was clearly stolen goods and provoked an invasion and siege of Syros by the Ghizi. Venetian arbitration eventually reconciled the feuding families and restored peace in the duchy, but only after considerable energy and treasure had been frittered away in the hostilities. Apparently, there were no casualties, so perhaps the fortifications were effective in keeping the small forces of opposing clans at a safe distance from one another (Fig. TWO-1.05, -1.06). There is no record, however, of the fate of the donkey!

Sanudo, his comrades, and their successors over the long life of the duchy derived their livelihood and wealth from the sea. Making the most of the islands' strategic locations within the shipping lanes of the Aegean archipelago, the Latin lords advanced their own commercial enterprises and

Fig. TWO-1.05 Naxos, citadel, 1969

Fig. TWO-1.06 Naxos, citadel, 1969

simultaneously preyed upon the commerce of others. Practicing a form of piracy acceptable at the time, they intercepted and exacted levies from passing merchant ships, a practice that enhanced their wealth and confirmed their importance as the gatekeepers of the Aegean sea lanes. Such easy pickings also attracted the attention and rapacity of Catalan, Genoese, and Turkish pirates, who raided the islands repeatedly, carried away treasure, and enslaved thousands of islanders. Since the war galleys used by the Mediterranean navies needed oarsmen, the captive Aegean islanders provided this much-needed labor, and as a result, a number of the islands became completely depopulated during this time. Some islands were recolonized in the fifteenth century with provision made for the security of the new inhabitants and cultivators. The Antiparos Kastro is an example of such provision and will be discussed in depth in Chapter FOUR.

This insecurity made life nearly intolerable on the islands. In the 1480s matters came to a climax under the rule of Duke Giovanni III. By this time the Ottoman Turks had established themselves on both sides of the Aegean littoral, forcing the duke to purchase his independence by paying *baksheesh*, or a gratuity, to the Sultan. This payment became an excuse for the duke to impose even heavier taxes on his own people, taxes that he apparently pocketed without providing the much-needed protection in return. In 1494 a mild revolt led by the Archbishop of Naxos got out of hand and led to the assassination of the despised duke. The people of Naxos then persuaded Venice to take over the administration of the duchy, which the Venetians returned to the late duke's son when he came of age.

During the reign of Suleyman the Magnificent, the Ottoman Turks emerged as a maritime power of the first order, challenging Charles V of Spain for supremacy in the Mediterranean. In the war of 1537, the Turkish admiral Kheireddin Barbarossa, probably a renegade Greek from the island of Lesvos, brought fire and sword to his fellow islanders. To this day, the magnitude of his cruelty is remembered in the folklore of the Aegean. Expelling the barons of most of the islands, including those of Astypalaia, Serifos, and Antiparos, Barbarossa sacked and depopulated Paros, laid siege to Naxos, and compelled the duke to surrender and pay an annual tribute of 5,000 ducats. The treaty of 1540 which ended the war did not return any of the islands to their previously independent lords, but when Giacomo IV succeeded his father as duke in 1564, the islanders of Naxos petitioned the Sultan to replace their local ruler, "a notorious debauchee" (Miller, *Essays*, 173). Although it is not known whom the islanders would have preferred, they were apparently surprised when the new Sultan Selim II appointed as duke Joseph Nasi, a Portuguese-Jewish banker who had served Selim well as his financial and political manager. Nasi remained in Constantinople and never visited his ducal domain. When he died in 1579, the duchy disappeared as a political entity and was replaced by direct rule from the *Sublime Porte*, the Ottoman government. Having successfully resisted the onslaught of Barbarossa in the 1530s, Tenos remained as the last Venetian outpost and observation point in the Aegean archipelago until 1715.

2.2 The Knights Hospitaller

While Dandolo and his associates from the Fourth Crusade were busy carving up Byzantine territory in Greece and the Aegean, the Kingdom of Jerusalem in the Holy Land continued to fight for survival. At the end of the thirteenth century, this battle ended in the loss of Jerusalem and the expulsion of the crusaders from the Levant. Among those expelled were the Hospitaller Knights of Saint John, who retreated to the Latin kingdom of Cyprus, where the Order had estates and properties. For the next twenty years, the brethren would rethink their mission and plan the future of their Order.

Still in existence today, the Sovereign Military and Hospitaller Order of Saint John of Jerusalem, Rhodes, and Malta is the only institution remaining from the era of the crusades. The Order was formed in the Holy Land and later spent 200 years in Rhodes and 260 in Malta, playing an impressive role in Aegean geopolitics despite its small size, both from the proximity of Rhodes and later, from the distance of Malta.

The trade routes to the eastern Mediterranean ports established by the Italian cities in the eleventh century opened the door for Western Europeans eager to make pilgrimages to the Holy Land. A Brother Gerard emerges from the obscure early history of these medieval pilgrimages as the founder of a hospice devoted to providing food and shelter to pilgrims. Dedicated to Saint John, Brother Gerard's hospice was well established when the crusaders conquered Jerusalem in July 1099. Beginning in the early twelfth century, the mission of the Order of Saint John expanded to include military protection for pilgrims as they traveled the road from the coast to Jerusalem. This military function of the Order took on a grand symbolic resonance: the Hospitaller Knights became "soldiers of Christ" as well as "servants of the poor." They were assigned to garrison castles, including, by 1142, the awesome Crac des Chevaliers, "the greatest and strongest of the castles of the Hospitallers, exceedingly injurious to the Saracens." By the time of the fall of Acre, their last stronghold in the Holy Land, and their retreat to Cyprus in 1291, the Hospitallers had established the military reputation of their crusading Order. More important for their future in the Mediterranean, however, they also had aquired secure revenue-producing bases and lands in Europe, whatever disasters might befall them in the East. This particular strength was to preserve the Order of Saint John during the challenging centuries that followed.

Their years in Cyprus allowed the knights to rebuild their ranks after the massive bloodletting in Acre. Their new island location occasioned a major shift in their war-making strategy, transforming the knights from a land fighting force to a sea fighting one, a change which was to characterize their war against the Moslems for the next several hundred years.

Their lot was not always easy in Cyprus. The Knights Hospitaller were uneasy "guests" of the Latin king Henry. Securing a territory of their own remained a major goal, and, naturally, the knights and their master, Foulques de Villaret (Fig. TWO-2.01), looked to the Aegean, where other

Fig. TWO-2.01 Foulques de Villaret, Italian picture from the 1930s

Latins, Venetians, Genoese, Catalans, and so on had recently made significant conquests. Securing papal approval and exploiting Byzantine weakness, in 1306 the knights joined a Genoese adventurer bound for Rhodes. In August 1309 the city of Rhodes opened its gates to them; by the end of 1310, the Knights Hospitaller controlled the island.

The conquest of Rhodes, which received papal confirmation, won for the Order of Saint John independent sovereign status, an important advance over their former status as providers of ecclesiastical and military services in the Holy Land (Fig. TWO-2.02). Exploiting the advantages of the location, relatively large size, and fertility of Rhodes, Foulques de Villaret's administration improved the structure of the Order. In addition, he ensured its future by building a formidable fortress-city, a base that helped to transform the Knights Hospitaller into the master seamen of the eastern Mediterranean.

The knights' lifestyle in Rhodes was the culmination of a long trajectory of change and improvement in the Order. In Acre all the knights had lived together in a sizable *auberge*, a large lodging house commanded by an

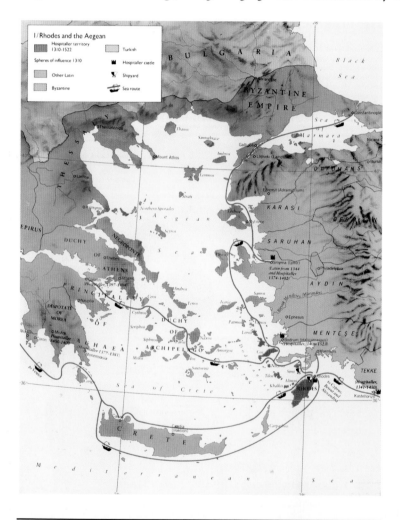

Fig. TWO-2.02 Hospitaller territory in the Aegean

officer. But in Cyprus, with no such facility available, groups of brethren lodged together in smaller residences according to their various nationalities, a practice formalized in the Tongue, or *Langue*, structure that governed military and communal life in the Order. By the time the knights established themselves in Rhodes, they were already organized into seven Tongues, which were, in order of precedence, Provence, Auvergne, France, Spain, Italy, England, and Germany. The head of a Tongue was its Pillar, or *Pillier*. Each Tongue maintained an inn, where members dined under their Pillar and offered hospitality to eminent visitors from abroad. Knights resident in the city of Rhodes lived in twos and threes in private houses in the *Collachium* area; most of these were located off the present-day Street of the Knights. The Tongue structure was reflected in the primary responsibility of the Order-- the defense of the walls of the city of Rhodes. Each of the seven Tongues was assigned to guard a particular segment of the fortifications, as indicated on the diagram below, covering the years from 1465 to 1522 (Fig. TWO-2.03).

The Order was divided into classes -- knights, chaplains, and sergeants -- reflecting the general division of Western European society from which the Order derived. Authority was concentrated in the hands of the knights, the

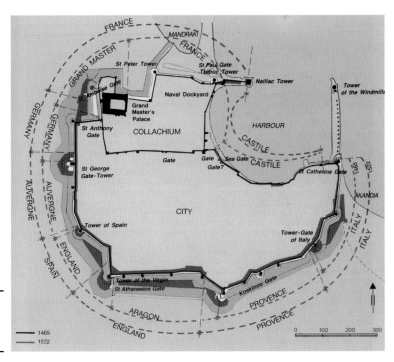

Fig. TWO-2.03
Rhodes,
fortifications

scions of noble families, who filled all major military and administrative offices, including that of the grand master, or *magnus magister*, the prince of this sovereign state. The knights' connections to the Roman Church and to the baronial families of Western Europe, whose extensive possessions produced men and revenues along with religious and political support, sustained the Order in Rhodes and, later, in Malta. The total number of knights remained small throughout their more than two-hundred-year residency in Rhodes. Reliable sources indicate the presence of eighty knights in the early fourteenth century and a maximum of 551 in 1513 when the Order was actively preparing to face its final -- and successful -- assault by the Turks. These numbers are surprisingly low considering the major role the Order played in eastern Mediterranean geopolitics. However, they indicate the magnitude of the religious, politica,l and economic support that Latin Europe provided the Knights Hospitaller of Saint John during their Rhodes residency.

The city of Rhodes, built on the Hippodamian orthogonal grid system of city streets, had seen prosperous days in classical and Hellenistic antiquity. Soon after the death of Alexander the Great in 304 B.C., Demetrios, one of his successors, won the sobriquet *Poliorketes* ("the besieger") for his original use of siege machinery, even though his specific machine, an ingenious assault tower, failed to breach the defenses of Rhodes. The departing Demetrios presented the tower to the undefeated citizens of the city, who used its materials to construct the Colossus of Rhodes, one of the Seven Wonders of antiquity, built to commemorate the siege.

A provincial capital during Byzantine times, as a city and a port, Rhodes was important enough to the commerce and communications of the empire to be strongly fortified. Anticipating the inevitable Moslem reprisals for their planned seafaring activities, the knights determined to augment the defenses of their newly acquired kingdom. Adapting their Holy Land experience with concentric fortification to the context of the Aegean archipelago, the knights extended their military presence to a number of the smaller Dodecanesian islands, making them in effect the outer defenses of the city of Rhodes. Telos, Kos (known to the knights as Lango), Kalymnos, Leros to the north, and Kastellorizo to the east provided them with valuable lookout points for hundreds of years.

Rebuilding Rhodes itself and augmenting its existing fortifications were equally important to the knights. The Byzantine governor's palace overlooking the port was reconstructed and became the grand master's residence. The walled Byzantine city in the north, much smaller than the older Hippodamian city, was emptied of the local population and became the

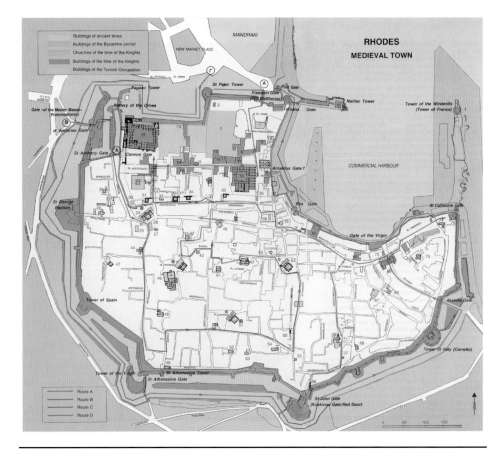

Fig. TWO-2.04 Rhodes

convent, or *Collachium*, of the Order. Its straight east-west main street, the present-day Street of the Knights inherited from the Hippodamian plan, became the spine of the Collachium, facilitating traffic between the Order's various inns and its hospital. The port, arsenal, and other related facilities developed on the eastern end of the Collachium (Fig. TWO-2.04, -2.05, -2.06).

Although the Byzantine walls were effective in defending the city from infantry assaults using catapults, battering rams, and the like, the introduction of gunpowder and firearms, beginning in the fourteenth century, radically altered warfare and rendered earlier fortifications useless. The cannon was invented in the fourteenth century; when iron cannonballs came into general use towards the end of the fifteenth, it became "the devastating

| Fig. TWO-2.05 Rhodes, Street of the Knights, 1970 | Fig. TWO-2.06 Rhodes, Street of the Knights, lithograph, 1825 |

weapon that rendered traditional fortification methods obsolete" (de la Croix 39), as became abundantly clear in 1494 when the French artillery of Charles VIII, armed with cannon and cannon balls, smashed through the strongest medieval walls of Italian cities. The new weapon introduced new parameters into the continual contest between defense and offense and dictated fundamental changes in fortification design:

> The urgency with which the problem [of the cannon] was viewed is indicated by the fact that not only military men, but artists, architects, and humanistic scholars eagerly applied themselves to the task of finding an answer to the threat. (de la Croix 41)

The effective use of artillery by the Turkish armies as well as the up-to-date information derived from their Latin European connections necessitated improved fortifications. The walls of Rhodes were again thickened and the ditch around them enlarged. The Order's Italian grand master, Fabrizio del Carreto, hired Basilio dalla Scuola, the chief military engineer to the Emperor Maximilian I. Carreto's Tower of Italy, a round tower with surrounding bulwarks and the last word in the northern Italian art of fortification, was the product of Basilio dalla Scuola's presence in Rhodes (Fig.

TWO-2.08). The new and formidable bastion of Auvergne in front of the Gate of Saint George was completed in 1521 and formed part of the final preparations for the expected Turkish siege that began in July 1522. Many believe the bastion of Auvergne to be the first true example of bastion design and "the model for one of the cardinal elements of fortress architecture for the next three centuries" (Sire 55).

Histories of the Sovereign Military Order of Saint John of Jerusalem, Rhodes, and Malta refer to three major sieges. The first two took place in Aegean Rhodes, the third in Mediterranean Malta, and all three occurred within a span of eighty-five years. The first siege began when a force of 70,000 men, assembled under the Sultan's standard and commanded by Mesic Pasha, landed on Rhodes in May 1480. The day after their arrival, the

| Fig. TWO-2.07 Rhodes, d'Amboise Gate, 1994 | Fig. TWO-2.08 Rhodes, Carreto Tower |

Tower of Saint Nicholas, a stronghold guarding the port, and the city of Rhodes itself came under heavy cannon bombardment by the troops of Sultan Mehmet II, "the Conqueror," who had used a cannon to breach the walls of Constantinople twenty-seven years earlier. The eighty-nine-day slaughter that followed ended with the Turkish failure to capture the city; it was, contemporaries said, as if the all-conquering sword of Mehmet II "had broken on the walls of Rhodes" (Sire 54). Guillaume Caoursin, the vice-chancellor of the Order and an eyewitness, reported on the siege and its vicissitudes. Accompanied as it was by some exceptionally vivid and informative illustrations of the siege (Fig. TWO-2.09, -2.10), Caoursin's report became an outstanding piece of promotion for the Order and brought fame and the new recruits who were so desperately needed for the future defense of the island. The knights' victory also affected the future of Latin Europe. Mehmet II, the Ottoman Sultan, had landed troops in Italy, ravaging Apulia and capturing Otranto, when Rhodes was besieged. His failure in Rhodes caused these troops to be withdrawn from southern Italy. When Mehmet II died the following year while preparing to lead another expedition against Rhodes, his death delayed a second siege for forty-two years.

By 1520, Suleyman -- known in the west as "the Magnificent" and to his people as *Kanuni* (or "lawgiver") -- had ascended the Ottoman throne. At the age of twenty-six, Suleyman was the head of a vigorously expanding empire. He would lead campaigns to capture Belgrade to secure an Ottoman presence along the Danube river and would lay siege to the Hospitallers' Rhodes to destroy its "Christian nest of vipers" and secure Ottoman control of the Aegean sea lanes. Suleyman's predecessor Selim had conquered Syria and Egypt. Rhodes was thus geographically encircled by Ottoman lands, which made the Knights' plunder of the trade between Constantinople and Alexandria all the more intolerable to the Ottoman Turks. Determined to ignore the then-usual limitation of campaigns to summertime and good weather and to lay siege until Rhodes fell, Suleyman raised an army much larger than that which had besieged the city in 1480 and landed on

| Fig. TWO-2.09 Caoursin, the siege of 1480 | Fig. TWO-2.10 Caoursin, fortification repair |

the island in July 1522.

At the time of Grand Master Fabrizio del Carreto's death in 1521, Rhodes could claim the most modern fortifications in the Christian world. Yet when Suleyman appeared before the gates, the defenders' numbers were small by comparison with the Sultan's. About 550 knights, 1,500 mercenary and Rhodian troops, and all the able-bodied citizens of Rhodes faced the daunting mass of 200,000 Ottoman troops (though contemporary reports may exaggerate). With the odds clearly against the defenders, their hopes for success rested on their cutting-edge fortifications -- bastions, ditches, and massive walls -- and on enough provisions and munitions to hold out for a year. To deal with the thousands of Turkish sappers and miners who were sinking shafts and placing charges under the walls of Rhodes, Grand Master L'Isle Adam had the services of Gabriele Tadini da Martinengo, a Venetian and one of the most accomplished military engineers of his time, whose techniques and inventions detected and frustrated enemy mines and miners.

Heavy bombardment, constant mining, crumbling bastions, breaches in the walls, assaults, retreats, and heavy losses on both sides ultimately exhausted the defenders, however. On Christmas Eve, Suleyman offered peace with honor, meaning that the knights and any Rhodians who wished to join them could leave the city unmolested. And so it was that on January 1, 1523, that "the survivors of the siege left their island home for ever" (Bradford 120), taking with them their arms, their belongings, and the archives of the Order. Eventually, Malta became their new home as the knights continued to war against their religious rivals for another two and one-half centuries, emerging victorious from the third siege, in 1565 in Malta.

The archives carried away from Rhodes in 1523 are preserved at the Royal Malta Library in Valetta on Malta. Research into the material in the archives (Tsirpanlis 426) has yielded incomplete sketches of the relationship between the knights of Saint John and the Rhodian population, but one can make certain speculations. The administrative authority inherited from Byzantium survived during the presence of the Order on the island as the knights acknowledged and cooperated with local representatives, particularly in matters regarding defense. Where jurisprudence was concerned, the Knights exhibited understanding and showed flexibility towards the local population, ratifying Byzantine privileges and taking over only the administration of defense.

During their early years on Rhodes, the knights appointed a Latin archbishop, thereby cutting off the local population's spiritual connection to the patriarch of Constantinople. Religious conflicts between the knights and the citizens of Rhodes were minimized, however, by agreements between the archbishop and the Orthodox metropolitan. It seems, too, that the large number of urban Rhodians who embraced the Western way of life on Malta became Uniates, which meant that they retained their Orthodox rites but were in communion with the pope. But the population at large clung faithfully to the traditions of the Orthodox Church (Fig. TWO-2.11) as an expression of their national consciousness and their resistance to their Roman Catholic masters.

"The Order's fleet not only fought the Moslems, it also transported merchandise" (Kollias 26). Forced to serve in this fleet, the Rhodians put this experience to good use by sailing their own vessels to other Mediterranean ports. While the knights were in power, Rhodes emerged not only as a center for the distribution of merchandise between East and West but as a manufacturing center, too, producing textiles, pottery, soap, sugar, and other goods. The economic interests that the Moslems of Asia Minor and the Christians of Rhodes had in common meant that commercial relations were not disrupted by the almost continual warfare between them. In addition, Rhodian Greek participation in the thriving economy of the island seems to

Fig. TWO-2.11 Saints Sergios and Bacchos as Knights, thirteenth-century icon

Fig. TWO-2.12 Buondelmonti, map of Rhodes

have been significant enough for an entrepreneurial and educated Greek middle class to arise with the tacit approval, if not the encouragement, of the knights.

There are even reports that Rhodians of both Greek and Latin descent studied at the University of Padua and returned to Rhodes to take up administrative positions within the Order as interpreters and diplomats. Interpreters were certainly needed, as important fifteenth-century peace treaties between the knights and the Ottoman Turks were written in Italian as well as in Greek, which was the official language of the Turkish sultans.

Early in the fifteenth century, when an interest in Greek antiquity began to develop in Italy, Cristoforo Buondelmonti visited Rhodes and, subsequently, made the island his base for exploring most of the other Aegean islands. Buondelmonti's major contributions to geographical knowledge of the Aegean archipelago, including his *Liber Insularum Archipelagi* (Fig. TWO-2.12), will be discussed later in this chapter under the heading "Greece Rediscovered." Rhodes also attracted Cyriacus of Ancona, another important figure in the rediscovery of Greece, who reportedly visited the island carrying Buondelmonti manuscripts about the region with him. In the forty-two years of relative peace between the two sieges (1480-1522) an "intellectual awakening was brought about by the coexistence of Greeks and Latins in Rhodes" (Tsirpanlis 426). The benefits of this harmonious coexistence disappeared when Rhodes fell to the Turks on January 1, 1523.

Although the Knights Hospitaller played a significant role in the Aegean, the Duchy of the Archipelago predated and outlasted them. For a considerable time in the fourteenth, fifteenth, and sixteenth centuries, the two groups inhabited the same geographic space, having come to the archipelago from different directions to pursue different interests. Expanding trade and profit brought the Venetians of the duchy, whereas the knights of Rhodes came to fight the "infidel" in religious wars. Often their interests merged, and collaboration ensued. Just as often, though, their interests diverged, and recriminations just short of warfare followed. Both the Order and the duchy functioned as independent entities, but in reality, both were dependent on major powers based outside the Aegean archipelago: the duchy, on the Venetian republic; the knights, on the pope and the European royalty in physical control of their estates.

The Venetians of the duchy intermarried with the local population, and their descendants remained on the islands during the Tourkokratia, the long period of Turkish rule. Today, their origin can be traced only in the Hellenization of their original Italian names. Because of their religious vows and their commitment to celibacy, the knights, by contrast, did not marry members of the local population. And for social and economic reasons as well as from a sense of mutual loyalty, the knights appear to have developed a more equal (and perhaps intimate) relationship with the Rhodian Greeks, which is suggested by the large number who followed them into exile in 1523.

For the purposes of this book, however, the most engaging aspect of the interrelationship between the Duchy of the Archipelago and the Knights Hospitaller of Rhodes appears in the intimate, mutually informing, and supportive relationship of the vernacular and formal architecture forms created by each within the larger family of the Aegean island towns.

Dependent on limited local means and resources and addressing issues at the local scale, the architecture of the Duchy of the Archipelago is represented by the vernacular, collective fortification forms that were integrated into the fabric of the towns of Antiparos, Sifnos, Astypalaia, and others. The duchy's collective fortifications thus provide the key to understanding the vernacular architecture of the Aegean island towns and will be discussed in detail in Chapter FOUR. By contrast, the Knights Hospitaller of Rhodes drew their inspiration and strength from power and wealth originating outside the Aegean region. Their presence is recorded in the formal architecture of the fortifications of the city of Rhodes. Detached from the fabric of the city, massive, extensive, and built to the designs of architects and engineers well versed in the art of fortification as practiced in Latin Europe, the walls of Rhodes addressed issues of warfare and commerce at the scale of the great Western European powers of the day.

But both forms of fortification meaningfully express the harsh and unrelenting conditions of life that prevailed in the post-Byzantine archipelago.

2.3 *Tourkokratia,* Turkish Rule

The capture of Rhodes in 1522 and the collapse of the Duchy of the Archipelago in 1566, both of which occurred during the reign of Suleyman, brought all of the Aegean islands except Tenos and Crete under Ottoman rule. As a result, the islands were incorporated into the same political structure as the other Greek-inhabited lands, where Tourkokratia, or Turkish rule, had begun in the preceding century (Fig. TWO-3.01). Tourkokratia, which lasted from the dissolution of the multinational Byzantine Empire in 1453 to the Greek Revolution in 1821 that led to the formation of a national state, "had a profound influence in shaping the evolution of Greek society"

Fig. TWO-3.01 Edward Dodwell, "Bazaar of Turkish Athens," early nineteenth century

(Clogg 3) and an equally profound influence on the shape of life and vernacular architecture in the Aegean islands. The period of Tourkokratia isolated the Greek world from such major historical movements in the West as the Renaissance and the scientific and industrial revolutions, although by the mid-eighteenth century, a nascent Greek mercantile class within the Ottoman Empire had begun to reestablish commercial and cultural contacts, and the ideologies of the Enlightenment and the French Revolution had begun to filter through. The merchant fleets of the Aegean islands became carriers of these new and inspiring messages.

Ottoman rule was based on the *millet* system, or the grouping of people by religious affiliation rather than by ethnic origin. The largest was the privileged Moslem *millet*. Non-Moslem "people of the book" were assembled into an Armenian *millet*, a Jewish *millet*, and an Orthodox *millet*, the largest after the Moslem.

Soon after the Turkish conquest of Constantinople in 1453, the Turkish Sultan Mehmet II, "the Conqueror," chose Georgios Gennadios Scholarios as the first patriarch under Ottoman rule, making him the head of the Greek Orthodox *millet*. The selection of Gennadios, an active opponent of reunifying the Orthodox and Roman Catholic churches, served the Ottoman interest in sustaining the rift between the two. The policy also had widespread support among the conquered Greek population of the Ottoman

Empire, particularly in the Aegean region where Latin rule had led the islanders "to prefer the Turban of the Prophet to the Cardinal's hat."

The patriarch's authority as head of the *millet* extended beyond religious affairs to regulating the daily life of Orthodox Christians and was granted in the expectation that he would guarantee the loyalty of the Orthodox *millet*. The consequences of infidelity could be brutal:

> When the sultan's authority was challenged then the hierarchs of the Church, in their role as both religious and civil leaders, were the prime targets of reprisals. Thus it was that, on the outbreak of the war of independence in 1821, the ecumenical patriarch, Grigorios V, together with a number of other religious and civil leaders, was executed in circumstances of particular brutality. (Clogg 11)

The *millet* system accepted the existence of a non-Moslem population, but it also imposed heavy taxes and subjected the captive Greek population to indignities meant to underscore their inferior status. "The main tax on non-Moslems was the *kharaj*, or capitation-tax, which literally entitled the tax-payer simply to retain his head on his shoulders" (Woodhouse 102). In addition, the Christian Orthodox subjects of the sultan could not challenge a Moslem in court, nor could they bear arms, ride horses, or wear the same clothes as Moslems. They were also forbidden to build or furnish churches and to ring their church bells. Granting tolerance to the "people of the book" in return for tax payments was a policy that began in the early centuries of Islamic conquest. (For more on the effect of this system on the Orthodox Church, see Bat Ye'or, *The Decline of Eastern Christianity under Islam*.) Because such taxation was a major source of Ottoman revenue, the *Sublime Porte*, as the Ottoman government was known, more often than not did not attempt to convert its non-Moslem subjects to Islam.

Among the forms of forced tribute exacted from non-Moslems, the most onerous was the *devsirme*, or Janissary levy. At irregular intervals, Christian peasant families were forced to surrender a male child aged six or seven to become a Moslem and a member of the slave bodyguard to the sultan, the Janissary Corps, the "nucleus of the first standing army in modern Europe" (Palmer 22). Brainwashed into absolute loyalty to the corps, most of the children from the *devsirme* tribute became lifelong soldiers, the most able rising to high rank in the Ottoman state. Several even became Grand Vizier.

Apparently, the *devsirme* was not applied to the Aegean islands. Nevertheless, the island populations suffered depletion and displacement as a result of the imposition of Turkish rule in the sixteenth century, frequently from piracy, as will be discussed below.

The devastating raids of the 1530s led by Kheireddin Barbarossa, the Algerian-based corsair who later became an admiral in the Turkish fleet (see p.29), linger in the islands' oral traditions, as in the account of the time when "Aegina alone (in the Saronic gulf) yielded the pirate six thousand prisoners and was left bare of inhabitants" (Zakythinos 34). Conditions improved in the eighteenth century, but piracy, Moslem and Christian, Mediterranean and local, remained a constant threat to the island populations for nearly three centuries.

In addition, the Aegean islands were subject to the special tax that provided crews for the imperial Ottoman fleet. Islanders served from April to October, when weather conditions were favorable for sailing for tax collection and general patrolling duties, but their annual recruitment did not entail conversion to Islam. As a result, this tax was not as devastating as the *devsirme* was to the mainland. Yet the hardships of life at sea -- disease and casualties from engagements with enemy vessels -- meant that considerable loss of life was attributable to this form of taxation. Islands such as Hydra (see Chapter SIX) "provided crews not in proportion to their population but in proportion to the number of ships they owned" (Zakythinos 31). By the late eighteenth century, when the Ottoman fleet was undergoing modernization, the number of islanders recruited from Hydra, Spetsai, and Psara alone reached 8,000, an enormous proportion of the three islands' populations. The office of the *Bash-Reis*, the Greek cocaptain of such ships who was in command of their Christian sailors, first appeared at this time. These new cocaptains, almost exclusively from Hydra, did much to improve the living conditions of their Greek crews. Since navigation was their primary duty, the Greeks' expertise eventually contributed to the development of the islands' own local naval and mercantile power, power that would play a pivotal role in the struggle for Greek independence in the 1820s and beyond.

Turkish rule in general, and in the Aegean islands in particular, was characterized by "vindictive oppression" alternating "with sudden relaxation" (Woodhouse 105). Following Barbarossa's devastations and the firm establishment of Turkish authority over the islands, "piracy seems to have abated...when a definite measure of economic recovery accompanied the gradual repopulation of deserted islands" (Vacalopoulos, *The Greek Nation* 77). Furthermore, the Ottoman *Porte* showed no interest in creating settlements or in posting garrisons or officials in the Cyclades Islands. Given the religious and administrative autonomy inherent in the *millet* system, institutions for self-government began to emerge all over Turkish-occupied Greece, and especially in the Aegean islands.

The prevailing form of self-government was the *Koinotis* (or "commune"), whose administrative details varied from place to place. The Koinotis "constituted a legal entity, independent of the administration of the ruling power, but nevertheless enjoying its toleration" (Zakythinos 57). The deed establishing the Mykonos Koinotis in 1615 has been preserved, along with similar documents from other islands. Called elders, *archons*, or notables, the officers of the Koinotis were elected to a year-long term by a general assembly of the local population. In Hydra, only ship owners and ships' captains were eligible for election.

The officers of the Koinotis had broad powers and responsibilities. Foremost among these was the collection and delivery of taxes to the Ottoman authorities. Other duties included supervising education and health services, inspecting markets, and managing communal affairs generally. Opening the gates of the Kastro at daybreak and closing them at dusk was another communal responsibility, and one that allows us to think of the Kastro as the physical expression of the Koinotis. From the eighteenth century on, we also hear of envoys from the Koinotis to the Ottoman *Porte* making special requests.

The origins and functions, as well as the political and spiritual implications of the Koinotis to the historical continuity of Greece, have been described as follows:

> The Greek communes of Turkish times did not derive from classical models... . They were the product of necessity and the natural consequence of the conqueror's easygoing ways and administrative deficiencies; but while the commune, being Byzantine in origin, has no direct connection with classical models, the whole shape of its subsequent development follows from a purely Greek line of thought and shows a Greek spirit. In a period of national suppression the Greek people, taking as their basis the tax-collecting machinery of their medieval empire, fashioned their own, without any outside intervention, without even any initiative on the part of their own intellectual or spiritual leaders, democratic institutions the conception and spirit of which brings them nearer than their medieval models to the sources of classical tradition. (Zakythinos 68)

Above all for our purposes, the Koinotis was protected by, and in turn sustained, the collective fortifications of the Aegean island towns, which formed the very core of the vernacular architecture of the archipelago.

2.4 Piracy

In *The Mediterranean and The Mediterranean World in the Age of Phillip II*, the French historian Fernand Braudel states the generally-held belief that "piracy in the Mediterranean is as old as history. There are pirates in Boccaccio and Cervantes, just as there are in Homer" (Braudel 866). This chapter looks at piracy as a distinctly Mediterranean institution and one that challenged the very existence of the Aegean island towns. For centuries, the threat of piracy remained the major force in shaping Aegean urban and vernacular architectural forms, forms that survive to this day. This critical threat to the archipelago's settlements is best understood when examined, as it is in the following paragraphs, over the period between the naval battle of Lepanto in 1571 and the fall of Algiers to the French in 1830.

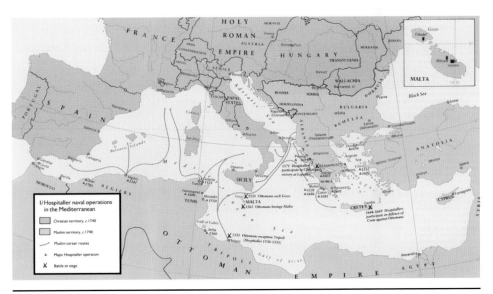

Fig. TWO-4.01 Christian and Moslem territory in the eighteenth-century Mediterranean

Following centuries of jihad and crusade, by the end of the sixteenth century the holy war in the Mediterranean had reached a stalemate (Fig. TWO-4.01), which the naval battle of Lepanto, fought in 1571 at the mouth of the Corinthian gulf in western Greece, only confirmed: it broke the spell of Turkish supremacy but offered few advantages to the victorious Christian

League. Fought on the grand scale of past battles--230 warships on the Turkish side, 208 on the Christian, each carrying hundreds of soldiers--and later commemorated in paintings of appropriately colossal scale (Fig. TWO-4.02), the battle killed thousands. As the last engagement between Christians and Moslems in the sixteenth century, Lepanto marked the end of one kind of warfare and the beginning of another: a small-scale, undeclared, eternal war, fought summer after summer, year after year, at sea or within sight of the coast, by hundreds rather than tens of thousands -- the *corso*, or the war of the corsairs.

At first, the corsair's enemies were those who worshipped a different god. Soon, however, such distinctions became blurred, as personal greed overrode religious beliefs. Each spring, dozens of ships set sail from their Christian or Moslem home ports to attack the shipping and the coastal regions of the Mediterranean. Ships and goods were plundered and sold as prizes. Victims who resisted were slaughtered on the spot; those who surrendered survived and were sold as slaves if poor, or held for ransom if rich. The corsairs plundered on land as they did at sea, so neither shipping nor the villages of the Mediterranean littoral were secure. Given their small size

Fig. TWO-4.02 Giorgio Vasari, "The Naval Battle of Lepanto," detail, sixteenth century

and long coastal exposure, the Aegean islands paid a heavy price in corsair depredations. After being plundered, many of the islands were abandoned, apparently for long periods.

"Piracy" and "privateering," "pirates" and "corsairs" are different terms suggesting the same set of cruelties. There are, however, distinctions among them that should be made. "Piracy" suggests violent sea action for private gain. "Privateering," although based on the ancient tradition of piracy, suggests institutionalized customs, agreements, and networks of intermediaries. As it eventually developed in the Mediterranean, the corsair war was an economic activity independent of religion and nationality that was practiced by rich and poor alike across the Mediterranean Sea. Particularly after the naval battle of Lepanto, Mediterranean privateering became "legitimate" war. Kings and other rulers licensed corsairs as privateers to augment their naval forces. In a formally declared war, corsairs would join the main royal forces in battle; more often, they would prey upon the enemy in smaller-scale operations.

The roster of corsair centers in the Mediterranean was a long one. But the most prominent were Valetta in Malta, and Algiers. Valetta became the headquarters of the Knights Hospitaller, the Christian Order of Saint John, who moved there under the protection of Charles V of Spain after the loss of Rhodes. On the Moslem side, Algiers became a corsair center in 1516 when Kheireddin, better known as Barbarossa and one of the most celebrated of the Barbary corsairs, seized the city, which owed allegiance to the Turkish sultan, and began its three-century-long history as the preeminent Moslem corsair port of the Barbary Coast and the Mediterranean (Fig. TWO-4.04).

Fig. TWO-4.03
Kheireddin, corsair
and Turkish admiral

Fig. TWO-4.04 Algiers

| Fig. TWO-4.05 Galley of Malta | Fig. TWO-4.06 Galley of Barbary |

As previously noted, Barbarossa also exemplified the blurred line between corsair and admiral (Fig. TWO-4.03): when he moved from Algiers to the Ottoman imperial seat of Constantinople, Sultan Suleyman the Magnificent appointed him *Kapudan-derya*, or "grand admiral of the fleet." Generally, though, both Algiers and Malta exploited their prominence and their distance from higher authority to increase their autonomy in dealing with friends and adversaries (Fig. TWO-4.05 –4.06).

Corsairs have appeared in many historical settings and diverse geographic locations. But the life and geography of the Mediterranean, an inner sea, provided ideal conditions for the corso to flourish as a profession. At best, agriculture and fishing yielded marginal livelihoods. For a young person of ambition the chance to achieve a better life through hard work was virtually nonexistent. The opportunities offered by life as a corsair were difficult to resist. In a sea crossed by hundreds of vessels and a landscape with a multitude of small harbors and inlets that provided secret places for refitting as well as shelter from the weather, the winter, and better-armed opponents, it was easy to imagine the corsair's life as leading to riches and fame.

And indeed the Italian term *corsale* identifies a person who is a corsair by profession and neither a criminal nor a fugitive. In maritime courts, a man would identify himself as such as readily as another would call himself a cooper, tanner, butcher, or baker. The corso was more often than not a lifetime profession, which the corsair entered at a young age. Good fortune offered rapid advancement. A young recruit with navigational skills and personal daring might soon become a corsair captain and go on to invest his profits in commerce, banking, and land. He might well found one of the many recorded dynasties of merchant corsairs. The potent combination of religious zeal with greed probably accounts for the profession's longevity:

Privateering was also of course an institution which served to enhance the glory of one's own God and to lead to the abasement of the God of one's rivals. Any institution which serves at one and the same time to make a person rich and to save his soul is never likely to suffer from a dearth of recruits. (Earle 18)

The preeminence of the Barbary Coast and Maltese corso was eventually challenged as other flags increasingly penetrated Mediterranean waters. The growth of English, Dutch, and French trade after 1750 was paralleled by an increase in these nations' naval strength. Commercial rivalries among the newcomers led them to negotiate treaties with the Barbary Coast corsairs which obligated the Western powers to pay tribute, often in kind (naval stores, guns, powder, and so on), in return for the corsairs' promise not to attack their shipping. Guns and other armaments paid as tribute actually enabled corsair attacks on rival merchant marines, yielding an additional commercial advantage to those paying the tribute.

The young United States was soon caught up in this web of tribute payments and trade intrigue. As early as 1785, the British encouraged the Algiers regency to declare war on the United States in the hope of driving American commerce out of the Mediterranean. Thomas Jefferson, first as United States Minister to France, then as Secretary of State, and eventually as President, dealt personally and at length with the vexing questions of whether to pay tribute and ransom for captured American sailors and whether to build a navy to blockade and punish the Barbary Coast corsairs. After being acrimoniously debated in the Congress, the issue was finally resolved in 1805. The United States Navy besieged Tripoli, and the United States Marines marched across the Libyan Desert, forcing a peace treaty to end the war as memorialized in the Marine Corps hymn. From the American perspective:

Americans had returned in triumph from the Mediterranean, having humbled the ancient enemies of Christian civilization, asserting their role as Americans in defending freedom. The victory over Tripoli ... had made the Americans the equals of any other people, not because of military power, but because that power was guided by a spirit of justice, and its goal was not conquest but freedom. The Americans, statesmen and sailors, leaders and common folk, were different from the "plundering vassals of the tyrannical Bashaw," as one poet had described the Tripolitans, and the European nations that countenanced the Bashaw's plunder and tyranny. ... The Americans were not only people to respect, people who, as John Paul Jones had said, deserved to be free; they had become people to emulate. …. the Barbary states would not disgrace the civilized world if the cabinets of Europe were inspired by "an American spirit." (Allison 34)

But it was France that dealt the final blows to the Mediterranean corsairs of both faiths. In 1798, on his way to Egypt, Napoleon ended the Christian corso of Malta. Decades later, in 1830, the restored French monarchy sent a punitive expeditionary force which landed in Algiers and cleared out the last of the Moslem Barbary Coast corsairs.

Such, in broad-brush form, were the realities of the corso in Mediterranean life generally. The same description applies to the corso of the Aegean archipelago but with a greater intensity that reflects the physical, political, economic, and religious peculiarities of this smaller but integral part of the Mediterranean. Certainly the corso had a direct and unmistakable effect on the life and architectural forms of the Aegean island towns.

By the early seventeenth century, nearly all of the Aegean islands had come under Ottoman control. The Ottoman Empire then extended from the Balkan peninsula to the gates of Vienna and across the shores of the eastern Mediterranean and North Africa to embrace the three regencies of Tripoli, Tunis, and Algeria, also known as the Barbary Coast. Since overland travel within the empire remained arduous and expensive, the Aegean Sea was the hub of imperial communication and trade. Few cities in Europe could match the Ottoman ports, which included Alexandria, Smyrna, Thessaloniki, and Algiers. None could compare in size with the imperial capital of Constantinople. The constant flow of ships carrying foodstuffs and raw materials to those urban centers turned the Aegean Sea into a major trade artery. Ships carrying such rich trade naturally became the corsairs' prey.

The geography of the Aegean archipelago determined the routes of the ships carrying such cargoes, and the common local knowledge of these routes made the corsair's job of locating prey easier, despite the risk of encountering the galleys of the Ottoman navy.

Under the *millet* system the Greek populations of the islands had substantial autonomy, since the Turkish presence was limited to annual visits by officials to collect taxes and take aboard the young Greek sailors whom the islands were required to provide as recruits for the Ottoman navy. The absence of Turkish civil or military authority from the islands prompted the Christian corsairs of the western Mediterranean to use many of the islands as forward bases of operation, despite the dangers of dwelling in enemy waters. On islands such as Kimolos (at that time also known as Argentiera), corsairs could obtain fresh provisions, take on water, bury their dead, and, crucially, maintain their ships. Ships required frequent careening for cleaning, caulking, repairing, and overhauling. Such overhauling was necessary but hazardous and a time of extreme vulnerability for both ship and crew. But the islands' small, hidden bays and the high points above them that allowed for the posting of lookout guards provided the best possible locations for such crucial maintenance and repair work. In addition, the Aegean winter was a dangerous time to sail. Some Maltese corsairs spent the winter months in protected island bays on the alert for an occasional prize. But most corsairs spending the winter months in Aegean waters were seeking the advantage of an early start on their spring operations.

Given their unusual autonomy from direct Ottoman authority, the islands and towns of the archipelago were also regular prey for Moslem corsairs from the Barbary regencies. Onshore raiding was one of their favored tactics. One or two ships would normally conduct such a raid. Landing a party of a few dozen corsairs who would march inland undetected, they would launch a surprise attack that would breach the gates of a town at dawn, take captives, seize treasure, and depart again as quickly as they had appeared. Stories of raids and the abduction of islanders to be sold in the Turkish slave bazaars abound in the folklore of the archipelago and have found their way into Greek literature, as in *Ftochos Ayios* (or *Poor Saint*) by Alexandros Papadiamantis, an important nineteenth-century prose writer and a native of the island of Skiathos in the northern Aegean. (For the *Ftochos Ayios* story, see Chapter FOUR.)

In addition, tales of the corso found their way into European literature more generally, as in Byron's *The Corsair* and Jules Verne's only historical novel, *L' Archipel en Feu (The Archipelago in Flames)* (Fig.TWO-4.07). Verne's *Archipelago* is set in the 1820s during the years of the Greek revolution. Its characters include a respectable banker who has secretly been financing a Greek corsair; his beautiful daughter, who desperately hopes that her father will refuse the corsair's offer for her hand; the corsair himself, who masquerades as a feared Moslem and is well known as such among the islanders upon whom he preys; his mother, a leader of the Greek revolution; and a handsome French naval lieutenant who has come to the archipelago to fight for Greek independence. The romantic plot culminates in the corsair's mother's denunciation of her son as a traitor and in a naval battle in which the corsair is killed -- at which point the banker's daughter gets her heart's desire and marries the French lieutenant. In writing the novel, the popular Verne responded to continuing and widespread public interest in the social and historical legacy of the Mediterranean corso several decades after its demise.

Both Christian and Moslem corsairs had devastating effects on the archipelago's population, but the islanders' relations with them, whether voluntary or forced, helped the islanders to develop and maintain their seamanship and fighting skills, assets which would serve them well later, in the struggle for independence.

In the century or so before Greek independence, when the Dutch and the English, with their purchased immunity from Barbary corsair attacks, increasingly carried goods from the Ottoman empire to the western Mediterranean and Atlantic ports, the local eastern Mediterranean trade fell largely into Greek hands. This port-to-port commerce within the Ottoman Empire was traditionally the main target of the Christian Maltese corsairs. As it passed into Greek hands, it raised difficult questions for both the Latin Christian corsairs and the Orthodox Christian Greek ship captains. In the context of the war against the Moslem "infidel," the pope, who also held religious authority over the Maltese corsairs, had always protected the Greeks as Christians. In addition, attacking Christian shipping contradicted the corsairs' oath. But under the new conditions, the Maltese corsairs began to challenge the Greek Orthodox captains as schismatics and heretics unworthy of the pope's protection and thus liable to Maltese corsair depre-

Fig. TWO-4.07 Jules Verne, frontispiece from *L'Archipel en Feu*

dations. In this confused situation, although the Latin corsairs retained some scruples against attacking ships with Greek captains or crews, they claimed the right of *visita* -- the right to stop and inspect any ship -- and would readily seize cargoes as Turkish trade. In such cases, the only remedy for Greek captains ironically lay with the courts of Malta, whose records indicate that Greek seamen occasionally won their cases and recovered goods confiscated by the Maltese corsairs.

In these complicated and ambiguous circumstances, every side involved -- Turkish merchants, Greek captains, and Maltese corsairs -- took risks in playing their roles within the commercial life of the eastern Mediterranean and Aegean Seas. In the same circumstances, the Greek population of the Aegean islands found opportunities to assert its autonomy, its religious beliefs, and its national identity in confronting its tormentors. With their traditional skills in seamanship and trade, the islanders developed the wealth and confidence to build and sustain the island towns and to manage sizable and robust merchant fleets. The captains and crews of these fleets, whose home ports were the Aegean island towns, were destined to play a dramatic role in the struggle for Greek independence in the 1820s. These same captains and crews also laid the foundation upon which the present-day Greek merchant marine has built its global preeminence.

Skillful seamanship, trading acumen, and a singular ability to rise to extraordinary circumstances contributed to the building of Hydra (Chapter SIX), a remarkable town that survives today in excellent condition. Although extraordinary, Hydra is not unique. Many other islands, including Mykonos, Patmos (Chapter FOUR), and Santorini (Chapter SEVEN), were similarly accomplished at mustering commercial fleets and building towns.

2.5 Greece Rediscovered

During the second half of the nineteenth century, the architectural profession in the Western world began to establish a process of formal education, abandoning the traditional model of apprenticeship. Located within an *Ecole des Beaux-Arts*, a polytechnic school, or a university-affiliated academic unit, this formal education ended with the granting of a degree or diploma that led eventually to licensed practice. As this shift took place, vernacular building, or "architecture without architects," emerged as a distinct category in architects' minds and eyes. At the same time what Siegfried

Giedion later called the "demand for morality in architecture" began to inform the observation and study of vernacular building. Many architects in the late nineteenth and early twentieth centuries saw the eclectic architecture prevailing at the time as an aesthetic "lie." Vernacular architecture, by contrast, provided "truthful" and unpretentious responses by builders whose education had not been contaminated by formal academic teaching.

Contrasts and contradictions between the formal architecture of the monuments of antiquity and the vernacular character of contemporary buildings were not absent from the reports of the limited numbers of antiquarians, collectors, diplomats, and architects who began traveling to Greece in the fifteenth century in search of relics of the past. In addition to the discovery and description of these monuments, the travelers and their reports launched a lengthy process frequently referred to as the "rediscovery of Greece," which also brought back to Western Europe information and images of contemporary life and the vernacular architecture of the Aegean islands.

In their rediscovery of antiquity, the humanists of the Renaissance had relied upon texts by ancient Greek authors. Greece itself, its physical world and its historical sites, was inaccessible to the artists and architects of the period, whose work necessarily developed in the absence of direct visual experience of the architectural prototypes of antiquity: none of the northern Italian Renaissance architects, for example, had seen the Parthenon. The rupture between the Roman Catholic and Greek Orthodox churches, aggravated by the seizure and looting of Constantinople by the crusaders in 1204, epitomized the long process of cultural and physical alienation between the two halves of the former Roman Empire. In addition, after the Greek peninsula fell under the domination of the vigorous and expanding Ottoman Empire, inquisitive "infidel" visitors were distrusted as spies. Access to Greece was thus restricted to a very small number of travelers from the West.

Some of the earliest, pioneering information that helped to launch the centuries-long rediscovery of Greece came from the two Italian humanists mentioned previously: Cristoforo Buondelmonti (born c.1385) and Ciriaco Pizzicolli (born c.1391), also known as Cyriac, or Cyriacus of Ancona.

Based in Hospitaller Rhodes, Buondelmonti, a Florentine monk, visited most of the Aegean islands in the first decade of the fifteenth century, possibly under commission to purchase Greek manuscripts. To record his travels, in 1422 he produced a manuscript titled *Liber Insularum Archipelagi (Book of the Islands of the Archipelago)* and enriched his descriptions with a great number of island maps. Widely circulated, this manuscript rekindled the interest of the contemporary scholarly community in the Aegean archipelago. The manuscript was translated from Latin into several languages, including Greek, and remained the basis of geographical knowledge of the Aegean archipelago until the end of the eighteenth century.

Buondelmonti's maps, laconically drawn in pen and watercolor, provide engaging information in visually inspiring terms. Although they lack the cartographic accuracy that was achieved in the nineteenth century, they show abstractly the essential outlines of islands, bays, and ports and indicate outstanding features on land, both natural and man-made. The drawing of the port, fortifications, towers, and windmills of Rhodes, for example (Fig. TWO-2.12), gives enticing and visually economical information that is useful to a visitor even today. The map of Santorini, which Buondelmonti identifies as Santellini, also stands out. Including Therasia and Kameni, the map displays the author's understanding of the volcanic activity that produced the complex and, abstractly but confidently, delineates the great rise of the caldera's cliffs, the most impressive diachronic feature of the landscape of this unique island (Fig. TWO-5.01).

Buondelmonti's *Liber Insularum Archipelagi* is in the medieval tradition of manuscript illumination meant for scholarly and library use rather than for use in Aegean navigation, for which there were marine charts, or *portolans*. Although he was based in Rhodes, the home of the Knights Hospitaller of the Order of Saint John, most of the islands Buondelmonti detailed

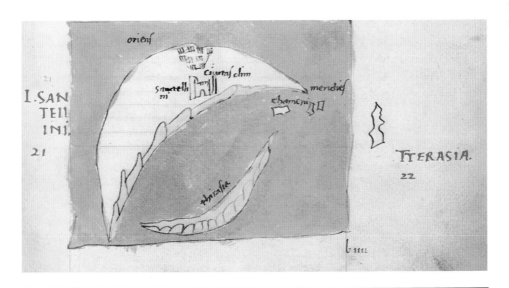

Fig. TWO-5.01 Buondelmonti, map of Santorini

in his manuscript were part of the Duchy of the Archipelago. The apparent ease with which he traveled from island to island indicates the continuing relations and communications between these two Latin Aegean realms, intercommunication that also informed the parallel development of formal and vernacular architecture in the archipelago.

Buondelmonti initiated a tradition of travel accounts that included pictorial information on the geography and antiquities of Greece. He was followed by Cyriacus of Ancona, a member of a merchant family in that city, a prosperous port in Adriatic Italy. Cyriacus traveled for more than four decades around the Aegean and the eastern Mediterranean littoral on family business. The monuments of the past that he encountered in his travels excited his curiosity and scholarly interest. Copying inscriptions at archaeological sites led him to believe that "the monuments and inscriptions are more faithful witnesses of classical antiquity than are the texts of ancient writers" (Etienne 26), a novel idea at the time. Put into practice, it established Cyriacus as the earliest archaeologist on record. With neither a formal education nor any instruction in drawing, he nevertheless pursued a primitive form of archaeology with vigor. His commercial travels often involved diplomatic missions, which, in turn, brought him into touch with the educated. He learned Greek by studying Homer and copying inscriptions, and drew classical temples, fragments, and figures from every site he visited.

Sadly, most of his notes, including his *Commentary upon Ancient Things*, were destroyed by fire nearly one hundred years after his early voyages. But enough has been preserved to allow us to understand his methods, talents, and contributions. Because of his pioneering commitment to the discovery of physical evidence from antiquity and his drawings of its monuments, many have thought of Cyriacus as the father of archaeology, a legitimate characterization, as he meticulously reproduced inscriptions from the archaeological sites he visited. But at the same time, his work was often uneven and not altogether reliable, as he was not above manufacturing fakes when they met his expectations better than the real things did.

In the visual record of Cyriacus's work, this unevenness intensifies. While his drawings of the Muses in Samothrace appear well proportioned and graceful (Fig. TWO-5.03), similar drawings from Delos (Fig. TWO-5.02) are crude and unsophisticated, despite the important information they transmit. A drawing of the western façade of the Parthenon that he executed during his visit to Athens in 1437 very clearly reveals Cyriacus's contributions and his limitations (Fig. TWO-5.04). He knows more about the site than most of his contemporaries, correctly referring to it as "the Acropolis," and he is intellectually attracted by its archaeological importance. However, his drawing of the western façade of the Parthenon exhibits a surprisingly limited comprehension of the aesthetic quality of the building. He is insensitive to its proportions, arbitrarily omits such important parts of its composition such as the metopes, and misrepresents others, such as the podium and the pediment.

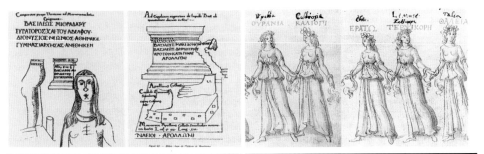

| Fig. TWO-5.02 Cyriacus of Ancona, drawing | Fig. TWO-5.03 Cyriacus of Ancona, drawing |

This criticism does not diminish the importance of Cyriacus's pioneering work and scholarly contributions to early antiquarianism and early archaeology. It does, however, point up the discrepancy between verbal and visual sensitivity, a discrepancy that seems to persist in the work of many of those who followed in Cyriacus's footsteps.

The art and science of collecting rare and precious objects flourished in the sixteenth-century Western European world. Manuscripts, coins, medals, statues, casts of busts and torsos all fulfilled the desire to possess objects of value. A fine art collection became a mark of prestige among the elite who could afford one, and its acquisition, a demonstration of political power. International politics and diplomacy became vehicles for amassing art collections, as the examples of the French and British ambassadorships to the *Sublime Porte* confirm. The collecting spirit promoted interest in and competition to acquire remnants of the past as scholarly evidence and as a means to the advancement of art. In addition, collecting increased the desire to travel in order to procure ancient treasures from such previously inaccessible places as the Greek peninsula and the Aegean archipelago.

Travel to Greece was in full swing by the seventeenth century. Better prepared than Buondelmonti and Cyriacus had been, the new visitors were systematic in their observations and brought better judgment to bear. During the second half of the seventeenth century, the focus of most visitors -- primarily French -- became, predictably, Athens:

The emergence of Athens in the consciousness of modern Europeans is unique. Unlike Rome, which continued to play a vital role almost uninterruptedly, Athens reentered the Western world, so to speak, more as a symbol of a bygone era and less as a place of current significance. In this instance cultural and intellectual considerations preceded political interests. (Augustinos 94)

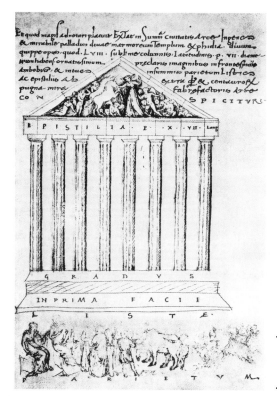

Fig. TWO-5.04 Cyriacus of Ancona, Parthenon

Among the French visitors to Athens was Father Jacques Paul Babin, a Jesuit missionary. His comments from the 1650s are of particular interest to this study. Knowledgeable and focused on the observation and recording of information, Babin belongs to the small group of travelers who visited and described Athens prior to the fateful Morosini bombardment of the Acropolis in 1687 (discussed in section seven of Chapter FOUR). Enough of the glory of the Acropolis was known to Babin to bring him there, but he found modern Athens, by contrast, small and disappointing. "Babin was one of the first to dwell on this antithesis and to juxtapose the two antipodal images," writes Augustinos (98). Babin himself writes of Athens:

Most of the streets resemble those of a village. Instead of these superb edifices, these glorious trophies, and these rich temples that were once the ornament of this city, one sees nothing but houses devoid of any magnificence, made from ancient ruins, having for their sole ornament some pieces of marble columns embedded in their walls without any order, in the same manner as the other stones. (Augustinos 98)

These comments indicate an awareness of the difference between formal architecture as represented by the buildings on the Acropolis and vernacular architecture as represented by the seventeenth-century fabric of the city that surrounded the writer. Babin also refers to the Athenian practice of using the physical remnants of previous epochs as a quarry for current building. Although discomforting to Babin and to archaeologists generally, such recycling continues to be common practice in the building of most Aegean island towns and does much to establish the intimate, tactile, and diachronic relationship between formal and vernacular architecture in the archipelago.

Even today, streets resembling "those of a village" can be seen when visiting the part of old Athens under the northeast corner of the Acropolis. Dating from the 1840s, this area, known as *Anafiotika*, or "the settlement of those who came from the island of Anafi," provides evidence of the transplantation of the Aegean vernacular architecture manner to a neighborhood

Fig. TWO-5.05 Athens, *Anafiotika*, 1997

Fig. TWO-5.06 Athens, *Anafiotika*, 1997

Fig. TWO-5.07 Athens, *Anafiotika*, 1997

in the shadow of an Acropolis much different from that seen by Father Babin (Fig. TWO-5.05,-5.06, -5.07).

Two other travelers, Jacob Spon, a physician from Lyon, and Charles-Francois Olier, the Marquis de Nointel, a French nobleman and ambassador to the *Sublime Porte*, emphasize the seventeenth-century French contribution to the rediscovery of Greece. Relying on Father Babin's eyewitness account and guided by Jean Giraud, the French consul in Athens, Spon embarked on the first systematic and meticulous exploration of Athenian archaeological sites (Fig. TWO-5.08). He identified buildings, organized topographic data, and established correspondences between descriptive texts and existing buildings. In the scientific spirit of his time, Spon, also an epigraphist, called the remains of antiquity "books whose stone and marble pages have been written on with iron points and chisels." His methodology stressed the importance of observation and reason, of seeing and thinking, a valuable lesson for travelers still resonant for present-day architectural education and practice.

Spon's work, published in 1678, two years after his return from Greece, painted a portrait of Athens for French and European readers of a small town of 8,000 people -- three-fourths of them Greeks, the rest, Turks -- hud-

Fig. TWO-5.08 Jacob Spon in Athens, 1676

dled under the protective mass of the Acropolis fortress. The "Athenians" were the Greek inhabitants of the town not its Turkish dwellers, of whom Spon and his contemporaries had little to say. Although the Greeks enjoyed a modicum of self-governance through their ecclesiastical authorities, the Turks were clearly in charge of the town, as Spon was well aware. He had to pay bribes -- nearly thirty pounds of coffee! -- to the Turkish authorities to be allowed to enter the citadel. There, under the surveillance of the garrison, he measured the Parthenon and identified the temple of Athena Nike, which was soon to be razed to make room for a gun emplacement. The Erechtheion was beyond his reach, as it housed the harem of the *disdar*, the fort commander. Between the temples, makeshift structures and dilapidated buildings housed the soldiers of the Acropolis garrison. Spon's verbal descriptions of these structures were confirmed by the drawings and paintings of such subsequent visitors as William Pars in 1765 and James Stuart and Nicholas Revett in 1787 (Fig. TWO-5.11) and present us once more with the symbiotic relationship between formal and vernacular architecture.

Spon's travels in Greece between 1674 and 1676 were bracketed by the fall of the Venetian city of Candia in Crete in 1669 and Morosini's bombardment of the Acropolis in 1687. The Venetian loss permanently altered the balance of power in the Aegean archipelago in favor of the Ottoman Turks; the bombardment made Spon one of the last Europeans to visit the Parthenon while the building remained intact. Before he left Athens, Spon visited the Saronic Gulf islands of Poros, Aegina, and Salamis, the latter two within sight of the Acropolis. "In his crisp and laconic manner," writes Augustinos, "he described the desolate state of these islands and the plight of their inhabitants, beset by poverty and preyed upon by pirates" (106).

As he observed the ravages of the corsairs, Spon almost fell victim to them on his way to Greece, a fate that actually befell a notable contemporary of his, the Marquis de Nointel, who survived an attack by Barbary Coast corsairs on the island of Chios in the northern Aegean. Nointel had been appointed the French ambassador to Constantinople, and his primary mission was to renew French capitulations and advance French interests in the Ottoman Empire.

[His] origins and personal qualities recommended him highly for this post: he came from an old, distinguished noble family, was well versed in foreign languages, was a seasoned traveler, and had a lively and abiding interest in the arts. Highly conscious of the importance of his mission, he was determined to surround himself with grandeur and sumptuousness, a style befitting the glory of his nation and also his predilection for splendor and magnificence. Furthermore, he was convinced that in order to deal successfully with the Ottomans, one should address them from a position of strength. This meant ostentatious opulence, a quality greatly valued by the Orientals, in his view, and a stance of superiority and steadfastness. (Augustinos 116-17)

Thus Nointel made grand entrances into Constantinople and all the other places he visited during his tenure as ambassador, including Athens. Having successfully completed his diplomatic negotiations, he set out to satisfy his personal interest in antiquities and the arts with a long expedition to the Levant. Upon his return in November 1674, his frigate cast anchor at Piraeus, then known as *Porto-Lione*. Accompanied by the local Turkish *Aga*, Nointel made a triumphant entry into Athens and was allowed to enter the Acropolis fortress nearly two years before Spon arrived in 1676. Impressed by the site and its buildings, Nointel was the first Western official to declare the artistic treasures of Athens superior to those of Rome, initiating a significant shift in cultural attitudes. By including scholars and artists in his retinue, Nointel made a further innovation that would be emulated in the future.

The *disdar*, the Turkish commandant of the Acropolis citadel, permitted Jacques Carrey of Troyes, one of the artists in the marquis's entourage, to make drawings of the sculptures and reliefs of "the temple of the idols" -- as the Moslems referred to the Parthenon -- drawings which became a unique and precious record of what was still in place before the calamity of 1687 (Fig. TWO-5.09).

Spon and Nointel represent Western Europe's emerging interest in the physical aspects of Greece. Although Spon's primary concern was intellectual and scientific and Nointel's, governmental and aristocratic, both provided important information and inspired interest in travel and study that fueled the continuing rediscovery of Greece. For this reason, Spon can be forgiven his harmless mistakes and misidentifications. Equally, we should be pleased that the French king did not take Nointel's suggestion that the treasures of the Acropolis be placed in his majesty's chambers or galleries, a suggestion not implemented for another hundred years and then by the ambassador of a rival country, Lord Elgin of Great Britain. So caught up were Spon and Nointel in discovery that Spon neglected the medical profession and Nointel, his ambassadorial duties to pursue their personal interests and impulses. Ironically, they died during the same year, 1685, the former in exile and penniless, and the latter bankrupt and in disgrace with his king.

In the eighteenth century, the European powers' efforts to advance their commercial and political interests in the Ottoman Empire gradually changed Turkish attitudes towards foreigners. Travel in the Greek peninsula and the Aegean islands became safer and easier and, for Europeans, fashionable. While merchants and traders continued to maintain a strong presence in the area, a number of artists and the sons of aristocratic families

Fig. TWO-5.09 Drawing of the west façade of the Parthenon from Nointel's visit in 1674

began to round off their studies and education with a "grand tour" to Greece. The grand tour fit well with the ideology of the Enlightenment, the most important Western European intellectual movement of the century, which promoted interrelated concepts of God, reason, nature, and man, issues also central in Greek antiquity. In short, "Greece, home of the arts and educator of taste, became the school at which Europe came to study" (Etienne 44 - 45).

The archaeological excavations at Pompeii and the discovery of Greek temples at Paestum in Italy in the mid-eighteenth century gave Western European scholars direct experience of Greek architecture and antiquity. Reports of this work inspired Johann Joachim Winckelmann (1717-68), the German scholar who definitively established the preeminence that classical Greek art has since retained in Western civilization. Although Winckelmann was never able to visit ·Greece himself, his work established the theoretical basis for the study and understanding of Greek antiquity.

The roughly contemporary London-based Society of Dilettanti, a club of aristocrats who had visited Italy and aspired to cultural activity, helped to build on Winckelmann's foundation by supporting the in situ work of James Stuart (1713-88) and Nicholas Revett (1720-1804).

Stuart and Revett first met in Rome and made plans for what eventually became the work they did together in Athens. Their aims, outlined in 1748, are still thought-provoking for those of us in the early twenty-first century who are concerned with the future of the Aegean island towns. Athens, they wrote, was:

the mother of elegance and politeness, whose magnificence scarce yielded to that of Rome, and who for the beauties of a correct style must be allowed to surpass her, as much as an original excels a copy, [but] has been almost completely neglected, and unless exact drawings from them be speedily made, all her beauteous fabricks, her temples, her theaters, her palaces will drop into oblivion, and Posterity will have to reproach us. (Stoneman 122)

Revett and Stuart worked together in Athens for two years, from 1751 to 1753, with Revett doing the measurements and Stuart, the paintings and the drawings. They were "determined to avoid haste and system, those most dangerous enemies to accuracy and fidelity" (Stoneman 122).

Before they returned to England, they also visited the islands of the Aegean archipelago, but on this part of their travels, the record is mute.

Professional commitment and their hopes for future architectural commissions in England prompted them to record their work in Athens in four volumes, *The Antiquities of Athens*, a publication which set new standards of exactness in architectural drawing (Fig. TWO-5.10). It took several decades to complete the four volumes, but the study became the basic architectural reference for a score of buildings in England, Ireland, and eventually, Scotland, setting the tone for the Greek Revival in Britain. Its influence even extended to American shores. President Thomas Jefferson owned a copy, and Benjamin H. Latrobe, true to the spirit of his time, declared himself "...a bigoted Greek in the condemnation of...Roman architecture... ."

To give scale to their drawings, architects often add human figures to their elevations and perspectives. Stuart took this practice a step further by drawing himself into many of his paintings (Fig. TWO-5.11), a confirmation not only of his physical association with what he was drawing but also of his personal and spiritual affiliation with the landscape of the site. This practice might also explain why, of the two authors, Stuart became the better known, even earning the sobriquet "the Athenian."

A young French aristocrat in the middle of the eighteenth century with a good classical education and a long family tradition of learning, would almost certainly have been aware of the work of Winckelmann, Stuart, and Revett and been motivated by them in planning his own grand tour of Greece. This was probably true of Marie-Gabriel-August-Florent, the Comte de Choiseul-Gouffier, who at the age of twenty-four, joined the royal frigate *Atalante*, which sailed to the Aegean archipelago to conduct geographical and astronomical observations in March 1776. Eager to cover as much territory as possible, Choiseul-Gouffier took along three artists and a personal secretary and produced, complete with archaeological illustrations, the richest record of contemporary life in the Aegean archipelago to date. Something of a maverick, Choiseul-Gouffier also chose to return to Paris not by sea, as was usual, but by land. This meant a long and hazardous crossing of northern Greece and Serbia, which were still parts of the Ottoman Empire, an overland trek to the Dalmatian coast, and from there, a long voyage to France.

Fig. TWO-5.10 Stuart and Revett, "The Antiquities of Athens," the Parthenon, 1787

Six years later, in 1782, the first volume of Choiseul-Gouffier's *Voyage pittoresque de la Grèce* appeared in print and was received with enthusiasm even beyond France. In addition to the rich descriptions he included of contemporary life in Greece and the Aegean islands, Choiseul-Gouffier espoused pioneering philhellenic views. In the frontispiece to his first volume, Greece is depicted in chains, "expiring" among the ruined tombs of Pericles, Themistocles, and other heroes of antiquity (Fig. TWO-5.12). "Let it be said clearly," Choiseul-Gouffier wrote in his introduction, that "there

Fig. TWO-5.11 James Stuart, "Stuart Sketching the Erechtheion," 1751

still exist in [Greece] men ready to revive the memories of their ancestors" (Tsigakou, *Rediscovery* 43), an early instance of giving a contemporary political significance to the well-established Western European admiration for Greek antiquity. Choiseul-Gouffier in effect advocated the liberation of Greece from Turkish rule, a view that would eventually lead to the Greek revolution and the emergence of the modern Greek state in 1830. (The revolution's effect on the evolution of vernacular architecture in the Aegean archipelago will be discussed later in this chapter. Its role in the devolution of some of the Aegean island towns will be discussed in Chapter FOUR.) Choiseul-Gouffier's sympathy with Greek independence was good for the national aspirations of the Greek people but had to be recanted later for political reasons. To secure the desirable post of French ambassador to the *Sublime Porte*, the post held a century earlier by Nointel and an assignment that combined prestigious service to the French king with opportunities to pursue his personal literary and artistic aspirations, Choiseul-Gouffier, like any good diplomat, opted to disavow his earlier sympathy with the Greek people whose daily lives he had so effectively depicted.

The French Revolution that began in 1789 put an end to Choiseul-Gouffier's ambassadorial tasks and cultural explorations. As an aristocrat with connections to the royal family, he was suspect in the eyes of the new regime and fled his post in 1792 to spend the next ten years in self-imposed but comfortable exile in Catherine the Great's Russia. He returned to Napoleonic France in 1802 when it was safe for him to do so. Out of politics and stripped of his wealth and titles, he refocused his attention on his earlier work and produced the second volume of the *Voyage Pittoresque de la*

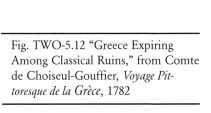

Fig. TWO-5.12 "Greece Expiring Among Classical Ruins," from Comte de Choiseul-Gouffier, *Voyage Pittoresque de la Grèce*, 1782

Grèce. In the end, he was luckier than such predecessors as Spon and Nointel. In the last two years of his life, he saw the restoration of the French monarchy and the return of his family estates and titles; however, he did not see the publication of the last volume of the *Voyage Pittoresque de la Grèce* published in his lifetime, as it appeared posthumously in 1822, exactly forty years after the publication of the first volume.

The *Voyage Pittoresque de la Grèce* was addressed to a late-eighteenth-century Western European readership and to its particular sensibilities and expectations, especially its preoccupation with the notion of the picturesque, best described in contemporary terms as "the kind of beauty which will look well in a picture." This definition seems to have guided the composition of Choiseul-Gouffier's illustrations. Ruins overtaken by nature (Fig.TWO-5.14), exotically clad natives dancing, and women in native dress posed in classical postures (Fig.TWO-5.13) conformed to his readers' idealized expectations but sugarcoated the islanders' hard life. Although Choiseul-Gouffier's visit had occurred immediately after a Russo-Turkish war (1768-74) that had included the occupation of a large number of the Aegean islands by a Russian fleet commanded by Alexei Orlov and harsh Turkish reprisals that followed the peace treaty and the departure of the Russians, these upheavals find no place in his idyllic illustrations. Even so, reliable information about the Aegean islands can be extracted from them. The rocky and unyielding terrain of the islands is presented convincingly. The defensive character of settlements built away from the edge of the sea and on hilltops is confirmed. Windmills, an historic source of energy in the region, are noted as integral parts of the settlements in nearly every illustration, and sailing ships and fishing boats are ever-present, underscoring the islands' historic dependence on the sea (Fig.TWO-5.15 -5.16).

Also important to the rediscovery of Greece was Thomas Hope (1769-1831), whose life straddled equally the eighteenth and nineteenth centuries. Hope's personal and artistic talents were perfectly suited to the tasks of promoting neoclassicism in English architecture and design and observing and recording Aegean vernacular architecture in a refreshingly direct and unprejudiced manner. The son of a Dutch banking family of Scottish origin, Hope inherited a considerable fortune made in business based in Amsterdam. After his eighteenth birthday, he spent eight years in one of the grandest grand tours of the day, studying architecture in the eastern Mediterranean and on the islands of the Aegean Sea. He fictionalized his experience in his anonymously-published novel *Anastasius* (1819), of which Lord Byron said "that his only two regrets were that he had not written it, and that Hope had" (Watkin 171).

As was apparently the case with Hope, the European warfare that followed the French Revolution diverted many grand tours from Italy to Greece.

Revolutionary France occupied and shattered Holland, so it was to England that Hope returned from his travels. There, his fortune and his experience of the grand tour helped him "to take by storm fashionable English society purely in order to influence its artistic taste" (Watkin xix). Like his younger contemporary Lord Elgin, Hope was snubbed at first as an out-

Fig. TWO-5.13 Women of Santorini, from Choiseul-Gouffier

Fig. TWO-5.14 Santorini, from Choiseul-Gouffier

Fig. TWO-5.15 Santorini (Oia), from Choiseul-Gouffier

Fig. TWO-5.16 Santorini, from Choiseul-Gouffier

sider,.But eventually, the architecture, furniture, fabric, and wallpaper that he designed gave him a decisive role in the formation of Regency taste and the Greek Revival (Fig.TWO-5.17).

Hope's biographer, David Watkin, focuses on the English period of his subject's creative life. In his preface, Watkin indicates that "the disappearance of [Hope's] personal papers and drawings has … helped to shroud his life and work in mystery" (xix). On the subject of Hope's (apparently lost) grand tour drawings of the Aegean island towns, Watkin continues insightfully:

> I believe it is to this [i.e., vernacular architecture] that Hope refers in his Downing pamphlet when, despite having argued so emphatically for the adoption of Greek Doric, he observes of himself that:

In bestowing (which few architects…can be supposed to have done) equal attention on the principle of most different and most opposite styles of architecture, I think I have learned to entertain for none an exclusive predilection, founded on ignorance and prejudice. Each species that has a distinct character of its own, also may display beauties of its own, provided that character be preserved… .

This last sentence Sir John Soane especially underlined in his own annotated copy of the pamphlet. And it was precisely this picturesque synthesis of accumulated civilizations built up around the memory of Greece and Rome which fired Hope's imagination. (Watkin 65, italics added)

Ten years after the publication of Watkin's biography, about three hundred fifty original watercolors and sepia drawings from Hope's grand tour

Fig. TWO-5.17 Thomas Hope, "Le Beau Monde," *Designs of Modern Costume*, 1823

came to light at the Benaki Museum in Athens. In light of this discovery, the italicized quotation from Hope becomes an appropriate and refreshing introduction to the spirit that guided his unique and very precious late-eighteenth-century visual record of the vernacular architecture of the Aegean island towns.

Unlike the Choiseul-Gouffier engravings executed by illustrators not present at the site, the Thomas Hope illustrations at the Benaki Museum are original watercolors and sepia drawings generated in situ. They were never intended for publication, and in their uniqueness, they present us with a direct, authentic, and unprejudiced visual document created by a gifted architect intent on communicating his discovery of the distinct character of the Aegean island settlements. Free from "selective eliminations or emotional confusions" (Tsigakou, *Thomas Hope* 32), Hope's drawings are site-specific, offering in effect a form of early "photographic" documentation of his subject. Elements in the "View of Skaros" drawing (Fig.TWO-5.18), including the outline of the large boulder, the horizon line, and the delineation of the island of Therasia in the background, can help today's visitor locate the very spot where the artist sat to execute the drawing sometime between 1787 and 1795. Placing a 1995 photograph next to the drawing (Fig.TWO-5.19) confirms the accuracy of Hope's observation. Similarly, the

Fig. TWO-5.18 Thomas Hope, Santorini, "A View of Skaros," c. 1795

Fig. TWO-5.19 Santorini, Skaros, 1995

monastery of Hydra in the "Town and Harbour of Hydra" is outlined in a form easily recognizable by today's visitor, notwithstanding the tile-roofed rather than flat-roofed houses, a nineteenth-century transformation that will be discussed in Chapter SIX.

At the same time, Thomas Hope also played an important role in the formation of early-nineteenth-century English taste in formal architecture.

Fig. TWO-5.20 Tournefort engraving, "Portara," Naxos, 1717	Fig. TWO-5.21 Thomas Hope, sepia drawing, Naxos, "View of the Town through the Gate of the Archaic Temple," 1787-99	Fig. TWO-5.22 Thomas Hope, watercolor, Naxos, "View of the Town through the Gate of the Archaic Temple," 1787-99

He contributed to the popularity of the Regency style, and "his zeal for Hellenistic ideals created the breeding-ground for the Greek Revival" (Tsigakou, *Thomas Hope* 27). By carefully recording its forms and character, Hope can also be described as the earliest observer, if not the discoverer, of the vernacular architecture of the Aegean island towns. In Hope's work and his personal, historical, and political circumstances, we see the two architectural themes -- the formal and the vernacular -- merge in the thought and work of a single individual. The merger is evident in Hope's watercolor "View of the Town of Naxos as Seen Through the Gate of the Archaic Temple, 1787-95/1799," where the two architectural genres appear in a mutually supportive relationship for the first time in an eighteenth-century work (Fig.TWO-5.21, -5.22). By contrast, just eighty years earlier, Joseph Pitton de Tournefort, a French scientist and botanist, had visited the same site in

Naxos but had recorded only the remnants of formal architecture on the island (Fig.TWO-5.20). It is apparent from this drawing that Tournefort was blind to vernacular architecture. He and his time were not ready for it.

As is evident from the foregoing discussion, the centuries-long rediscovery of Greece accelerated during the late eighteenth and early nineteenth centuries and found its natural conclusion in the long revolutionary struggle of the Greek nation for liberation from Ottoman rule and the emergence of Greece as an independent state in 1830. The magnitude of this struggle and its direct and indirect consequences for the substance and character of the vernacular architecture of the Aegean islands before their ultimate "discovery" in the twentieth century require further discussion in the remaining section of this chapter.

2.6 Athens, the Cultural Capital of the New State

Fig. TWO-6.01 R. Muller, "View of the Acropolis from the Pnyx," 1863

Peace in the southern Greek peninsula and the Aegean archipelago, the incorporation in the 1830s of a number of the Aegean islands into the new Greek state, and the geographically symmetrical French conquest of Algiers in the 1830s effectively ended the era of piracy in the Mediterranean. This geopolitical change decisively affected the character of the Aegean island towns. With piracy a threat of the past, some old settlements that had been high density and constricted expanded beyond their former defensive perimeters. Others, released from defensive restrictions on their physical size, relocated themselves over a period of years to more accessible sites nearby.

Athens was a small, war-devastated village in the 1830s, dominated physically and spiritually by the imposing combination of the natural landscape and the man-made buildings of the Acropolis with its reminders of Periclean glories (Fig.TWO-6.01). The Turkish garrison had not yet evacuated the Acropolis citadel when the young King Otho, the seventeen-year-old son of King Ludwig of Bavaria, landed in the provisional capital of Nafplion in February 1833 to assume the throne of Greece. But given the important roles played by the major powers Britain, France, and Russia in liberating Greece from Ottoman rule, together with the ardent pan-European admiration for Periclean antiquity, it was virtually inevitable that Athens would become the capital of the reborn state.

Fig. TWO-6.02 Karl Krazeisen, "Greeks Fighting among Classical Ruins,"1829

The same enthusiasm for Periclean antiquity was expressed in the political and architectural ideologies of the new state (Fig.TWO-6.02) as an interest in reclaiming the heritage of a glorious past, a past that was also admired by the major powers that supported its rebirth and protected its fragile, early existence. On December 1, 1834, King Otho accordingly made his official entry into Athens. As the administrative and cultural capital of the emerging state, the new Athens was planned and built in the spirit of neoclassicism that prevailed across Western Europe during this period. Such public buildings as the Royal Palace -- now the Parliament Building (Fig.TWO-6.03) -- the Academy, the University, the National Library, the National Technical University, and the Arsakeion are important, but not the only, examples of contemporary neoclassicism. Countless private buildings, ranging from upper-class mansions in the city center to unpretentious houses dispersed throughout, also partook of the neoclassical spirit well into the

Fig. TWO-6.03 Athens, Parliament Building

| Fig. TWO-6.04 Athens, Thermopylon Street,1970 | Fig. TWO-6.05 Poros, 1998 | Fig. TWO-6.06 Hydra, 1963 |

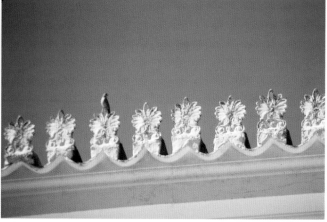

| Fig. TWO-6.07 Sifnos, 1988 | Fig. TWO-6.08 Sifnos, Artemon, 1988 |

twentieth century, as did buildings throughout the archipelago (Fig.TWO-6.04, -6.05, -6.06, -6.07, -6.08).

The formal culture emanating from the capital of the Moslem Ottoman Empire was always alien to the Greek Christian population of the islands. During the long period of Tourkokratia, therefore, the culture and architecture of the Aegean island towns developed independent of the Ottoman capital and, indeed, autochthonously. The emergence of a Greek state with

Fig. TWO-6.09 Serifos, 1973   Fig. TWO-6.10 Patmos, 1999   Fig. TWO-6.11 Patmos, 1999

Athens as its capital ended this disjunction and served to establish cultural homogeneity within its borders and institutional avenues for disseminating the formal culture of the capital to the islands. Thus, neoclassicism became the architectural language and vocabulary of the buildings, the schools, and the city halls the new state built to promote the official national culture and its functions in the island towns (Fig.TWO-6.09, -6.10). The neoclassical architectural themes expressed by such buildings entered into and were absorbed by the nineteenth-century language of Aegean vernacular architecture (Fig.TWO-6.11). Examples of these "intrusions" being assimilated and transformed by the local vernacular abound. Eighteenth-century travelers described Hydra as a town with the flat roofs typical of the Aegean vernacular tradition. But tiled roofs and other neoclassical elements characterize the nineteenth-century town that survives today. Throughout these towns, the entry gates to private houses also incorporate the recognizable two-column and pediment-over-door neoclassical theme and demonstrate the widespread assimilation of the formal architectural messages that emanated from the post-liberation administrative and cultural capital of Athens. (For further discussion of this issue, see Chapter FIVE.)

2.7 Greek Antiquities, Western European Rivalries

National and military rivalries between the European nations and, in particular, between Britain and France during the early nineteenth century found expression in a rush to plunder the antiquities of the Greek peninsula and the Aegean islands. The Ottoman Empire had no cultural or political interest in preventing or limiting this plunder; on the contrary, as it faced military defeat and loss of territory, the *Sublime Porte* often used permission to acquire antiquities as a bargaining chip in dealing with its European adversaries. Sultan Abdul Hamid II's late-nineteenth-century exclamation, "Look at these stupid foreigners! I pacify them with broken stones" (Marchand 188) sharply illuminates the geopolitical context of the plunder.

Already urgent during the two decades before the struggle for Greek liberation, this rush to plunder was further accelerated by a specific architectural phenomenon -- the building of grand public museums all over Europe in such cities as London, Paris, and Munich. To enhance their institutional prestige and the glory of the states that built them, the directors of these museums were eager to add to their collections original and prestigious items from Greek antiquity. In the context of this competition, one might conclude that Great Britain was victorious over France not only at Waterloo, where Wellington defeated Napoleon, but also when the British Museum won an acquisition battle with the Louvre: at the same time that an act of Parliament enriched the British Museum with the Elgin marbles in 1816, the Louvre was ordered to empty itself of the works of art that Napoleon had looted from other European countries. Happily for France, four years later, on the Aegean island of Melos, luck and the quick clandestine operation of a group of French navy officers salved the national pride by bagging the statue of the Venus of Melos for the Louvre.

As a new state, Greece quickly took decisive early steps to safeguard its antiquities by prohibiting their export. An archaeological service was established as early as 1834. A year later, King Otho's Bavarian garrison withdrew from the Acropolis citadel, and plans for building a royal palace on the Acropolis designed by Karl Friedrich Schinkel, a German architect known for his neoclassical work in Berlin, were apparently abandoned. The archaeological service officially opened the Acropolis to the public in 1835, and it has been a prime tourist attraction ever since.

Well into the second half of the nineteenth century, the admiration for Greek antiquity continued to find expression in the formal architecture of the period. Although neoclassicism was in decline in England after the

1830s, it remained fashionable in Scotland and Bavaria. In Greece, it lasted to the end of the century and beyond. This European peregrination of neo-classicism as a formal architectural style gave birth to the unusual design of the church of Saint George in the old Venetian fortress at the port of Corfu (*Kerkyra*). Built in 1840 by the British administration of the Ionian Islands for the use of its troops, this Anglican Church in the form of a Doric temple (Fig.TWO-7.01, -7.02) is a rare, if not unique, example of an architectural style reimported from the British Empire to the land of its origin. Corfu, historically free of Ottoman Turkish rule and a Venetian possession until 1799, together with the six other major Ionian Islands, was by geography and culture relatively closer to Europe than the rest of Greece and, by the geopolitical accident of becoming a British protectorate, a likely site for such a transplantation. The building was converted to a Greek Orthodox church following the departure of the British garrison in 1864 and is used today as a museum.

The greater ease of travel in a newly independent Greece and the continued European interest in Hellas and archaeology attracted a wave of European visitors more scholarly than the grand tourists of pre-revolutionary days. The second half of the nineteenth century saw the publication of scholarly archaeological reports, often by Germans. Admiration for Hellas, deeply rooted in German secondary and university education, led in 1875 to the first formal agreement with the Greek state for politically disinterested German excavations to take place in Olympia. Subsequent agreements concerning other sites with French, British, American, Austrian, and Italian

Fig. TWO-7.01 Joseph Schranz, "View of the Port of Corfu," 1826

Fig. TWO-7.02 Corfu, old Venetian fortress, Saint George, 1996 archaeological missions internationalized the maturing science of archaeology and augmented the work of the Greek archaeological service. These agreements also established a topography of excavation sites that covered the whole country, not just Athens, a topography much like the one prevailing today. In a subtle way, late-nineteenth-century archaeology brought the distinctive character of the Greek landscape, including the Aegean islands, to national and international attention.

This heightened archaeological activity produced surprising results in the work of Heinrich Schliemann (1822-90) and Sir Arthur Evans (1851-1941). Although very different personalities, Schliemann and Evans both brought their personal wealth and unflagging enthusiasm to the task of revealing the extraordinary treasures of the hitherto-unknown Mycenaean and Minoan civilizations, pushing back the Greek past dramatically. Although their discoveries blurred the focus on classical antiquity, that focus nevertheless was strong enough to reach its apogee at the first modern Olympic games, which were staged in Athens in 1896 at the remarbled Panathenaic stadium.

Energies devoted to the building of the modern "European" Greek state using reimported architectural prototypes could not mask for long the native reaction against the "worship of all things foreign." At the same time, in Greece itself the quest continued for an authentic neo-Hellenic identity based on a conception of Greek history as a continuum linking the ancient, medieval, and modern periods that led eventually to the rediscovery and rehabilitation of the nation's Byzantine past. In literature, the arts, and the intellectual life of the country, an awareness gradually developed that Byzantine accomplishments were much closer to nineteenth-century Greece, historically and culturally, than were those of classical antiquity. This development led in turn to the realization that the post-Byzantine period, the period of Tourkokratia, had had a profound influence on the evolution of neo-Hellenism. It was during Tourkokratia, for example, that the most recent features of the vernacular architecture examined here evolved.

2.8 The Twentieth Century

The early-twentieth-century Modern movement in architecture denounced the imitation of classical styles as well as the practice of eclecticism and sought inspiration instead in a more distant past uncontaminated by academic attitudes and manners. In this spirit, Charles-Edouard Jeanneret, better known as Le Corbusier, or Corbu, produced a serialized set of travel notes and sketches for a French newspaper in 1911. As Corbu's architectural work and writings exerted a profound influence on subsequent generations of young architects, it did not escape their attention that his *Journey to the East*, published before World War I, included drawings and observations not only of formal but also of vernacular architecture from the Balkan peninsula and from Greece, where the young Corbu had also sought inspiration.

But the earliest systematic study of vernacular architecture in Greece and the Aegean archipelago was made by A. J. B. Wace and R. M. Dawkins and appeared in the October 1914-March 1915 issue of *The Burlington Magazine for Connoisseurs*. Archaeologists both, Dawkins had already published work stressing "the relationship between social organization and the use of space in the island of Karpathos" (Philippides "Historical Retrospect" 34); Wace was later to become a celebrated figure in the study of the Mycenaean age. One hundred years after Thomas Hope, men such as these, whose primary interest was in the ancient world, again observed and recorded examples of Aegean vernacular architecture.

Their relatively short article in *The Burlington Magazine* presented a wealth of new material in the form of drawings and photographs of fortified Aegean settlements, perhaps the first ever to be published (Fig.TWO-8.01). These drawings included the organization of interior space, the built-in furniture, and the arrangements of household items characteristic of individual houses in the region. The article, entitled "The Towns and Houses of the Archipelago," and the article that preceded it, entitled "Ethnography," appeared under the rather inappropriate general heading "Greek Embroideries I and II," which betrays the folkloric interests that motivated the authors' early, systematic study of vernacular architecture.

Fig. TWO-8.01 Wace and Dawkins, Antiparos from the northeast, c.1914

Folklorists, in fact, generated many of the initial studies of vernacular architecture. A folklore society was established in Greece as early as 1908; its annual publication *Laografia* (or *Folklore*) first appeared in 1909. Folklorists were primarily educators and philologists who emphasized written evidence and texts, the importance of access to antiquity, and the continuity of Greek traditions. Such attitudes were often enriched by a "geographical approach" in which "architecture [was] not divorced from the natural factors determining the nature of the space, that is, the topography and the climate" (Philippides, "Historical Retrospect" 35).

The traumatic experience of the Asia Minor "catastrophe" of 1922, when a million and one-half Greek people were expelled from their ancestral homes in Asia Minor to be resettled on the Greek mainland, together with the encroachment of interwar Modernism, intensified the earlier emphasis on a "return to the roots" movement. Architects, including Aristotelis Zahos, joined the folklorists Angeliki Hatzimihali and George Megas to become leading figures in this 1920s movement. Professor Dimitris Pikionis (1887-1968), my former teacher, was a product of this climate of ideas. Pikionis's thought and teaching are better understood and appreciated today than during his lifetime, especially his love and respect for the natural environment and for the way humankind relates to it and his understanding of the Greek vernacular tradition as an autochthonous source of inspiration for the future course of Greek architecture. Pikionis also recognized the formidable burden that the architecture of Greek antiquity represented, notwithstanding its inspirational potential during its nineteenth-century neoclassical reemergence.

In his 1935 article *"E laiki mas techni k'emeis"* ("We and Our Folk Art"), Pikionis outlined ways of looking at and thinking about vernacular architecture. He considered "unaffectedness" one of the great merits of the folkvernacular tradition and, by extension, of ancient and medieval architecture. Although one might fail to find "great art in it," one would certainly find "natural, that is true art" (Philippides "Historical Retrospect" 38). This article introduced a new era in which vernacular architecture was no longer seen as a simple shell surrounding folk man but as material for philosophical reflection. An understanding of vernacular architecture could not be arrived at by applying the "conventional criteria of formal architecture. On the contrary, understanding demanded perception in depth" (Philippides, "Historical Retrospect" 38).

Pikionis's appointment in 1930 to the faculty of the School of Architecture at the National Technical University in Athens brought his insistence on the meaning and significance of vernacular architecture to the minds' eyes of his students. An immediate result was the formation of teams of young graduates who, under Pikionis's leadership and with the sponsorship of the Society of Greek Vernacular Art, traveled to the western Macedonian region of northern Greece beginning in the summer of 1935 to record and study examples of the vernacular architecture of the area. Measured drawings, photographs, and color reproductions of decorative elements were collected during repeated summer expeditions from 1935 on except during World War II, and were published after the war as *Archontika tes Kastorias (Mansions of Kastoria*, 1948) and *Spitia tes Zagoras (Houses of Zagora*, 1949) (Fig.TWO-8.02, -8.03, -8.04). These summer expeditions launched a tradition of research and publication in the School of Architecture eagerly embraced by its students and continued by its graduates. The result was a plethora of publications on vernacular architecture in the decades following World War II that continues today.

To illuminate the varied and evolving perceptions of vernacular architecture that have developed in Greece and in the United States, brief reference should be made to a number of important publications and exhibitions.

Vernacular architecture was presented and discussed, albeit briefly, as the peer of formal architecture in a 1940 book, *Architektoniki os Techni (Architecture as Art)*, by the architect and philosopher Professor Panayiotis A. Michelis, an influential teacher at the School of Architecture in Athens. In this important book, the basic reference on architecture theory in Greece for the next decades, Michelis (1903-69) for the first time raised the question of what vernacular architecture has to offer to the creation of a regional or even a national architecture.

Fig. TWO-8.03 Zagora, decoration

Fig. TWO-8.02 Kastoria, house

Fig. TWO-8.04 Zagora, School of Rhigas

Another important architect of the post World War II period, Aris Konstantinidis, attempted to answer the same challenging question in his architectural work and writings. Well known outside Greece for the high quality of his buildings, Konstantinidis exhibits in both his work and writings "a determined effort to deduce lessons from vernacular architecture of value to modern architectural practice, in a much more systematic fashion than anything attempted by Pikionis" (Philippides, "Historical Retrospect" 42). Elsewhere, Konstantinidis articulates what was already known about the vernacular: it compensates us for our "lost innocence."

The most ambitious undertaking on the subject, however, has been that of Melissa, the Athenian publishing house that began in the early 1980s to produce a multivolume set of studies of *Greek Traditional Architecture*. Edited by Dr. Dimitri Philippides, an architect and member of the architecture faculty at the National Technical University in Athens, the set is the collective work of more than fifty contributors, most of them architects, each of whom has written one or more monographs focused on a particular island in the Aegean and Ionian Seas or on a region of the Greek mainland. By 1992 more than fifty-five monographs had been made available in Greek, English, and German. The aims of the publication are stated in the general preface:

> The first of these [aims] is to disseminate information and thereby promote research into vernacular architecture by giving, for the first time, as complete and systematic a picture as possible of the architecture of the main regions of the country... .The second aim of the publication is conservation: that is, to contribute through the texts and illustrations to the preservation of the image of a group of monuments that is in danger of disappearing completely. This will make it clear that, even in their mutilated condition, and abandoned as they are to their fate, these monuments of vernacular architecture are worth preserving intact not only in our memories, but also in reality, so that they will be able to communicate their message to the generations to come. A third aim, no less important than the first two, is to clarify certain attitudes to the nature of research, and to discount a range of misconceptions, which even today impede the work of scholars. At the same time, it is hoped that new approaches to the phenomenon will be encouraged through a variety of researches, and that it will be possible to come to some firm conclusions about the potential of each line of approach and to stimulate further investigation. (Rayas, *Traditional Architecture* 6)

An exhibition titled "Architecture Without Architects" mounted by the Museum of Modern Art in New York from November 1964 to February 1965 was the first major event to introduce vernacular architecture to the wider public in North America. In the exhibition catalogue, Bernard Rudofsky, the producer and designer of the exhibition and the catalogue author, acknowledged the help of the John Simon Guggenheim Memorial Foundation and the Ford Foundation in underwriting his research. More pointedly, he cited in the acknowledgments the support of major figures in the by-then well-established Modern movement:

These grants might never have been given without the enthusiastic recommendations of the architects Walter Gropius, Pietro Belluschi, Jose Luis Sert, Richard Neutra, Gio Ponti, Kenzo Tange, and the Museum's Director Rene d'Harnoncourt, all of whom hail from countries rich in vernacular architecture. (Rudofsky, *Architecture Without Architects* i).

Such prominent supporters, together with the prestige of the Museum of Modern Art as a venue, gave legitimacy to and acted as a sort of grand entry for vernacular architecture into the previously exclusive domain of formal architecture. Examples of vernacular architecture from all over the world contributed to the richness of the catalogue, with Rudofsky's black-and-white photographs of the Aegean islands and of Santorini, in particular, comprising an important part of the study.

With an international audience ripe for more information, it is unsurprising that my study of vernacular architecture in Greece could be published in the United States a few years later. *Hydra: a Greek Island Town*, examines vernacular architecture at the "urban" scale of a small town, rather than in the context of a single edifice:

This book [*Hydra: a Greek Island Town*] depicts the systematic broadening of the evolution of a traditional urban center in relation to particular historical events. It also essays a new method of analyzing the layout of the settlement, with diagrams and photographs, in a technique that reconstructs the movement of a pedestrian walking through the streets and squares of the town. (Philippides, *Historical Retrospect* 46- 47)

Thus began a period of wider interest in vernacular architecture in general and that of the Aegean island towns in particular. Since the 1960s, Western European and North American prosperity and affordable mass transportation have allowed hundreds of thousands of visitors to discover the islands. Architects and architecture school faculty have also discovered the rewards of first-hand observation, study, and publication on such an exciting subject. American, British, Japanese, Canadian, Greek, and other publishers have produced a multitude of studies taking various analytical and theoretical approaches. The special vocabulary and language of vernacular architecture; its specific strength in the relationship of building to site; and such issues as community and privacy, human scale, the character of public spaces, and building materials and methods of construction have all become themes for exploration, analysis, and presentation, and together have helped to reveal the timeless qualities of the vernacular architecture of the Aegean islands.

THREE

▷ ◁

THE AEGEAN
ARCHIPELAGO

▷ ◁

Fig. THREE-1.01 N. Visscher, map of the Aegean Sea, 1682

The history and geology of the Aegean archipelago have a unique relationship. Historically, the Aegean Sea is one of the oldest regions of the
globe – Homer describes it; geologically, it is one of the youngest. Its
numerous islands, the mountain peaks of a collapsed landmass, provide
physical evidence of its geological provenance.

The Aegean islands and Crete nurtured the great civilizations of antiquity from which much of contemporary European culture derives. Today the islands comprise the southernmost geographical points of the European Union; at the time of writing, the island of Kastellorizo in the Dodecanesian complex serves as the Union's easternmost landmass.

The name of the Aegean Sea may derive from Aegeus, the mythological king of Athens and father to Theseus. Having slain the Minotaur in Crete and freed Athens from its yearly tribute payment to King Minos, Theseus mistakenly used a black sail signifying mourning on his return instead of the agreed-on white sail signifying victory. Anxiously waiting on the rocky shores of Attica for his beloved son's return, Aegeus spied the black sail and in desperation, flung himself into the sea, which has been known as the *Aigaion Pelagos*, or the "Sea of Aegeus" ever since. Another version of the etymology of the word, deriving from *aiges*, i.e., "waves," suggests an image of this great body of water as eternally moving and perennially self-transforming. This visual and aural image inspired Odysseus Elytis (1911-96), the "poet of the Aegean" and the 1979 Nobel laureate, whose verse celebrates the "luminous Aegean" archipelago, "interwoven with the wind, the waves, the pebbles, the stones and the vegetation of the islands" (Yiatromanolakis, "Aegean and Greek Literature" 446).

Portolans, or navigational charts of the Aegean, were developed when the Byzantine emperors granted trading privileges to navigators from other lands, including Venice, Genoa, and Pisa. Modeled on Byzantine prototypes and drawn on parchment in manuscript form, portolans (Fig. THREE-1.02) recorded the cumulative observations of the seamen who regularly traveled the intricate sea lanes of the region. Although assembled primarily for navigational use, they also had antiquarian and scientific interest and were acquired by the libraries of princes and the learned. Portolans augmented contemporary geographic knowledge and led eventually to the art of cartography. The two maps of the Aegean shown below (Fig. THREE-1.03, -1.04) are from the sixteenth and the nineteenth centuries, respectively, and represent an increasing sophistication in producing accurate cartographic representation, which eventually included the capacity to print multiple copies.

Beginning in the Renaissance, the term "archipelago" came to be identified with the area defined by the Aegean Sea. "Archipelago" derives ultimately from the combination of the Greek *arkhi* ("chief") with *pelagos* ("sea"), but its more immediate source in English is the Italian *arcipelago*. Etymologists have speculated that rather than coming directly from the Greek *arkhipelagos*, the Italian term itself might have been a corruption of *Aigaion Pelagos*, or the Greek "Aegean Sea." The term appears repeatedly on

Fig. THREE-1.02 [Antonio Millo],
the Aegean Sea, c. 1580-90

Fig. THREE-1.03 A. Ortelius,
"Hellas-Graecia, Sophiani," 1579

Fig. THREE-1.04 W. Smith,
map of the Aegean, 1843

portolans and early northern Italian marine charts to designate the area between the peninsula of Greece and the coast of Asia Minor (Fig.THREE-1.01). The Dutch cartographers whose work facilitated the trading privileges newly acquired from the Ottoman Empire by Dutch, French, and English traders also used the term "archipelago" on their seventeenth-century maps. Choiseul-Gouffier, the late-eighteenth-century French ambassador to the *Sublime Porte*, designated the Aegean Sea *Egiopelago ou Archipel*. But the maps the British Navy published in the nineteenth century are the earliest cartographically correct images of the region, nearly identical to those in use today.

Today the term "archipelago" has acquired a more generic usage and refers to any body of water abounding with islands or, more specifically, to any group of islands and interconnecting waters that form an intrinsic geographic and political entity. In this sense there are a number of archipelagos in the Mediterranean. Those with a relatively large number of islands are grouped around the Balkan Peninsula and include the Dalmatian coast islands and the Ionian Islands off the west coast of Greece. An enclosed archipelago, the Aegean Sea boasts the largest number of islands in the region within its shores, grouped into such distinctive clusters as the Cyclades and the Dodecanese. These groups of islands provide the focus for the chapters that follow. A distinguished European ecologist has best summed up the distinctive quality of the Aegean islands:

> There are archipelagos in the northern parts of the continent, too, but they are usually young areas, only recently liberated from ice and colonized by plants and animals, and their severe climate has discouraged exploitation by man. By contrast, the mild climate of the Greek archipelagos has for centuries favored man... . (Curry-Lindahl, *Europe* 84)

As an arm of the Mediterranean, the Aegean Sea can be seen as a bay with the mainland of Greece defining its western and northern edges and the Asia Minor Turkish coast delineating its eastern edge (Fig.THREE-1.05). To the south, a chain of islands -- from west to east, Kythera, Antikythera, Crete, Kasos, Karpathos, and Rhodes -- articulates entry to and from the larger body of the Mediterranean Sea. At its northeastern corner, the Aegean is connected by a water chain formed by the straits of the Dardanelles (the Hellespont), the Sea of Marmara (*Propontis*), and the Bosporus, which leads to the Black Sea (*Euxeinos Pontos*). This connection to the Black Sea has been historically important to the life, commerce, and culture of the Aegean islands. A meridian twenty-five degrees east of Greenwich runs through the

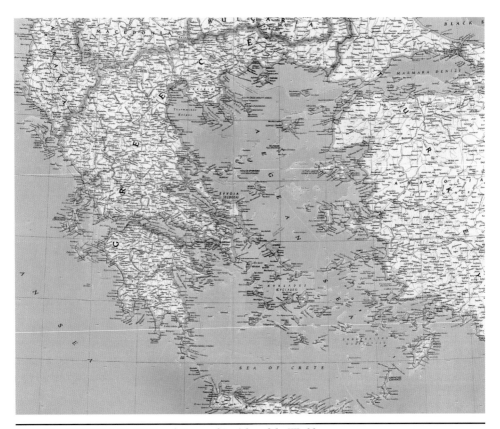

Fig. THREE-1.05 *National Geographic Atlas of the World,*
Greece and the Aegean, 1992

middle of the Aegean. Extended northward this meridian passes through downtown Helsinki, Finland; extended southward, it touches Johannesburg, South Africa.

Roughly four hundred miles from north to south (a distance comparable to that from New York City to Cape Hatteras in North Carolina) and two hundred miles at its widest, the Aegean contains some eighty-three thousand square miles of land and water. By comparison, the land area of Greece, including all of the islands, is about fifty-one thousand square miles, fifteen percent less than the total land area of the state of Florida.

Crete, the largest island in the region, boasts a number of mountain summits higher than two thousand meters. Mountains of 1,000 meters are not unusual and can be found on such islands as Andros (Fig.THREE-1.06) and Naxos in the Cyclades; Rhodes (Fig.THREE-1.07) and Karpathos in the Dodecanese; and Ikaria, Samos, and Chios in the northern Aegean. Sea

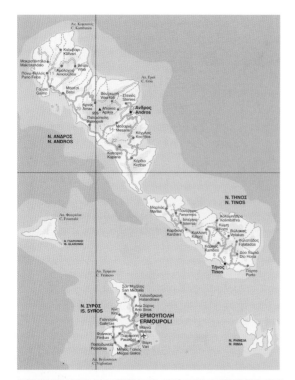

Fig. THREE-1.06 Andros

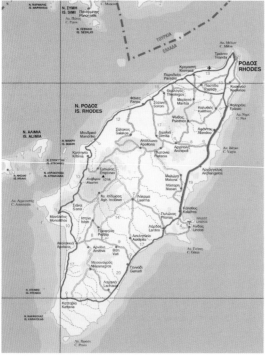

Fig. THREE-1.07 Rhodes

depths of 1,000 meters are frequent. Greater depths occur north of Crete, with the deepest perhaps thirty-five hundred meters.

A submerged block of the earth's crust forms the floor of the Aegean Sea. Folded rocks of limestone extending from the mountains of Greece to the mountains of Turkey mold submarine ridges. Traceable on the sea floor, these ridges provide the foundation of most of those Aegean islands that emerge on the surface as island chains. The chain of Kythera, Antikythera, Crete, Kasos, and Rhodes is one of the easiest to see on the map. Almost touching Attica and Evvoia, the Cyclades extend south and then eastward towards the promontories of Asia Minor (Fig.THREE-1.08, -1.09, -1.10, -1.11).

From early geological and historical times, volcanic activity has convulsed and remade the region. Santorini is an extreme and unique example of the effects of this volcanic activity and will be discussed at greater length in Chapter SEVEN.

The collapsed landmass that produced the Aegean Sea has also given us,

Fig. THREE-1.08 Poliegos,1994   Fig. THREE-1.09 Poliegos, 1994

Fig. THREE-1.10 Folegandros, 1994   Fig. THREE-1.11 Naxos, 2000

sui generis, the Aegean shoreline, which mediates between landscape and seascape and between the visible and invisible worlds that compose the Aegean archipelago (Fig.THREE-1.12, -1.13). Land and water meet in an extensive, undulating shoreline that meanders to yield bay after bay, inlet after inlet, beach after beach, and port after port, all geographic features on both sides of the shoreline that have supported a visible network of islands and towns and challenged the navigators of an invisible network of sea lanes. These two networks have historically facilitated the tasks of seamen who sailed in the archipelago and built the towns on the island heights and promontories that we see today.

No other area of the Mediterranean has a shoreline as extensive as the Aegean's in comparison to the size of the land it encloses. This unique ratio is essential to understanding the visual implications of the archipelagic landscape/seascape. A similar ratio of shoreline to enclosed land describes the larger surrounding region, that is, the continental shores that delineate the Aegean Sea as well as the islands within. The same is true of the peninsula of Greece, a medium-sized country that nevertheless accounts for approximately thirty-five percent of the total length of the Mediterranean shoreline. This thirty-five percent of shoreline translates into 17,000 kilometers, a surprising length, nearly one-half the 37,000-kilometer shoreline of the continent of Australia. Two-thirds of the length of the Greek shoreline is accounted for by that of islands; the Aegean archipelagic shorelines make up a major percentage of this figure (Fig.THREE-1.14, -1.15, -1.16, -1.17).

A naturally formed area of land that is surrounded by water and remains above water at high tide is the geographic and legal definition of an island. By this definition, numerous islands large and small, inhabited and uninhabited, emerge from the Aegean's waters, particularly in the Cyclades region, to form an intricate relationship between land and sea. The proximity of the islands to one another (Fig.THREE-1.18, 1.19) accentuates a relationship in which the sea clearly predominates and further defines the physically unique and visually inspiring character of the region.

Greece contains 9,835 islands and islets within its borders (Yiangakis 7). This figure includes islands in both the Ionian and the Aegean Seas, with a majority in the latter. Of these islands, 115 have year-round populations, ranging from fifty people to 100,000. With a population of 550,000, Crete is unique among the group. Of the 115 inhabited islands, eighty-three lie in Aegean waters and constitute such geographic and administrative groups as the Cyclades, the Dodecanese, the Northern Sporades, the islands of the Northern Aegean, and others.

Subtropical in climate, the islands experience hot, dry summers and mild, wet winters. Temperatures in the Cyclades complex can range from

Fig. THREE-1.12 Serifos, 1973   Fig. THREE-1.13 Serifos, 1973

Fig. THREE-1.14 Folegandros, 1994   Fig. THREE-1.15 Folegandros, 1994

Fig. THREE-1.16 Sifnos, 1994   Fig. THREE-1.17 Folegandros, 1994

| Fig. THREE-1.18 Naxos, from Paros, 1973 | Fig. THREE-1.19 Paros, from Naxos, 1969 |

the low forties (Fahrenheit) in the winter to the low nineties in the summer. Light afternoon breezes make for cooler nights even in the hottest summers. Rainfall is extremely rare in the summer and is heaviest in December and January. In its plant and animal life, the archipelago affords numerous examples of species isolation and adaptation to a space-limited environment.

The sun is almost ever-present throughout the region as high-contrast black-and-white and color photographs confirm, and Greece claims the largest number of cloudless days per year of any country in Europe. But it is the wind that has the greatest impact on Aegean life. The meltemi, an intense wind that blows from the northwest during the summer, usually in August, interrupts sea traffic and isolates the islands from one another and from the mainland, often for days at a time. Trees twisted into tortured shapes by the wind offer testimony to its force as well as its persistence (Fig.THREE-1.20, 1.21, 1.22, 1.23). Within the towns the narrow and irregular streets provide protection from these forceful winds and from the sun. The arrival of the afternoon breezes concludes siestas and commences the second half of the day.

In the days of sailing ships, the Aegean winds determined the maritime calendar. Mild weather in May began the season for trade, corso, or both; to avoid winter storms, the sailing season ended in late October. A historian of the region suggests a possible origin for the term "meltemi" and notes its role in producing the clarity of light characteristic of the archipelago:

In July and August the Etesian winds (called from the Greek *etos*, a year, because they were regular annually) blew from between northwest and northeast strong and steady, declining slightly at nightfall but picking up again shortly after sunrise and reaching their maximum in the early afternoon. It was then that the rowers at the galley benches could take their ease, while the Rhodian seamen hoisted the high-shouldered lateen sails and the galley plunged forward at top speed. Because this was the season of fair weather, *Bel Tempo*, the Etesians were also called *Beltemp* (later corrupted to *"Meltem,"* as they still are known). During the summer months, except for a little early morning mist, there were no fogs and visibility was usually crystal clear. The northerly winds broomed the atmosphere and produced that extraordinary clarity of Greek light which makes an object several miles distant as sharply defined as one a few cables away. (Bradford, *The Knights* 74-75)

Fig. THREE-1.20 Crete, 1997   Fig. THREE-1.21 Folegandros, 1994

Fig. THREE-1.22 Santorini,1995   Fig. THREE-1.23 Santorini,1995

Information on the population of the Aegean islands during the Tourkokratia period is limited at best and unreliable at worst. We can be certain, however, that the numbers were relatively small. Fortified towns protected populations probably numbering in the hundreds. The population of Kastro, the capital of the prosperous island of Sifnos, apparently did not exceed 3,000 people at any given time. A recent and authoritative study of the social structure and economy of the Koinotis of Serifos describes the population of the island as between 1,000 and 3,000 people between the sixteenth and the early nineteenth centuries, with a number of peaks as well as valleys (Liata 32). In 1770 at the beginning of its great adventure as a major Aegean naval power, the town of Hydra boasted 3,500 people.

Migratory movements, including Albanian colonization of the islands, helped to replenish populations devastated by war and piracy. Venetians and other Italians were absorbed during the existence of the Duchy of the Archipelago from the thirteenth to the sixteenth centuries, as family names from the Cyclades Islands confirm. Migration, often coerced, from one island to another readjusted the balance between natural resources and the numbers of inhabitants, as was apparently the case with the colonization of Antiparos in the fifteenth century (discussed in detail in Chapter FOUR). Available data indicate a periodic "internal Aegean diaspora" (Asdrahas 243), and turbulent times often resulted in population movements from Crete to the coast of Asia Minor.

Population figures from the Cyclades indicate stability between the census of 1861 -- the earliest reliable census taken by the new Greek state -- and that of 1891. The natural population increases of the nineteenth and early twentieth centuries were counterbalanced by precipitous declines after World War II, when young people pursued employment in the growing metropolitan area of Athens and in West Germany, Australia, and Canada. Exceptions to this general population decline include Mykonos, where an active international tourist industry has produced an eighty-two percent increase in year-round population, from 3,400 to 6,200 in the forty-year period between 1951 and 1991. By contrast, Paros, more than twice the size of Mykonos and an island with a great deal of agricultural activity and less dependence on tourism, has seen a modest six percent increase in population from 9,000 to 9,600 during the same forty-year period.

Farther from the Athenian metropolis than the Cyclades, the islands of the Dodecanese as a group registered an overall thirty-five percent increase, from 121,000 to 163,000 during the period from 1951 to 1991. Within the Dodecanese, however, smaller islands experienced population declines during that period, while such larger islands as Kos, Kalymnos, and Leros saw substantial population increases. Rhodes, the largest and most accessible island, blessed with attractive living conditions, tourism, and archaeological riches, has experienced a remarkable population increase of sixty-seven percent, from 59,000 to 98,000 during the same forty-year period from 1951 to 1991.

The island of Aegina in the Saronic Gulf, only a thirty-five minute hydrofoil ride from the port of Piraeus, is now virtually part of metropolitan Athens. Not surprisingly, then, its year-round population has increased by a third, from 8,800 to 11,600 during the period from 1951 to 1991. By comparison, Hydra, which is on the same hydrofoil line but is twice as far from Athens, has experienced a fifteen percent decline in year-round population from 2,800 to 2,400, despite its many tourist attractions, although the summer tourist season temporarily triples or quadruples this number.

Population shifts in the Aegean islands have also occurred in the larger context of a Greek internal migration that intensified after World War II, a phenomenon which renewed and increased the population in urban centers at the expense of the mountain villages and the smaller islands, and so, dramatically altered the physiognomy of the country.

| Fig. THREE-1.24 Folegandros, 1994 | Fig. THREE-1.25 Sikinos, 1994 |

Historically most of the islands possessed only "moderate agricultural wealth" (Asdrahas 242 and Fig.THREE-1.24,-1.25), prompting them to exchange agricultural as well as manufactured products and to provide services to one another in order to produce additional wealth. Sifnos, a relatively fertile island self-sufficient in cereals, also traditionally made cotton cloth that absorbed the cotton production of nearby islands. It exported honey, wax, onions, and sesame seeds, but also "drank wine imported from Melos" (Asdrahas 245). Santorini exchanged its wine for wood from Folegandros, but it lacked cereals and sent its ships to purchase them from Amorgos. Late-eighteenth-century customs records from Patmos illustrate the exchange of products among the islands: iron, cotton, onions, cheese, wine, and wax were exported by Samos; soap, hides, sponges, cotton, canvas, and salt, by Symi; olive oil, by Crete and Mykonos; rafters and planks, from Kastellorizo, and so the list goes on.

"Some islands specialized in one main activity," writes Asdrahas (247). The focus on sponge diving on Kalymnos, Symi, Chalki, and Kastellorizo is an example. The men of Melos were known as the best pilots, and those of Symi, as the best divers; both were much sought-after for the recovery of sunken ships. The ship-owners of Mykonos took building timber from

Fig. THREE-1.26 Mykonos, 1991   Fig. THREE-1.27 Tenos, 1986   Fig. THREE-1.28 Sifnos, 2000

Mount Athos to Alexandria, and on their way back, carried coffee and rice to sell not only in the islands but also on the mainland.

These exchanges enhanced the interdependence of the islands. The Aegean archipelagic environment, with its visible islands and invisible network of sea lanes, led each island to focus on its own resources, on the one hand, and allowed all to share products, attitudes, and traditions, on the other. In this context, one can admire the unity of a shared vernacular architecture and, at the same time, appreciate the uniqueness of each island, as expressed in the handrails of Mykonos (Fig.THREE-1.26), the dovecotes of Tenos (Fig.THREE-1.27), or the bell towers of Sifnos (Fig.THREE-1.28).

In Chapter ONE the Mediterranean Sea was referred to as "a vast botanical garden enclosing a salt water lake" (Carrington 197). Olive trees and grape vines have a primacy in this garden (Fig.THREE-1.29, -1.30, -1.31, -1.32) and their products, olive oil and wine, have historically done much to sustain life in the Aegean archipelago.

In *The Metamorphosis of Greece since World War II*, the historian William H. McNeill incisively discusses land cultivation in a country which empha-

Fig. THREE-1.29 Peloponnesos,
grapevines, 1998

Fig. THREE-1.30 Ithaki,
olive trees, 1997

Fig. THREE-1.31 Crete,
grapevines, 1982

Fig. THREE-1.32 Ithaki,
olive trees, 1997

sizes specialized crops such as olive oil and wine, both of which have helped to make market behavior prominent in Greek life. In his second chapter, entitled "An Ecological History of Greek Society to 1941," McNeill explains why farming for the market played such a large role in Greece:

> The basic fact was that specialized crops brought a bigger return from a given amount of land than could be secured by raising only items for domestic consumption. The reasons for this are both geographic and economic. The two principal commodities Greeks raised for sale at a distance were olive oil and wine. Olives and vines both require long hot summers for maturation; and olive trees cannot withstand prolonged temperatures below freezing in winter. Hence there is a geographic boundary beyond which olive oil cannot be produced – a boundary that does not include all of the present Greek state by any means, but only those (mainly coastal) regions where winter temperatures are mild enough to allow olive trees to flourish. Grape vines are hardier, but only some soils and climates produce a wine good enough to sell at a price that makes vineyards more profitable than grain fields. Hence the limits upon wine production were always more economic than climatic, though the regions where vineyards can produce a commercially profitable wine are climatically defined.
>
> Both to the north, around the western and northern shores of the Black Sea, and to the south, in Egypt, lie grain-rich lands where olives will not grow and where vines cannot produce wine like the best that comes from the Aegean basin. Since these regions are connected with the Aegean coastlands by sea, ships can easily carry wine and oil in one direction and grain in the other; and the cost of such transport is small in proportion to the value of the goods in question. Obviously, for such currents of trade to flourish, someone must produce and be willing to part with a large amount of grain. This has usually meant that local landlords, having discovered the delights of wine and the manifold uses of oil as food, unguent, and fuel for lamps, somehow compelled humbler members of society to raise more grain than they needed for their own support. Such landlords then took possession of the surplus grain and proceeded to exchange it for oil and wine. Once such a current of exchange had become established, other commodities could be swept into the trade net; and the geographic range of profitable exchanges might ramify very widely indeed, east-west as well as north-south. But the fundamental pattern was defined by a north-south axis, allowing oil and wine to

be exchanged for grain across climatically defined frontiers.

Terms of trade across this climatic boundary persistently favored the oil and wine producers. After all, grain could be raised in the Aegean regions; olive oil and good wine could not be produced in the regions with which the Greeks traded. Hence bargaining advantages tended to rest with the Greeks. In addition, production of wine and oil required a wait of several years between the time the vines or trees were planted and the coming in of the first harvest. Such a capital cost was heavy indeed for small producers, and, to make such sacrifice bearable, the price pattern had to favor the man who had waited several years without return. The further fact that both wine and oil carry well, and can be stored for years in jars or barrels without spoilage, also gave those who sold these two commodities a market advantage against dealers in grains whose stock in trade was intrinsically a wasting asset. Rats, mice, insects, and fungi were in perpetual competition with men as grain consumers; and their ingenuity in securing access to human grain-stores repeatedly overcame the obstacles men were able to put in their paths. Hence grain dealers were ordinarily under pressure to sell before losses from spoilage became too great, while wine and oil dealers could afford to wait indefinitely until the price was right. These simple facts assured Aegean wine and oil producers of a persistent advantage in terms of trade. A plot of land put into olives or vines could usually produce a quantity of oil or wine exchangeable for more grain than could have been raised on that same piece of land--quite a lot more grain. Dense rural populations, living on relatively small plots of land--as little as three or four acres per family was often adequate to keep body and soul together--thus became possible in the parts of the Aegean coastlands where olives and vines flourished best.

The resulting pattern of rural life allowed for abundant leisure. Even with traditional methods of cultivation and harvesting, in which human muscles did all the work, there were many weeks of the year when no useful tasks could be performed in the fields. This was the time devoted to talk about public affairs in ancient times. In ages when direct participation in political decision-making was not permitted to mere peasants, Greek cultivators still used these times of leisure for talk. Conversation, poetry, and speech-making consequently remained highly developed arts among men of Hellenic speech, rural and urban alike.

It is useful, perhaps, to think of wine- and oil-exporting villages as semi-urban communities. The villagers were like townsfolk in depending on imported grain at least for a part of their year's food; and they were like townsfolk in enjoying favorable terms of trade because both offered commodities in comparatively short supply. Finally, these villagers were also like townsfolk in depending on the availability of surplus grain in some distant place... .Yet in olive and vine regions, landlords did not monopolize marketing functions. Even when the rental basis was sharecropping, the cultivator had to go to market with his share of the harvest, for only by so doing could he hope to have access to the grain (and other things) needed to support his family through the year. Grain farmers, by contrast, when landlords and tax collectors had skimmed off their share, had enough left over to feed themselves throughout the year. They therefore had little need to enter the market, save for the occasional purchase of a tool or some other extraordinary object. The Greek wine and oil producer, on the other hand, had to buy and sell to live at all. Hence the great importance of market skills and the centrality of commercial calculations in traditional Greek rural behavior. (McNeill 31-35)

Developments in the Aegean islands for the last several hundred years are more easily understood in light of McNeill's analysis. Extensive and undulating island shorelines provided ample space for the long summer maturation required by olives and vines. The central location of the Aegean traders and the traditional north-south, Black Sea/Egypt pattern of trading olive oil and wine for grain became important again as the eighteenth-century sea trade of the Ottoman Empire passed into Aegean hands. The captains of Hydra were following the same geographic pattern when they broke the British blockade of Western European ports during the Napoleonic Wars, an enterprise whose consequences for the vernacular architectural forms of Hydra will be discussed in Chapter SIX. Last but not least, the cultivation of olive trees and grape vines continued to allow the "abundant leisure time" McNeill mentions, even as the defense needs of post-Byzantine times induced high-density building and living. Leisure time away from the fields in a high-density, relatively urban environment continued to promote McNeill's "conversation, poetry, and speech-making...[as] highly developed arts among men of Hellenic speech," practices still easily observed today in the daily life of the Aegean island towns.

Historically, sea lanes rather than land paths have provided inexpensive and relatively safe transportation within the Hellenic world. The passenger-car ferries, hydrofoils, and catamarans of recent decades have altered the nature of travel, opening up the Aegean islands to local and international tourism, which, in turn, has radically transformed the islands' economies as well as their towns. Some islands have been affected more than others. Distance by sea from the Athens-Piraeus metropolitan complex has played an additional role in the intrusion of tourism into the islands. Some of the more distant islands, which in the past served as places of political exile, have been spared the consequences of rapid development, but, as a result, have suffered heavy population losses. More recently, airstrips and airports built on land formerly reserved for cultivation have made some islands more accessible. Airstrips on Melos, Astypalaia, Skyros, Santorini, and other islands have shortened travel time from Athens considerably. Crete, Rhodes, Mykonos, Skiathos, and several of the other islands feature international airports with their own connections to major European cities, which have begun to render these islands independent of Athens. And helipads for emergency medical evacuation serve almost every inhabited island as part of an extensive national health care system.

Most islands feature more than one high point with an easily detectable whitewashed building at the summit; reaching the top, however, can be difficult. A hike to the summit demands a start very early in the morning, particularly during the hot and dry summer months (Fig.THREE-1.33, -1.34). An hour or two of sharp climbing in treeless terrain covered by the typically Mediterranean *macchia* -- that is, shrubs and evergreen bushes -- on donkey trails and occasionally on cobbled paths ends in a revealing, uplifting, and rewarding experience, acoustically, spatially, and visually.

Fig. THREE-1.33 Sifnos, 1986   Fig. THREE-1.34 Sifnos, 1986

The islands' summits are almost always windy. The massive whitewashed masonry structure of a deserted monastery can provide much-needed protection from the wind, particularly when it reaches buffeting force (Fig.THREE-1.35, -1.36). The wind also carries the sounds of people, animals, and machines to the summits, but electricity, available for the last four decades in all the islands, has deprived the scene of the once vital and characteristic sound of windmills.

Reaching the summit yields an arresting view of the island -- its periphery, its ridges and valleys, its size and scale, and its distance from other islands. The relationship between settlement and port where there is only

Fig. THREE-1.35 Sifnos,
Profitis Elias, 1986

Fig. THREE-1.36 Sifnos,
Profitis Elias, 1986

one settlement on an island becomes clearer from a bird's eye perspective, as does the intimate interdependence between a settlement and its site. Summits also offer commanding views of the seas encircling an island, and in the past, allowed islanders to alert the guardians of their settlement gates to heighten their defenses when unfamiliar ships were sighted (Fig.THREE-1.37, -1.38, -1.39, -1.40, -1.41, -1.42).

Breathtaking views of an island's rugged scenery are also revealed from its summit. Rocky segments of coast alternate with short, sandy beaches in a continuous undulation of bays and promontories. Exposed craggy ridges and bare hills contain occasional green patches and valleys in a terrain crisscrossed by endless terraced fields -- testimony to the labor of countless generations of islanders attempting to extract sustenance from an unyielding land.

The view from a summit also yields a comprehensive understanding of island topography as it relates to human habitation. Viewed from sea level, a typical 550-foot island hill (Fig.THREE-1.43) can be visualized as a diagram (Fig.THREE-1.44) that roughly divides the hill into four zones of possible land use.

Fig. THREE-1.37 Sifnos, 1986   Fig. THREE1.38 Sifnos, 1986

Fig. THREE-1.39 Sifnos, 1986   Fig. THREE-1.40 Sifnos, 1986

Fig. THREE-1.41 Sifnos, 1986   Fig. THREE-1.42 Sifnos, 1986

The lowest of the four zones, ZONE 1, includes most of the agriculturally productive land and access to the sea and fishing. Oleander bushes, prickly pears, and agave plants -- the last two, imports to the Mediterranean from the New World -- often form rough hedges that discourage trespassing and provide a border for this zone (Fig.THREE-1.45, -1.46, -1.47, -1.48).

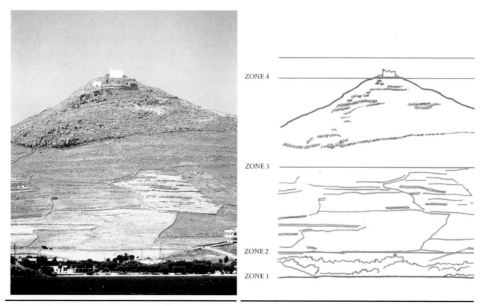

| Fig. THREE-1.43 Paros, 1973 | Fig. THREE-1.44 Paros, diagram |

The next layer of land, ZONE 2, is green and full of wild flowers in the spring, burnt brown in the summer (Fig.THREE-1.49, -1.50), and divided into odd shapes by dry stone walls that delineate property and enclose grazing areas for mules, donkeys, and goats. Property walls also flank tight mule

| Fig. THREE-1.45 Aegina, prickly pears, 1997 | Fig. THREE-1.46 Spetses, oleander, 1991 |

Fig. THREE-1.47 Paros, donkeys, 1973

Fig. THREE-1.48 Paros, agave, 1973

tracks forming networks of paths still in use on most of the islands (Fig.THREE-1.51, -1.52). Although Toyotas in abundant numbers have by and large replaced mules and donkeys on the paved roads, the animals still serve faithfully on stepped paths and uneven tracks and in narrow passages (Fig.THREE-1.53). Goats are ever-present in the island landscape. Although useful animals in many ways, their grazing habits have proved catastrophic to the land (Fig.THREE-1.54), and some argue that where goats have been banished, the effect has been salutary. In Ayion Oros, a monastic community on a peninsula jutting into the northern Aegean, the monastic rules have forbidden the presence of females of any kind, including goats, for mil-

Fig. THREE-1.49 Astypalaia, spring, 1970

Fig. THREE-1.50 Astypalaia, summer, 1971

Fig. THREE-1.51 Kythnos, 1973

Fig. THREE-1.52 Kythnos, 1973

Fig. THREE-1.53 Folegandros, 1994

Fig. THREE-1.54 Kythnos, 1973

Fig. THREE-1.55 Crete, 1997

Fig. THREE-1.56 Crete, 1997

lennia. "The result is an environment of equilibrium, with a richer wild vegetation than anywhere else in Greece" (Curry-Lindahl 89).

ZONE 3 is a no-man's-land. Rocky, unproductive, and of no apparent use, this land is either barren or covered with the shrubs and evergreen bushes typical of Mediterranean macchia vegetation in areas where, many centuries ago, deciduous forests flourished (Fig.THREE-1.55, -1.56).

The fourth and highest layer in the diagram, ZONE 4, is furthest from daily use and visitation and is dedicated to spiritual, religious, and annual feast day celebrations. Occasionally a monastery or a nunnery but more

Fig. THREE-1.57 Ios, 1973

Fig. THREE-1.58 Melos, 1988

often a one-room chapel, a whitewashed building at the top (Fig.THREE-1.57, -1.58) is generally dedicated to the Prophet Elias (a replacement for the Helios of antiquity with his four-horse chariot), who was traditionally thought to emerge over the mountain peaks to initiate the new day. On his feast day, July 20, islanders flock to the mountaintop to honor him as the patron saint of rain, thunder, and lightning, and, thereby, to celebrate centuries of cultural continuity.

FOUR

▷ ◁

COLLECTIVE FORTIFICATION: KASTRO

▷ ◁

As larger islands with fortified cities, Crete and Rhodes played pivotal roles in the perennial wars between the Venetians and the Knights Hospitaller, the Latin Christians, on the one hand, and the Ottoman Turks, on the other. The massive and sophisticated fortifications in the cities of Rhodes and Candia (present-day Irakleion) indicate the scale of sixteenth- and seventeenth-century warfare in the region and the immense human and material resources invested by besiegers and defenders alike.

The smaller islands suffered the ravages of war as well, but seldom were major resources invested in protecting or conquering their towns. Defenses were based on locally available means, however limited, and had also to address the small-scale threat of a raid by a single ship or by two corsairs joining forces. And the towns had to be defended from assaults originating in rivalries among the local lords and the warfare that resulted from such assaults. An incident in Skaros on the island of Santorini from the late fifteenth century illustrates the point. The lordship of Skaros had become a matter of dispute between two Venetian families, the Pisani and the Crispi. The latter illegally entered and occupied the town:

> But when [the Pisani] emissaries arrived at Santorini, they found that John III had strengthened the defenses of Skaros, and were compelled to retire ignominiously under a heavy shower of stones. (Miller, *The Latins* 614)

Detached, freestanding fortification walls were beyond a small island's resources. An ingenious and alternate building configuration was adopted instead that rendered expensive detached fortifications unnecessary: individual houses were assembled with shared walls to produce a continuous and solid defense perimeter penetrated by a limited number of controlled gates. Inside the enclosure, narrow paths led to individual houses, public places, and other buildings. For all practical purposes, a small town thus became a collective fortification, a compact monolithic structure much like an extended single building. Depending on the topography of a particular site, a free-flowing or a geometric periphery outlined the town. The site and its specific topographical features emerge thereby as extremely important elements in the defense of a small Aegean island town.

4.1 Site, Serifos

Fig. FOUR-1.01 Sifnos, 1973

Serifos, a relatively small island in the Cyclades complex, measures thirty-seven square kilometers and was home to 1,095 people, according to the 1991 census. The size and resources of the island have traditionally supported one town also called Serifos but often called Chora, a common practice in the region. Located on the south side of the island, the town provides a first-rate example of how important site features could be used to enhance the defenses of a small Aegean town (Fig. FOUR-1.01).

Built on a 200-meter-high hill, the contemporary town, parts of which apparently date from the era of the Duchy of the Archipelago, commands a view of the bay of Livadi below and of a wide sweep of the sea from east to west. Within this sweep, the northern tip of Sifnos, southeast of Serifos at a distance of eight miles, is easily visible. Antiparos, thirty miles to the east, and Kimolos, twenty-five miles to the south, are also within sight.

Building the town on a 200-meter-high hill within sight of passing sailing ships was a necessity. Historians have pointed out that during the years of piracy, "coastal villages were razed, and those inhabitants who escaped moved either to more secure villages in the interior or to larger islands" (Vacalopoulos, *The Greek Nation* 71). The island of Serifos had little interior, and the islanders were forced to adopt an alternative-- to stay on the island and build their town on the site most easily defended, a hilltop.

Given the excellent visibility characteristic of the Aegean, any corsair intent on assaulting Serifos would have been likely to be observed from its heights. Early detection provided precious warning to the islanders and perhaps discouraged attackers who would have been aware that they had been spotted. Had a corsair band nonetheless landed in Livadi, the villagers' ability to observe their movements on land from the heights would still have been a major advantage to the defenders. While the attackers expended considerable energy marching uphill, the defenders would have met them, rested, at the top of their defensive walls and from behind their secured gates.

Observing sea approaches from high ground remained crucial to survival throughout the turbulent centuries of piracy and well into the early nineteenth century. As a result, an extensive network of observation points was built throughout the Aegean archipelago, either located within towns as at Serifos, or built as freestanding structures above settlements as on Mount Ere on the island of Hydra (see Chapter SIX). Called *vigla* (from the Latin *vigilare*, or "keep awake, watch"), Aegean observation structures appear in Buondelmonti's fifteenth-century island maps. Smoke and fire from a vigla also served to communicate between islands, thus serving the shared defensive needs of the archipelagic community as a whole.

No ship in the Aegean Sea can remain out of sight of land for long given the proximity of the islands, particularly within the Cyclades and the Dodecanese groups. The heights of Serifos and similar Aegean observation points thus constituted a vital information-gathering network recording inter-island and long-distance sailing ship traffic, at first for defense, but later for commercial purposes. Of course, observation points could also be used for more sinister purposes. Corsairs could use them to send word of approaching victims to their ships lurking in the bay below, as the memoirs of a seventeenth-century English prisoner indicate happened more than once on the trade route between Alexandria and Constantinople during his captivity. Last but not least, in more lawful times observation points also served joyous social purposes, as when watchmen spotting an island-owned vessel returning from a long commercial voyage would rush to the town below to bring the good news to the families of the captain and the crew hours before the ship's arrival in port.

The collective fortifications created by building houses attached to one another produced a continuous, solid, and hard-to-penetrate defense perimeter. Every Aegean town that survived the days when pirates menaced the archipelago used this collective fortification system at least in part but adapted it to its particular   physical and political circumstances. Some of these adaptations have survived in better shape than others. Some have been abandoned. Antiparos and Sifnos are still inhabited, and despite removals, additions, and alterations, the provenance of the original collective fortification of each can easily be traced and recorded. Astypalaia has been deserted since World War II in favor of a new town built below its single, original edifice, a new town on which construction had been begun perhaps as early as the middle of the eighteenth century. Kimolos is currently in the final stages of abandonment. Both structures, the old Astypalaia and Kimolos, are disintegrating fast. Skiathos and Skaros in Santorini were abandoned in the nineteenth century in the decades after piracy disappeared from the archipelago. We know their remarkable sites and can make good guesses about their specific vernacular forms. The following pages examine in detail all six towns as well as Patmos, where the Monastery of Saint John the Theologian served as the dominant fortification. This examination should provide a better understanding of the collective fortification principle under which these towns were built as well as of the particular site and geopolitical conditions to which this ingenious building system was adapted in these seven cases.

4.2 Antiparos

Kastro, derived from the Latin *castrum*, is Greek for "castle" or "fortress." In the Aegean, the term was used mostly but not exclusively in the Cyclades complex of islands. There, it identified a collective fortification or a fortified

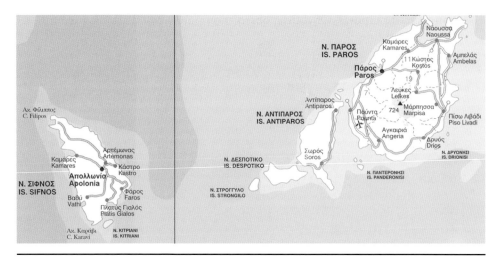

Fig. FOUR-2.01 Sifnos and Antiparos

place such as the residence of the local Latin lord during the Duchy of the Archipelago period and, by implication, referred to the capital or main town of the island. *Chora*, which means "place," is another term for a principal town, a term that is still in use. Often a Chora has grown around a Kastro, as happened in Antiparos and in Astypalaia.

Antiparos is the largest of a group of islands clustered near the southwest coast of the much bigger Paros and has a surface area of thirty-five square kilometers and a high point of 300 meters (Fig. FOUR-2.01). Despite the absence of a tourist industry, Antiparos has defied the regional trend of the last several decades by retaining and even increasing its population to 800 people, according to the 1991 census. The earliest records of Antiparos as a fief within the feudal structure of the Duchy of the Archipelago date from the late-fourteenth century. Cristoforo Buondelmonti, the Florentine monk mentioned in Chapter TWO, refers to Antiparos in the early decades of the fifthteenth century as a deserted island.

The Antiparos Kastro was built between 1440 and 1446 (Phillipa-Apostolou, *To Kastro tes Antiparou* 14), when the island was granted as a fief to Giovanni Loredano on his marriage to Maria Sommaripa, the daughter of a family prominent in the duchy. His marriage brought Loredano to the duchy:

> ...thus a great Venetian family obtained a footing in the Cyclades. This infusion of new blood was of great benefit to the island, which had long been uninhabited: for the energetic Venetian repopulated

it with new colonists, and built and resided in the castle, whose gateway, now fallen, still preserved, in the eighteenth century, his coat of arms." (Miller, *The Latins* 605)

The castle was built as a protected residence for the colonists. Apparently from islands nearby, these colonists were to introduce olive tree cultivation to Antiparos to enhance the value of the Loredano fief. This simultaneous colonization and fortification took place as the politically and militarily fragmented Aegean archipelago was once more in the process of violent transformation. The Ottoman Turks, steadily advancing across the Balkan Peninsula, were to breach the walls of a depopulated Constantinople in 1453 and to reach Athens in 1460. The Turkish pirates, newcomers to the Aegean, had begun to raid the islands. The Duchy of the Archipelago was to cede more and more of its independence in exchange for Venetian protection. And the Knights Hospitaller of Saint John were to continue to defend Rhodes from the Turks until the knights' defeat in the siege of 1522.

Today, the town of Antiparos (the only town on the island) is flanked by two bays and located on flat ground forty meters above sea level near the northern tip of the island. Located on the east bay, the town port faces a shallow strait separating Antiparos from Paros. On the west side, the bay opens up to the larger Aegean Sea. Since the island of Sifnos and its medieval capital of Kastro are visible about fifteen miles away (Fig. FOUR-2.02), broad strategic thinking about the defense needs of the duchy as a whole probably influenced the choice of the site for the Antiparos Kastro. Although concealed by twentieth-century buildings on all four sides, the fifteenth-century Antiparos Kastro is still an inhabited part of a very much alive twenty-first-century town (Fig. FOUR-2.03).

In the dry and often parched landscape of the Aegean, access to water was a sine qua non, particularly for those within a defense enclosure. The location of the Antiparos Kastro building was certain to have been influenced by the need for water, and, indeed, an old filled-up well has been located inside the Kastro, and a contemporary well, drilled within the perimeter of the fortified enclosure, provides water for the present community.

The flat site of the Antiparos Kastro made possible the application of the concept of collective fortification within the perimeter of a perfectly square building. Each side measures 176 feet. The enclosure contains twenty-four one-level units of habitation on each of the two upper floors. The top floor on the west side is missing with no indication of why or when it was removed. The length of each unit runs parallel to the external wall and varies from eighteen to thirty-six feet. Party walls eighteen feet in length sep-

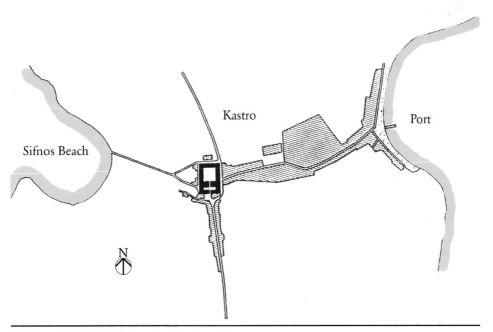

Fig. FOUR-2.02 Antiparos, site plan

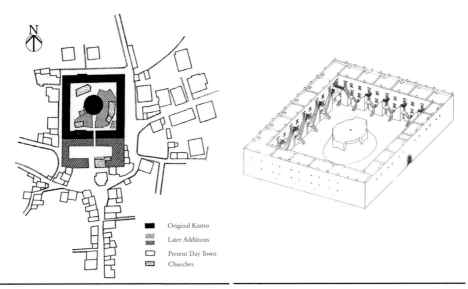

Original Kastro
Later Additions
Present Day Town
Churches

Fig. FOUR-2.03 Antiparos, Kastro

Fig. FOUR-2.04 Antiparos, Kastro, axonometric drawing of original building

arate the units. Access to the units is from the internal court, up massive stone steps to the lower habitable floor and lighter wooden stairs to the upper floor. In the original building, the external masonry perimeter wall -- between five and six feet thick -- was pierced by openings whose limited number and restricted dimensions are reminders of its original defensive purpose (Fig. FOUR-2.04, -2.05). Alterations made in the last one hundred fifty years or so to the west, north, and east walls of the original building have resulted in a proliferation of larger openings -- balconies, loggias, doors, and windows -- in these walls. Despite their incompatibility with the original concept of collective fortification, these alterations have not harmed the visual integrity of the massive external wall, which retains a surprisingly commanding presence. A gate on the south wall, shut during the night and opened in the morning, originally controlled access to the com-

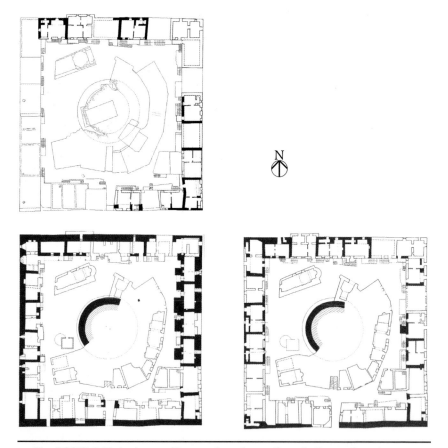

Fig. FOUR-2.05 Antiparos, Kastro, plans, lower floor (left), top floor (upper left). The black walls are part of the original building.

Fig. FOUR-2.06 Antiparos, Kastro, courtyard elevation drawing, looking north

Fig. FOUR-2.07 Antiparos, Kastro, courtyard views, looking north, 1993

plex, but this practice had been abandoned by 1882, according to J. Theodore Bent, who visited Antiparos that year. Today, that gate survives as a frame and a passage and continues to provide access to the central court (Fig. FOUR-2.06, -2.07) and to a good number of the units, as intended in the fifteenth-century plan (Fig. FOUR- 2.08, -2.09, -2.10, -2.11). However, remodeling has often prompted an abandonment of the original plan by providing unit access directly from the surrounding streets (Fig. FOUR-2.12, -2.13, -2.14).

In the geometric center of the courtyard, rising eighteen feet above the ground, there is a building with a round foundation with a diameter of sixty feet. No information about the building or its purpose has survived, although the structure may have extended above the flat roofs of the enclosure to support either a residence for the local feudal lord or a keep, a stronghold for observation and last-resort defense. French and Italian defense examples that might have found their way to Antiparos by way of its Venetian overlords and the stronghold towers of the nearby Ayion Oros monasteries might have served as the prototypes for such a structure. But this round-based building erected at the same time as the square enclosure was clearly meant to enhance the defenses of the Kastro.

Imported design ideas and construction techniques were used in building the Antiparos Kastro, but the building materials were local. A combination of natural and cut stone was used to produce the massive external walls. Corners were built with large blocks of marble cut in ways that suggest that

Fig. FOUR-2.08 Antiparos, Kastro, internal courtyard, 1993

Fig. FOUR-2.09 Antiparos, Kastro, internal courtyard, 1993

Fig. FOUR-2.10 Antiparos, Kastro, gate looking north,1993

Fig. FOUR-2.11 Antiparos, Kastro, internal courtyard, 1993

Fig. FOUR-2.12 Antiparos, Kastro, exterior walls,1993

Fig. FOUR-2.13 Antiparos, Kastro, exterior walls,1993

Fig. FOUR-2.14 Antiparos, Kastro, exterior walls,1993

they were recycled from an older building, although there is no evidence that such a building existed on Antiparos. On nearby Paros, however, a great number of marble building blocks from antique Greek temples were recycled to erect the thirteenth-century fortifications (Fig.EIGHT-1.09). Considering the proximity of the two islands, the recycled marble blocks found in the external defense wall of the Antiparos Kastro may well have originated on Paros.

Roughly shaped wood beams, closely spaced, span the distance between the bearing walls. A local species of tree – the *fithes*, a member of the juniper family -- is the source of this rather poor-quality building material, which compensates for its irregular shape by being surprisingly durable.

Together with the Metropolis church built in 1603, the houses attached to the south side of the original Kastro constitute the first expansion of the original collective fortification. This expansion, which suggests a population increase, occurred several decades after the devastating Barbarossa raids of 1537 and the establishment of Ottoman rule in most of the Aegean islands after 1580. The additions increased the capacity of the expanded Kastro to about one hundred dwelling units. Assuming an average of four to five persons per family and, thus, per dwelling unit, the Kastro could now accommodate four to five hundred inhabitants, and, indeed, travelers to Antiparos from the fifteenth to the mid-nineteenth century record populations ranging from two to six hundred.

The newer dwelling units do not adhere to the discipline of the original fifteenth-century edifice. But since they are attached to the south wall and built as extensions of the east and west external walls, they attest to a continued need to protect the inhabitants and, by inference, suggest the continuing threat of piracy. At this time, entry to the enlarged complex was relocated southward, on the axis of the old gate. The cul-de-sacs on the right and left of this axis, which echo the central space of the original building, reinforce the likelihood that this early-seventeenth-century addition, despite its somewhat awkward attachment to the disciplined geometry of the original edifice, remained focused on defense.

Chapels and other buildings were added within the perimeter of the original edifice later. Two chapels are part of a string of single rooms arranged in a curvilinear manner around the south and east sides of the round-based central tower -- probably destroyed during the Ottoman conquest, its demise signaling a change in the overlordship of Antiparos, as in that of the Aegean archipelago generally. A third chapel, also dating from the seventeenth century and called the chapel of Christos, stands free of the larger structure at the northwest corner of the inner court of the original edi-

| Fig. FOUR-2.15 Antiparos, Kastro, internal courtyard, 1993 | Fig. FOUR-2.16 Antiparos, Kastro, internal courtyard, Lion of Venice, 1993 |

fice (Fig. FOUR-2.05, -2.07). On the domestic scale typical of the Aegean islands, this barrel-vault-and-dome-covered chapel asserts its place in a difficult location with gentleness and conviction. Its west wall makes a masterful and sophisticated architectural concession -- rare in such a chapel's geometry -- to its powerful and immediate neighbor. Its genial presence introduces an additional architectural scaling element that helps to register the magnitude of the complex. Together with the two other chapels, it also celebrates the reemergence of the occupants' Greek Orthodox faith in the era following the downfall of the island's Venetian Roman Catholic overlords.

A detailed and insightful study of the fifteenth-century Antiparos Kastro by Philippa-Apostolou (1978) demonstrates convincingly that a grid was used in the design and construction of this exceptional example of Aegean vernacular architecture. This grid was based on the *passo*, a Venetian unit of measurement equal to five feet eight inches, or 1.78 meters. Controlled by this grid, such dimensions as the thicknesses of the walls, the heights of the doors, the dimensions of the rooms, the lengths of the external walls, and so on are all multiples of the Venetian *passo*. Like most other architectural units of measurement, the passo was inspired by human scale and is similar to the *modulor* (six feet), a much-debated unit of architectural measurement proposed in the 1940s by the French-Swiss architect Le Corbusier (Charles-Edouard Jeanneret).

The presence of a grid strengthens the argument that the Kastro was conceived and built as a single building rather than in stages to realize the colonization and fortification plans of Giovanni Loredano, the Venetian holder of the fief of Antiparos. The use of the grid also demonstrates the ability of the vernacular architecture builders of the Aegean islands to absorb new building techniques imported from elsewhere.

The seventeenth-century additions to the fifteenth-century edifice, along with more recent additions and the continuous tenancy of the Kastro even today, demonstrate that Antiparos is a living organism, constantly recycling architectural elements and redesigning spaces and, in its daily dynamism, keeping its precious heritage alive rather than reducing it to another museum.

4.3 Sifnos

Located on the east coast of the island of Sifnos (Fig. FOUR-2.01), the Sifnos Kastro crowns a dome-like hill that stands 250 feet above sea level (Fig. FOUR-3.01). Forming a peninsula jutting out of the landmass of the island (Fig. FOUR-3.02), the north and east sides of the hill rise precipitously from the sea, which on the south side forms a small bay called Seralia. Buondelmonti uses the name to identify the bay on his fifteenth-century map of Sifnos. The most vulnerable side of the hilltop settlement was the western side where, in the past, footpaths led to its guarded gates. Today, those same gates continue to defend the Kastro by keeping vehicular intruders out (Fig. FOUR-3.03).

The natural features of the site as well as its commanding views of the sea have invited occupancy and fortification throughout Aegean history. Indeed, the northern and highest sector of the Kastro contains the remnants of an ancient Greek acropolis first excavated by the British School of Athens in the 1930s.

In the early thirteenth century, Sifnos became part of Marco Sanudo's Duchy of the Archipelago. With many other islands, it reverted to Greek hands when Licario, an Italian admiral in the service of the emperor, restored Byzantine rule in the area during the later part of the century. Nearly one hundred years later and two years before the Knights of Saint John installed themselves on Rhodes in 1309, Januli da Corogna, an adventurer

Fig. FOUR-3.01 Sifnos, Kastro, 1985

Fig. FOUR-3.02 Sifnos, Kastro and central island settlements, 1973

of Spanish origin who belonged to the knights, seized Sifnos, renounced his allegiance to the Order, and declared himself an independent sovereign. His seizure initiated a period of more than three hundred years of Latin rule on the island, which passed by marriage from the da Corogna to the Gozzadini family, who were eventually dethroned by the Turks in 1617. The main features of the architecture of the Kastro we see today date from the three-hundred-year period of Latin rule.

The building components of the Antiparos Kastro were assembled on a flat and virgin site as a single building erected in one stage. Both the site and the single-stage process allowed a rectangular, geometric defense perimeter

Fig. FOUR-3.03 Sifnos, Kastro, 1985. Note the cars parked outside the settlement.

to emerge. Similar building components were assembled on the same collective fortification system in the Sifnos Kastro to produce a continuous defense perimeter. But Sifnos's hilltop site and its previous occupancy resulted in a non-geometric, free-form perimeter built in more than one stage. Although both were built to the characteristically compact scale of Aegean vernacular architecture, the fortifications differ in size. The original structure of the Antiparos Kastro occupies an area 175 feet square, or 31,000 square feet in total, while the elongated final plan of the Sifnos Kastro, with its long axis running from northwest to southeast, measures 230 x 780 feet, or 180,000 square feet (Fig. FOUR-3.04).

The Sifnos Kastro seems to have been built in four distinct stages each of which enlarged the defense perimeter (Philippa-Apostolou, *To Kastro tes Sifnou.*). The *Mesa Kastro* (or "inner fortification," a term still in use by the inhabitants) at the north end of the settlement (Fig. FOUR-3.04, area A; –3.05) encloses the fourteenth-century structures of the early da Corogna rule, which were built on top of the ancient acropolis, a quarry with enough high-quality building material to be recycled to erect a fortified residence for the local ruler and a government seat. Churches, both Latin and Greek, large enough for official functions reinforce the hypothesis that the site included a government seat. Additional confirmation is provided by the existence within the site of a heavy masonry foundation measuring twenty-two feet square, suggesting a defense tower or a keep like the one in Antiparos that

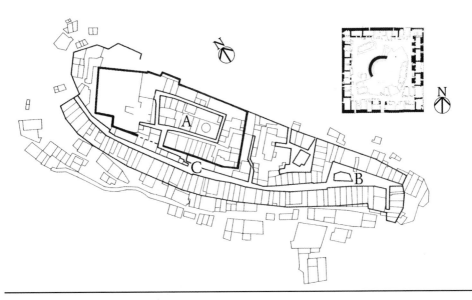

Fig. FOUR-3.04 Sifnos Kastro and Antiparos Kastro, plans drawn to same scale

could be used as a stronghold for observation and last-resort defense.

Two additions were attached to the southeast side of the Mesa Kastro (Fig. FOUR-3.04, areas B and C). Their dates are unknown. Each has retained its independent entry, and neither is physically integrated with the Mesa Kastro. Extending from the south tip to the north end of the earlier fortified enclosures and facing west, an arch-like row of dwelling units sharing party walls formed the third and last enlargement of the Sifnos Kastro and was the most characteristic and significant (Fig. FOUR-3.04, area C).

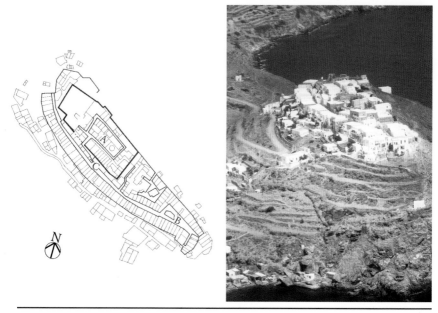

Fig. FOUR-3.05 Sifnos, Kastro, plan and aerial view, 1971

This third addition increased the size of the Kastro substantially and was built to house the common people rather than the nobility at a time when the Hellenization of the Latin lords had advanced appreciably. As it extended to embrace the older fortifications, the new enclosure became one of the most legible and best-preserved applications of the collective fortification system. Two levels of individual properties provide a continuous, massive external wall with a minimum number of openings, each of minimal dimensions (Fig. FOUR-3.08). Three gates incorporated into the lower level of the new enclosure control access to the interior of the Kastro. The gates guide pedestrians and beasts of burden to a path bent to follow the inner side of the enclosure. Leading to the Mesa Kastro and the other parts of the town, this path gracefully provides access to the individual dwelling units comprising the external arch-like enclosure. Steps made of stone masonry blocks lead to the upper floor of each dwelling unit (Fig. FOUR-3.07), underscoring the concept of horizontal property as well as the minimal internal dimensions of the dwelling units. In a manner typical of most Aegean settlements, these massive blocks of steps articulate the curved inner path of the Kastro and, by their use, introduce a domestic scale subtly but clearly into the public space.

At its south end the path runs into the only sizable public space inside the Kastro. Because of the drop in site elevation, the two levels of this public space allow for small pedestrian bridges that cross over the path and provide direct access to the upper-level dwelling units. The quality of this small public space is dramatically enhanced by the presence of the Theologos church whose south elevation acts as a sort of stage set and gently dominates the public space in front of it (Fig. FOUR-3.09, -3.10). The domestic scale

Fig. FOUR-3.06 Sifnos, Kastro, typical enclosure unit, 1986

Fig. FOUR-3.07 Sifnos, Kastro, interior path and idividual dwelling units, 1960

of the church and the unpretentious composition of its south façade merge easily with the building fabric of the Kastro. Yet the delightful and distinctly Sifniote bell tower also sets the church apart in a masterful exhibition of the contradictions typical of the manners of the vernacular architecture of the Aegean island towns.

Fig. FOUR-3.08 Sifnos, Kastro, southeast corner, 1960

Fig. FOUR-3.09 Sifnos, Kastro,
Theologos church, 1997

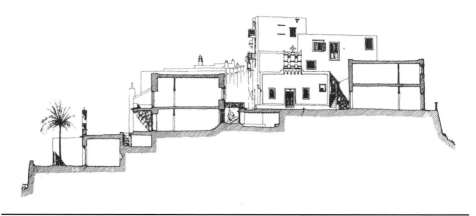

Fig. FOUR-3.10 Sifnos, Kastro, section drawing through the Theologos church area

The flat roofs of buildings throughout the Aegean served as rainwater catchments. The roofs of the arch-like row of dwelling units on the west side of the Sifnos Kastro serve that purpose even now. Important elements in a region of limited annual precipitation, drainpipes and cisterns directed and stored rainwater in an area often located within the foundation of a house (Fig. FOUR-3.06). Flat roofs could also serve as continuous ramparts when needed, allowing defenders to move their forces quickly from point to point and to concentrate them as circumstances required (Fig. FOUR-3.11, -3.12, -3.13).

A number of gates controlled access to the various enclosures of the Kastro. The octagonal post inscribed with the names of the da Corogna and Gozzadini families that still stands today seems to have been part of a gate controlling access to the Mesa Kastro. There are traces of perhaps two other gates on the eastern side of the Kastro enclosures. Three gates -- the Venieri, Chandaki, and Portaki -- survive reasonably intact only because they were incorporated into the lower level of the last enlargement, and are still a living part of the Kastro.

Fig. FOUR-3.11 Sifnos, Kastro, flat roofs and interior path, 1960

Fig. FOUR-3.12 Sifnos, Kastro, flat roofs as ramparts, 1985

Fig. FOUR-3.13 Skyros, flat roofs, 1971

The design of these gates borrows from the formal military architecture then in Byzantine and Latin use and adjusted to local circumstance. Each of the first two gates, Venieri and Chandaki (Fig. FOUR-3.14, -3.15), replaces a lower-level dwelling unit. Party walls shared with other units define the width of the gates. Doors of some type, probably metal or timber, blocked entry at the outer and inner walls. If the enemy breached the external doors, the defenders at the upper level could reduce the attackers' enthusiasm before they could breach the second pair of doors by pouring boiling oil on them from above.

Gates were closed at sundown and opened at sunrise. As fears of piracy diminished, the gates came to be used as public, semi-enclosed spaces for neighborhood social gatherings, a custom that has lasted until recent times. To accommodate participants at such gatherings, stoops -- that is, raised platforms for seating -- ran the length of the gate enclosure on both sides (Fig. FOUR-3.15) and may explain the current reference to the Venieri gate as the Loggia Venieri. Roughly shaped wood beams, the fithes mentioned earlier, support the ceiling and again confirm the domestic scale of the gate enclosure.

The name Portaki (or "little door") appropriately characterizes the smallest of the three gates at the southeast end of the Kastro. Small indeed, with its door of domestic dimensions and a lintel that is flat rather than arched, the external opening seems to represent an attempt to remain unobserved (Fig. FOUR-3.16) and probably served special or private rather than public functions. Restricted in its internal dimensions, too -- no room here for

Fig. FOUR-3.14 Sifnos, Kastro, Venieri gate, 1985

Fig. FOUR-3.15 Sifnos, Kastro, Chandaki gate,1997

Fig. FOUR-3.16 Sifnos, Kastro, Portaki gate, 1986

| Fig. FOUR-3.17 Sifnos, Kastro, from the southwest, 1988 | Fig. FOUR-3.18 Sifnos, Kastro, from the northwest, 1986 |

double rows of stoops -- the entry path follows a set of narrow steps as they rise to meet a loggia built with unexpected flair on the left. A squat column supports two substantial arches. The wall recession behind both offers the equivalent of the loggias of the other two gates. The small-scale assembly and the interplay of spaces -- some covered, others semi-enclosed or uncovered -- and the elements borrowed from formal architecture but executed in the most sensitive vernacular manner make this diminutive gate and the internal path emerging from it one of the most rewarding urban experiences inside the Sifnos Kastro.

Like other Aegean islands, Sifnos has lost population during the last fifty years. The present population of about two thousand who remain year-round seems to have stabilized in the last twenty-five years or so. The majority of the inhabitants are concentrated in the more spacious central island settlements of Apollonia and Artemon; fewer than one hundred live permanently in the Kastro today in as many of the old housing units.

4.4 Astypalaia

Larger than Sifnos but not as fertile, Astypalaia consists of two halves united by a narrow isthmus that together measure ninety-seven square kilometers (Fig. FOUR-4.01). The rocky and mountainous terrain, with elevations of 1,600 feet in one half and 1,200 in the other, includes little arable land. Like Antiparos, Astypalaia supports only one settlement, also known as Chora, which had a population of about one thousand people in the 1991 census.

Located in the southern half of the island, Chora -- not unlike the Sifnos Kastro -- sits atop a promontory pointing southeast, facing the major north-

Fig. FOUR-4.01 Astypalaia

Fig. FOUR-4.02 Astypalaia, promontory, Kastro and Chora, from the south, 1995

south Aegean sea lanes (Fig. FOUR-4.02, -4.03, -4.04). The strategic positions of island and promontory invited early settlement, the historical record of which is fragmented. The ancient name Astypalaia (*Asty*, or "city"; *palaia*, or "old") has survived with few of the usual alterations, although the island was called Stampalia during the era of the Duchy of the Archipelago. Historically and geographically, Astypalaia belongs to the Dodecanese island complex, and, in consequence, its more recent history has differed from those of Antiparos and Sifnos. Astypalaia remained part of the Ottoman Empire after Greek independence in 1830 and came under Italian administration from 1912 to 1943 before it was returned to Greece with the rest of the Dodecanese Islands in 1947.

The name of the Querini-Stampalia Palace on the Grand Canal in Venice is a reminder of the prominent Venetian families who sought adventure in the Aegean islands and of the Duchy of the Archipelago. Whether Astypalaia became a fief of the Querini family as early as the thirteenth century is not clear. The island had changed hands a number of times before it "was laid waste in the time of Murad I (1362-89)" (Vacalopoulos, *Origins of*

Fig. FOUR-4.03 Astypalaia, from the air, 1971

Fig. FOUR-4.04 Astypalaia, from the air, 1971

the Greek Nation 69-71). It was not until 1413, while Buondelmonti was traveling in the area, that Giovanni Querini recolonized Astypalaia with islanders from Tenos and Mykonos. The Kastro at the top of the promontory was built then to provide protected residence for the colonists. The Querini family preserved the Venetian presence on the island until 1541 when Astypalaia also became part of the Ottoman Empire, eighteen years after the conquest of Rhodes.

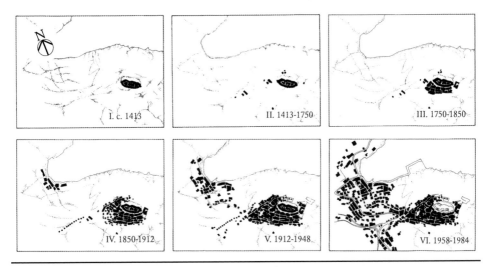

Fig. FOUR-4.05 Astypalaia, six stages of development

The Astypalaia Kastro was built at the top of a massive rock formation crowning the promontory 400 feet above sea level. Erected in one stage, it follows the collective fortification system of the vernacular architecture tradition common to the Aegean island towns (Fig. FOUR-4.06, -4.07, -4.08, -4.09). The Kastro is defined by a completely enclosed defense perimeter, with access to the interior limited to one powerfully built gate. The Astypalaia Kastro is no longer inhabited, the last occupants having moved to the Chora below at the end of World War II and the Italian administration (Fig. FOUR-4.10, -4.11).

The natural rock edge extends upward to merge with the man-made external walls of the Kastro enclosure, which is long and narrow (Fig. FOUR-4.13). Measuring 150 x 400 feet, the Astypalaia Kastro encloses 60,000 square feet, about one-third as much space as the Sifnos Kastro. Buttressed in places, the formidably tall external walls undulate gently on the southwest side where the gate is located, to become irregular on the northeast side.

The effects of desertion are apparent in the ruins of the interior, where the walls of some dwelling units survive (Fig. FOUR-4.12). Many of the top floors have collapsed since the early 1950s. However, the pace of deterioration has been slowed by recent repair work. Sharing party walls, dwelling units on three levels originally lined the peripheral defensive wall and were

Fig. FOUR-4.06 Astypalaia, 1970

Fig. FOUR-4.07 Astypalaia, 1971

Fig. FOUR-4.08 Astypalaia, 1971

Fig. FOUR-4.09 Astypalaia, 1995

accessible from interior paths, as in Sifnos. The remnants of foundations confirm the presence of similar units in the central, now open, area of the Kastro. Narrow and irregular pedestrian circulation paths were important contributors to the apparent high density of building in the fifteenth-century Kastro. Measured drawings of the fortification trace the size and scale of about thirty of the original units of habitation. Superimposing similarly-sized units on a drawing of the periphery and the interior of the Kastro indicate that there were perhaps seventy-five units per level. Assuming three levels of such units and four or five persons per family brings the full occupancy of the Kastro to about one thousand, a number larger than but still comparable to the likely numbers inhabiting the Antiparos and Sifnos Kastra.

Amidst the ruins of the Astypalaia Kastro, two whitewashed churches are still in use and survive in excellent repair. Saint George, built in 1790 and freestanding today, was part of the tightly knit urban fabric of the Kastro (Fig. FOUR-4.14). Attached to its west end is a covered space called *blatsa*

| Fig. FOUR-4.10 Astypalaia, Kastro, plan, lower level | Fig. FOUR-4.11 Astypalaia, Kastro, plan upper level |

| Fig. FOUR-4.12 Astypalaia, Kastro, interior view, 1995 | Fig. FOUR-4.13 Astypalaia, Kastro, exterior walls, 1995 |

by the people of Astypalaia (perhaps a corruption of the Italian *piazza*), an echo of a public space from the eighteenth-century days of the settlement.

Sitting atop the gated entry to the Kastro and dedicated to *Panayia* ("All-Holy Mother"), the other whitewashed church, built in 1853, is still important in the religious life of the citizens of Astypalaia. Its spectacular location and the treatment of its two exterior elevations make this building symbolic of the nineteenth-century transformation of Astypalaia, when it began to spill out of its defensive enclosure and into the town below. This church also offers insights into the vernacular architecture forms of the Aegean island towns as they evolved in the nineteenth century.

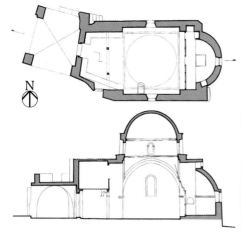

Fig. FOUR-4.14 Astypalaia, Kastro, Saint George, plan, section and view from the east, 1995

N

The 1853 Panayia church replaced an earlier building on the same location (Fig. FOUR-4.15). The strategic placement of the gate along the southwestern wall of the Astypalaia Kastro and the uniqueness, size, and elaborate interior passage space that remains strongly suggest that the former building was a tower guarding access to and defending the gate (Fig. FOUR-4.16, -4.17, -4.18).

It is tempting to contemplate the symbolism of the replacement of a fortification by a church. By 1853 the defense tower was obviously an unpleasant reminder of the fear of corsairs and of Latin domination. But when the church was built, twenty years had passed since the French landings in Algiers and the elimination of the Barbary corsairs, and the British and French fleets and the expeditionary armies allied with the Ottoman Empire were crossing the Aegean to make war on Russia in the Crimean peninsula. The changed geopolitics of the mid-nineteenth century Mediterranean gave the citizens of Astypalaia, still under Ottoman rule, a new sense of security. Thus, the elimination of the tower and its replacement with a church, a building that reasserted the islanders' traditional devotion to Eastern Orthodoxy.

In a remarkably sophisticated and "current" architectural manner, each of the two exposed elevations of the Panayia church responds to its context, and each is radically different from the other. The east elevation is addressed to the domestic scale of the Kastro interior. Apart from the unusual, large arched gate opening under the church (Fig.FOUR-4.16), and the massive masonry pier at its southeast corner (possibly a remnant of the earlier tower structure) all the other elements -- apse, dome, whitewash, and so on – are typical of the post-Byzantine vernacular architecture of the Aegean islands. Indeed, in scale, composition, and architectural vocabulary, both of the Kastro churches, Panayia and Saint George, speak the same language. The west elevation of the Panayia church is addressed to the larger, more ambitious public scale of the Kastro exterior and to the growing settlement of Chora

Fig. FOUR-4.15 Astypalaia, Kastro, interior space with the Panayia church over entry gate, 1971

Fig. FOUR-4.16 Astypalaia, Kastro, interior, 1971

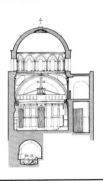

Fig. FOUR-4.17 Astypalaia, Kastro, Panayia church, section

Fig. FOUR-4.18 Astypalaia, Kastro, gate under church, 1971

below (Fig. FOUR-4.19, -4.20). Part of the larger exposed stone surface of the defense enclosure, this elevation is enriched by the four windows of the church, which alert the observer to the existence of a different use of space behind this short segment of the wall. The windows are framed by such formal architectural components as pilasters, arches, and pediments cut in stone in a unique example of the assimilation of formal architecture elements into the vocabulary of vernacular architecture.

Both elevations of the Panayia church along with its location atop the gate that links the domestic and public worlds of Astypalaia appear to celebrate the ongoing relocation of the town from the Kastro above to Chora below. Astypalaia had remained within the tight confines of the Kastro after its transition from Latin to Turkish rule and up to the middle of the eighteenth century. Prosperity and an increase in population made possible by better conditions for seaborne trade finally allowed for expansion and hesitant building outside the Kastro during the second half of the eighteenth century.

In response to the topography of the new site and under the protective mass of the fortification, an assembly of dwelling units began to emerge on the southwest side of the Kastro in successive rings. The floor plans of these units remained the same as those of their predecessors inside the fortifica-

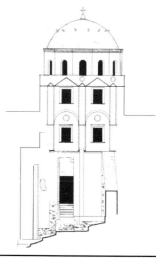

Fig. FOUR-4.19 Astypalaia, Kastro, Panayia church over gate, west elevation

Fig. FOUR-4.20 Astypalaia, Kastro, Panayia church and gate from the west

tion. Yet the adaptation of the units to the new site offered a welcome reduction in building density as well as ventilation and better views over the roofs of the ring of dwellings below. Further expansion moved northward and downhill as the site dictated, towards the bay area of Pera Yialos (Fig. FOUR-4.21, -4.22). Commercial buildings serving the island's sea trade appeared in Pera Yialos before and during the period of Italian administration (1912-1943). Adjusting to the intricacies of the site, a natural path zigzagged to form a physical spine connecting Chora and the Kastro on the hill with the Pera Yialos port area. Flanked by houses and surfaced in a step-

Fig. FOUR-4.21 Astypalaia, Kastro, Chora, and port, 1971

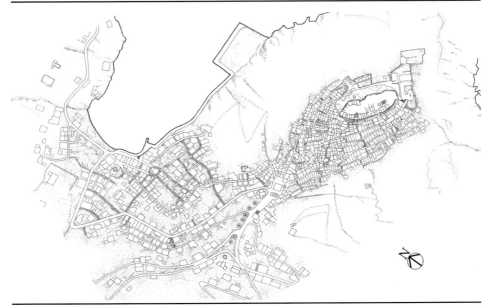

Fig. FOUR-4.22 Astypalaia, Kastro, Chora, and port

| Fig. FOUR-4.23 Astypalaia, spine | Fig. FOUR-4.24 Astypalaia, spine, 1971 |

ramp-step sequence for use by pedestrian and beast-of-burden traffic, the ample width of this passage underscores its importance as a spine and as a vibrant architectural element in the new, three-part articulation of the settlement: Chora - spine - Pera Yialos (Fig. FOUR-4.23,-4.24). Unfortunately, overbuilding on both sides and "improvements" to allow motorcycles to override the steps of the spine have diminished the integrity of this precious architectural enrichment of the urban form of Astypalaia.

4.5 Kimolos

| Fig. FOUR-5.01 Kimolos | Fig. FOUR-5.02 Kimolos, 1999 |

Fig. FOUR-5.03 Kimolos and Psathi port, 1971

Fig. FOUR-5.04 Kimolos and Psathi port, 1994

Fig. FOUR-5.05 Kimolos, Kastro, and Chora, 1999

Fig. FOUR-5.06 Kimolos, Kastro, and Chora, 1999

Kimolos (Fig. FOUR-5.01, -5.02) is visible from Antiparos, twenty-five miles away. Both are small islands, Kimolos measuring forty-one square kilometers, and Antiparos, thirty-five. They share the typical serrated Aegean shoreline. Kimolos's high point is 1,200 feet, Antiparos's, 900. Each island has a single town. Both islands are nearly attached to, and have developed in the shadow of, their larger neighbors, Melos in the case of Kimolos, and Antiparos in the case of Paros. Unique in the Aegean for its mineral wealth, including obsidian, Melos embraces a large, deep, and sheltered bay frequently used as a first stop by sailing ships entering the archipelago from the western Mediterranean. Known since antiquity for its high-quality marble, Paros is agriculturally one of the richer islands of the Cyclades. Kimolos produces "Kimolian earth," or chalk, known to every schoolboy and schoolgirl in Greece as *kimolia*. Unique stalactite caves have also always attracted visitors to Antiparos.

Located about seven kilometers from the port of Psathi and seventy meters above sea level, the Kimolos Kastro site possesses a commanding

Fig. FOUR-5.07 Kimolos, Kastro, 1971   Fig. FOUR-5.08 Kimolos, Kastro, 1999

Fig. FOUR-5.09 Kimolos, Kastro, 1971   Fig. FOUR-5.10 Kimolos, Kastro, 1999

view of the sea approaches to the island and the port below. The site thus gave the inhabitants the advantage of fighting a corsair raiding party on land from higher ground (Fig.FOUR-5.03, -5.04). In this respect, the Kimolos Kastro site resembles the site of Serifos more than it does that of Antiparos.

Since the 1830s, the town of Kimolos has grown beyond the protective walls of the late-sixteenth-century Kastro. Since the beginning of the twentieth century, building outside the Kastro has occurred at the expense of the original fortification, as in Astypalaia (Fig. FOUR-5.05, -5.06). Indeed, the Kimolos Kastro, unlike the Antiparos Kastro, ceased long ago to function as the core of the present town. Instead, it is in the last stages of a long process of abandonment by its inhabitants. Roofs have caved in, walls have collapsed, and windows and doors have rotted away (Fig. FOUR-5.07, -5.08, -5.09, -5.10, -5.19, -5.20). Sad as the situation is, enough physical evidence survives to allow for a fairly accurate understanding of the Kastro's likely original form. The Kimolos Kastro, like those already discussed, is an application of the collective fortification principle. Built approximately one hundred fifty years after the Antiparos Kastro, the Kimolos Kastro, in its conception as well as its application, illustrates the continuity and change that characterize the vernacular architecture of the archipelago.

Attached to each other by their long sides, the 123 units of horizontal habitation on each of the two levels of the Kimolos Kastro compose two concentric quadrilateral building blocks. The four unequal sides of the external building block, each defined by an imperfect line, form an enclosure whose longest side measures seventy-four and one-half meters and whose shortest measures fifty-six and one-half. The external enclosure, the defining element of this collective fortification, allows entry through two gates, one on the east wall, the other on the south (Fig. FOUR-5.11, -5.12, -5.13, -5.14, -5.15). Both gates lead to a four-sided, open-air space, a public street that mediates between the two concentric building blocks. This street functions as an internal pedestrian circulation spine for the fortification, as it provides access to the two levels of housing units on each of its four sides. Massive masonry steps become the "joints" that connect the spine to the upper-level horizontal units. An appendix-like element, comprising six units and a church and located at the center of the smaller internal enclosure, completes the plan of the Kastro (Fig. FOUR-5.16).

The topography of the site is the primary cause of the irregularities in the external and internal long walls of the Kastro. As it drops eight meters from its north to its south side, the inclined site contributes significantly to the architectural character of the fortification. An axonometric reconstruction (Fig. FOUR-5.17) explains the three-dimensional form of the Kimolos Kastro by outlining the roofs of individual units as they descend to follow

| Fig. FOUR-5.11 Kimolos, Kastro, south gate c. 1914 | Fig. FOUR-5.12 Kimolos, Kastro, south gate c. 1971 | Fig. FOUR-5.13 Kimolos, Kastro, south gate c. 1999 |

the slope of the site. The north wall, which rests on the edge of a precipitous three-meter drop, would have been least vulnerable to assault.

Knowledgeable builders created the Antiparos Kastro. The irregular enclosure of the Kimolos Kastro shows an equally firm understanding of the collective fortification principle. Its peripheral walls, unequal in length and not rectilinear, might seem to suggest less competence in its execution, but this bent and uneven periphery is misleading. The builders of the Kimolos Kastro were heirs to the Byzantine building tradition, which had demonstrated frequently that it did not greatly value the perfection of straight lines and exact ninety-degree angles. This tolerance for inexactitude is demonstrated in the Katapoliani plan on page 219 (Fig.FIVE-2.49). The Katapo-

Fig.FOUR-5.14 Kimolos, Kastro, east gate, 1971

Fig. FOUR-5.15 Kimolos, Kastro, east gate, 1999

liani basilica on the nearby island of Paros had had a major architectural presence in the archipelago since the sixth century age of Justinian and was almost certainly a sight familiar to the eyes and minds of the vernacular architecture builders of the Aegean islands. The apparent inability of the builders of the Kimolos Kastro to construct straight peripheral walls of equal length may in fact reveal a more sophisticated understanding of defense than perfectly straight walls would have. The geometric clarity established by a perfectly square enclosure with gates at the mid-point of each

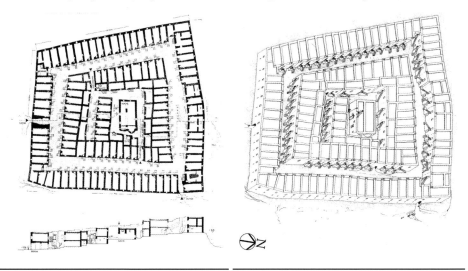

Fig. FOUR-5.16 Kimolos, Kastro, plan and section

Fig. FOUR-5.17 Kimolos, Kastro, axonometric reconstruction

side and streets corresponding to those gates could in fact work in favor of those hoping to breach the external defenses of an Aegean Kastro by making their next steps easier. An irregular, non-geometric internal town organization, on the other hand -- one characterized by a labyrinth of hidden accesses and unexpected turns -- had the potential to confuse attackers and thus heighten the defenders' chance to repulse the enemy. A maze of irregular streets, cul-de-sacs, and dead ends well known to the locals but unfamiliar to invaders is the most prominent feature of the urban structure of Aegean towns. Without having been specifically planned, this feature worked well for defense. Thucydides certainly thought so. In his description of the outbreak of the Peloponnesian War, he tells of a Theban force:

> [making] an armed entry into Plataea...while it was still peace time and...no sentries were on guard. Now the Theban troops marched

into the marketplace and grounded arms there... . As for the Plataeans, when they realized that the Thebans were inside their gates and that their city had been taken over... they were ready enough to come to an agreement... . But while negotiations were going on they became aware that the Thebans were not there in great force and came to the conclusion that, if they attacked them, they could easily overpower them... . They decided therefore that the attempt should be made, and, to avoid being seen going through the streets, they cut passages through the connecting walls of their houses and so gathered together in numbers... . When their preparations were as complete as could be, they waited for the time just before dawn, when it was still dark, and then sallied out from their houses against the Thebans. Their idea was that if they attacked in daylight their enemies would be more sure of themselves and <u>would be able to meet them on equal terms, whereas in the night they would not be so confident and would also be at a disadvantage through not knowing the city so well as the Plataeans did.</u> They therefore attacked at once... . As soon as the Thebans realized that they had fallen into a trap, they closed their ranks and fought back... . Twice and three times they succeeded in beating off the assault, and all the while there was a tremendous uproar from the men who were attacking them, <u>and shouting and yelling from the women and slaves on the roofs, who hurled down stones and tiles;</u> at the same time it had been raining hard all night. Finally they lost heart and turned and fled through the city, <u>most of them having no idea, in the darkness and the mud, on a moonless night at the end of the month, of which way to go in order to escape, while their pursuers knew quite well how to prevent them from escaping. The result was that most of them were destroyed...</u> Such was the fate of those who entered the town. (2 124-26, emphasis added)

A description of fighting inside the breached walls of a small Aegean island town of the seventeenth century would probably differ only in lacking Thucydides's eloquence.

A very high percentage of the dwelling units, the basic building blocks comprising the Kastro, are of the monochoro, or single-space, type. Long and narrow, and articulated by thick stone masonry walls enclosing less than two hundred square feet of living space per family, these units met the need to house and protect the maximum number of people within the minimum amount of space and thus keep the defensive perimeter as short as possible. Indeed, the Kimolos Kastro, which was built in one stage, unlike that of

Sifnos, was conceived to accommodate many more inhabitants than the Antiparos Kastro -- 800 as opposed to 250 for Antiparos.

The geometry of the external enclosure of the Kimolos Kastro dictated the architectural plans of the irregular dwelling units at the four corners. Four units on the north side of the enclosure were deliberately made larger than the rest. Privileged by their size, three of them also assumed prominence by their orientation towards the sun, the sea, and the widest part of the pedestrian circulation spine -- also a privileged public place, since it was apparently the marketplace for the Kastro.

An Orthodox church, sympathetic in scale to its immediate context, was built in the geometric center of the Kimolos Kastro, instead of a central tower, as at the Antiparos Kastro. The presence of a church is symbolic of a

Fig. FOUR-5.18 Kimolos, Kastro, entry to dwelling unit, 1999

Fig. FOUR-5.19 Kimolos, east gate from inside, 1999

Fig. FOUR-5.20 Kimolos, Kastro, 1999

Fig. FOUR-5.21 Kimolos, Kastro, 1999

Fig. FOUR-5.22 Kimolos, Kastro, 1999

major cultural change taking place in the Aegean islands by the sixteenth century, the diminishing presence of the Roman Catholic Venetian over-lords and their replacement by native Greek Orthodox families.

The Kimolos Kastro was completed after the 1580 treaty that brought Kimolos and a number of other Aegean islands under the control of the Ottoman Turks, who replaced the Venetian feudal system with a measure of autonomy for the island, including such privileges for the Orthodox Church as the right to repair buildings and to ring church bells.

Seventeenth-century travelers consistently describe Kimolos as a pirate port where goods and money changed hands quickly. At this time, indeed, Kimolos was also known as *Argentiera*, or, "the silver-island," a reference to the money that circulated constantly in its marketplace. The island offered corsairs a well-protected bay where their ships could be beached for repair and cleaning, and proximity to Melos with its busy port at the southwestern entry to the Aegean archipelago. These assets together with the island's newly granted autonomy allowed local leaders to rise to prominence as naval merchants and, eventually, to build the Kimolos Kastro.

A well-researched and persuasive article by W. Hoepfner and H. Schmidt in the *Bulletin of the German Archaeological Institute* presents important infor-mation about when the Kimolos Kastro was built and the identity of its builder. Apparently, the Kastro was completed by the end of the sixteenth century and, probably, by 1592 -- that is, before the end of the Elizabethan era in England. The builder of the Kimolos Kastro, so similar in form to Antiparos's, was Ioannis Rafos, a Greek merchant from Kimolos who seems to have had strong ties to the Greek Orthodox Church.

An icon in the collection of the Byzantine Museum in Athens that measures 11 x 13 inches (Fig. FOUR-5.23) is instructive on the career of Ioannis Rafos. An enthroned Christ, flanked by the Virgin Mary and Saint John the Theologian, is depicted in the upper half of the icon. The lower half is occupied by Ioannis Rafos himself, kneeling in prayer. An impressive galley in front of him, flanked by steps leading to a windmill, is crowned by the façade of the Kastro, with the inscription "Kimolos" above it. Island tra-dition makes it likely that the icon was commissioned by Rafos himself to underline his status as a well-to-do merchant and ship owner as well as the founder of the Kastro and to emphasize his Orthodox faith by beseeching Christ, the Virgin Mary, and Saint John the Theologian to protect the island, the Kastro, and his ships.

Read in the context of Kimolos's shift from Venetian to Ottoman con-trol, the icon also helps to explain the rapid building of a sizable and com-plete edifice like the Kastro. Apparently, it served to keep Rafos's crews together during the winter months of inaction by offering them a safe and protected residence. The units of the Kimolos Kastro, more tightly packed than those at Antiparos, suggest that the occupants spent a good part of the year at sea. The four larger units on the north wall may have been assigned to ships' captains. The largest of these, closest to the northwest corner, displays above its entry door a coat of arms drawn in the Venetian manner but including in its design a cross of the type associated with the Orthodox Church (Fig. FOUR-5.22). This dwelling may well have housed Rafos himself. The western dress he wears in the picture on the icon as well as the decoration of doors and window jambs in the Kastro's interior façades (Fig. FOUR-5.18, -5.21) reflect northern Italian tastes and implicitly assert legitimacy by suggesting continuity with the years of Venetian rule. The relative size of Rafos's house, if the house was his, and its incorporation within the main block of dwelling units rather than sequestration in a separate tower indicate the change in rule represented by the building of the Kastro. Rafos, a native Greek rather than a Latin lord, lived within rather than apart from the community, a version of the more egalitarian relationship of an Aegean

Fig. FOUR-5.23 Icon, enthroned Christ with Virgin Mary and Saint John the Theologian, Byzantine Museum, Athens

ship's captain to his crew than that of a feudal lord to his serfs.

Since pirates were still present on the island, we must assume that Rafos and his crews cooperated with them, an illustration of the blurred line between merchant and pirate in the seventeenth-century life of the Aegean archipelago.

4.6 Skaros in Santorini, Kastro in Skiathos

Fig. FOUR-6.01 Skiathos

Fig. FOUR-6.02 Santorini

Comparable in size to both Sifnos and Astypalaia and more than twice the size of Antiparos, Santorini is best known as the product of the volcanic violence to which the island has been subjected repeatedly, most recently in 1956. With a year-round population of about ten thousand, according to the 1991 census, Santorini today sustains a number of settlements, as it did during the era of the Duchy of the Archipelago, when it claimed five fortified towns: Skaros, Oia (or, Saint Nicholas), Pyrgos, Emporio, and Akrotiri (Fig. FOUR-6.02).

Skaros appears on the Buondelmonti map of Santorini from the 1420s (Fig. TWO-5.01). The Barozzi, the first ducal family on the island, used Skaros as the seat of their government, a status it retained throughout the existence of the Duchy of the Archipelago. For reasons both internal and external, Skaros's citizens began to leave it for less crowded and, presumably, equally safe accommodations nearby beginning in the seventeenth century, which led to its complete abandonment after the 1830s.

The Antiparos Kastro and the Sifnos Kastro have been continuously inhabited. Chora now extends the life of the abandoned enclosure of the Astypalaia Kastro. But only the powerful character of the site and the overgrown foundation walls confirm the existence of fortified settlements in Skaros on Santorini and in the Kastro on the northern Aegean island of Skiathos, which, like Skaros, was deserted after the 1830s (Fig. FOUR-6.01). Historical and literary documents referring to both settlements provide insights into the life and architecture of these now deserted islands.

Alexandros Papadiamantis (1851-1911), the son of a Greek Orthodox priest, was perhaps the greatest Greek prose writer of his time. His stories, set on his native Skiathos, are notable for their careful observation of daily life, their loving descriptions of folk traditions and the natural environment, and their powerful portrayal of the dignity and harshness of traditional Aegean island life. "Papadiamantis did for his island what Thomas Hardy... did for [his] homeland," as Constantinides observed in *Tales From a Greek Island* (xi).

Ftochos Ayios (*Poor Saint*) is among Papadiamantis's nearly two hundred works of short fiction. The story is particularly useful to an understanding of the vernacular architecture of the Aegean islands, since the narrative gives us revealing information about both life and architectural form in the fortified settlement of the Kastro on Skiathos.

Subtitled "A Tale from Skiathos," *Ftochos Ayios* speaks of a place on the island where the earth was red and fragrant, giving rise to a legend that a poor shepherd had attained sainthood by shedding his blood on the spot when he was killed by corsairs. The corsairs were said to have taken revenge on him for warning his fellow islanders in the Kastro of the corsairs' secret landing on the island, thereby frustrating their plans. Set in the early years of the eighteenth century, the story vividly portrays the hazardous life of the islanders, the constant threat from corsairs roaming the Aegean, and the islanders' defenses against this threat.

Papadiamantis describes Kastro as having been built on a craggy and forbidding promontory at the extreme north point of the island (Fig. FOUR-6.03). A drawbridge over a deep chasm is said to have connected the promontory to the island and controlled the only entry into the town (Fig. FOUR-6.04, -6.05). A guard performed the daily duty of raising the drawbridge before sunset and lowering it again after sunrise.

Papadiamantis's island tales were not illustrated, but there is a picture of a settlement similar to the Skiathos Kastro as Papadiamantis describes it in a drawing of a contemporary settlement, the "View of Skaros" (Fig. FOUR-6.06) in the collection of Thomas Hope (1769-1831). Hope, the Dutch-born British traveler, student of architecture, and collector and patron of the arts discussed in Chapter TWO, visited Greece twice before the end of the eighteenth century and produced a number of watercolors and sepia drawings, 350 of which are in the collection of the Benaki Museum in Athens. Fani-

Fig. FOUR-6.03 Skiathos, Kastro, 1971

Fig. FOUR-6.04 Skiathos, Kastro,
drawbridge, 1995

Fig. FOUR-6.05 Skiathos, Kastro, drawbridge,
1971

Maria Tsigakou points out in *Thomas Hope, Pictures from 18th Century Greece* that "in order to have in his possession a more complete portfolio of Greek views, Hope also acquired works other than his own" (30). For this purpose, he hired artists and apparently purchased drawings by the French consul in Athens, Louis Sebastien Fauvel. Tsigakou adds that, "I believe that the "View of Skaros" must be attributed to Fauvel as there are great similarities [with known Fauvel drawings] in the handling of the pen as well as in the lettering" (30). I accept this judgment. But since the Skaros drawing is part of a much larger collection by Hope, he must have considered it an important record of his observations, and I will refer to it in the paragraphs that follow as Hope's drawing.

Hope's pencil drawing is of the fortified town of Skaros during the last decades of its occupancy. The drawing is of particular merit and quality, clearly the work of an accomplished artist sensitive to issues of scale, proportion, and perspective and to the intimacies between site and subject.

Important and enlightening similarities exist between Papadiamantis's story and Hope's drawing in their portrayals of the landscape and of the man-made settlements. Papadiamantis calls the Kastro "a nest of seagulls," a rock rising abruptly 650 feet above the sea and joined to the rest of the island by a movable wooden bridge. In the Hope drawing, Skaros also rises precipitously from the sea. Crowned by a massive rock connected to the rim of the caldera by a narrow ridge providing access to the gate of the settlement, the Skaros of the Hope drawing also resembles "a nest of seagulls"(Fig. FOUR-6.09, -6.10, -6.11, -6.12, -6.20, -6.21, -6.22). In fact, Skaros was situated at the top of a promontory rising nearly one thousand feet from the sea and in the caldera of the Santorini volcano, due east of the present-day village of Merovigli (Fig. FOUR-6.07, -6.08).

Today's visitor to the site, confronted by the forbidding topography and perplexed by the unexpected smallness of the settlement, would readily agree with Papadiamantis that it is "a wonder" that people "managed to live on this waterless and inhospitable rock." Papadiamantis explains "the pressing need to do so: the fear of the Barbary corsairs and of the Venetians and the Turks crowded and piled them up on this naturally unconquerable promontory."

Hope's drawing confirms this. Heavy masonry-walled, barrel-vaulted houses typical of the vernacular architecture forms of present-day Santorini crowd against one another (Fig. FOUR-6.13, -6.14). Minimal in square footage, they form a defensive perimeter over an abrupt site-fall to the sea on both sides of the pictured settlement. Church cupolas with the characteristic Santorini lantern, which can be seen on today's Ayios Menas in Fira on Santorini (Fig. FOUR-6.15, -6.16, -6.17), enrich the building typology of the settlement and, together with the dwelling units, compose the enclosed town.

According to a seventeenth-century visitor, Skaros contained nearly two hundred houses sheltering as many as one thousand people. Massing so many units within the tight confines of the Skaros rock was only made possible by constricting the size of the individual dwelling units, which were similar to those comprising the external defensive walls of the Sifnos, Antiparos, and Astypalaia Kastra. Flights of steps for negotiating the uneven site are recorded in the Hope pencil drawing as scaling elements and are integral to the architecture of the Skaros settlement.

The Aegean climate allows outdoor living for most of the year. Scarce

Fig. FOUR-6.06 Thomas Hope, pencil drawing on paper, "View of Skaros," c. 1795

Fig. FOUR-6.07 Santorini, Skaros, 1995

Fig. FOUR-6.08 Santorini, Skaros, 1995

resources and limiting economic conditions dictated dwelling units of minimal size in any case. These small units, together with the high building density within the collective defense enclosure of Skaros, made for a shortened and consequently more easily defended perimeter -- all conditions accurately observed and recorded in the Hope drawing with a degree of truthfulness and understanding not always found in illustrations by other eighteenth-century visitors.

The authenticity of Hope's drawing is also underscored by the outline of the Skaros rock and of Therasia island in the background -- both elements of the unaltered natural landscape easily recognized by today's observer (Fig. FOUR-6.18, -6.19). The feeling of authenticity is strengthened by the artist's use of pencil, which suggests that the drawing -- unlike the lithographs that illustrated other travel accounts -- was executed in situ, allowing for accurate measurement and the portrayal of both the natural landscape and of man-made architectural forms.

At its lower left side, Hope's drawing depicts the entry to the fortification. A drawbridge leads to an arched gate flanked by two tower-like struc-

Fig. FOUR-6.09 Skiathos, Kastro, 1995   Fig. FOUR-6.10 Skiathos, Kastro, 1971

Fig. FOUR-6.11 Santorini, Skaros, 1995

Fig. FOUR-6.12 Santorini, Skaros, 1995

tures, the only flat-roofed buildings in the drawing, that form ramparts from which defenders could fight attackers from below. Small openings in the larger tower on the right provide for observation and firing, and perhaps identify a room for the guard (Fig. FOUR-6.06). A nearly identical entry gate is described by Papadiamantis in *Ftochos Ayios* in the scene in which the shepherd rushes to warn the gatekeeper of the corsairs' appearance on the island.

In the story, the shepherd finds himself in front of the fortification at daybreak. Anxiously, he observes the rocky gap between the island and the

Fig. FOUR-6.13 Thomas Hope, "View of Skaros," detail

Fig. FOUR-6.14 Santorini, Oia, 1992

Fig. FOUR-6.15 Thomas Hope, "View of Skaros," detail

Fig. FOUR-6.16 Santorini, Fira, Ayios Menas, 1982

Fig. FOUR-6.17 Santorini, Fira, Ayios Menas, 1973

site of the town -- "a land abyss hovering above a watery abyss," where "vertigo conquers a person." To his relief and despite the sun's rise, the drawbridge is still up! He calls the gatekeeper, who eventually responds, unseen from behind an embrasure, by asking whether the shepherd wants a rope and net dropped to him so that he can be hoisted up to the rampart. The shepherd refuses and shouts a warning to the gatekeeper not to drop the bridge that morning and then rushes back to tend his goats. As he returns to his flock, the corsairs, who by now realize that it was he who frustrated their raid, seize him and kill him on the spot. Hence the legend that the earth was colored red by his blood and turned fragrant and holy by his sacrifice.

In other parts of *Ftochos Ayios*, Papadiamantis provides useful information about the corsair raid, which, as described, is typical of Barbary corsair operations throughout the archipelago and confirms that the Skiathos Kastro and similar fortifications were designed for defense against such sudden, unexpected, small-scale raids rather than against naval and land sieges by regular military forces. The raid described in *Ftochos Ayios* involves a small corsair ship, which lands a third of its crew of fifteen to eighteen just before daybreak in a small, distant, and uninhabited bay, invisible from the Kastro. The plan is to surprise the islanders at sunup by positioning the corsair ship before the Kastro to provide a diversion for the land party, which is to cross the drawbridge, breach the gate, and enter the town.

The tales of hidden treasure that circulated as a result of the endless conflicts in the Aegean and Mediterranean Seas motivate the corsairs. They also hope to enrich themselves by capturing men, women, and children to be sold in the Algerian and Turkish slave markets. Indeed, the capture of slaves, common practice throughout the Aegean archipelago for several hundred years, had devastating effects on the population and the economies of the islands and on the towns whose defenses had been breached.

Papadiamantis's captivating prose and vivid descriptions paint a literary portrait of the vicissitudes of life in the Skiathos Kastro in the eighteenth

Fig. FOUR-6.18 Thomas Hope, "View of Skaros," c. 1795

Fig. FOUR-6.19 Santorini, Skaros, 1995

century. Thomas Hope's drawing "A View of Skaros," by a talented artist from another culture, gives reliable visual testimony to the architecture that sheltered a life much like that Papadiamantis portrayed at the end of the same century. Hope and Papadiamantis also offer concurring testimony to the effects of piracy in the Aegean Sea during the post-Byzantine centuries.

The capture of Malta by Napoleon in 1798 and the French landings in Algiers in 1830 eradicated piracy from the Mediterranean Sea. Freed from the need to defend against it, the inhabitants of Skiathos and Skaros, now parts of a newly independent Greece, descended from the fortified towns to more accessible locations closer to the sea. Today the fortifications are in ruins, but legends and drawings remain to testify to the harsh conditions of life within them in earlier centuries.

| Fig. FOUR-6.20 Skiathos, Kastro, gate, 1971 | Fig. FOUR-6.21 Skiathos, Kastro, gate, 1971 | Fig. FOUR-6.22 Skiathos, Kastro, gate, 1971 |

(Note: The work of Alexandros Papadiamantis has been brought to the attention of the English-speaking world as *Tales from a Greek Island* in an excellent translation by Elizabeth Constantinides. The volume is a selection consisting of twelve works of short fiction. Unfortunately, *Ftochos Ayios* is not among them. The translations of the quotations from *Ftochos Ayios* are mine.)

4.7 Patmos

Like most of the Aegean islands, Patmos, in the Dodecanese complex, is small -- thirty-four square kilometers, or about the same size as Antiparos. The island is elongated, with a deeply indented coast that is mostly bare and rocky and rises to a height of 269 meters. Chora and Skala, the two major settlements, have a combined population of about twenty-five hundred. A four and one-half kilometer drive from Chora, Skala (or "ladder," "landing place"), the younger of the two settlements, is located at the deep end of the bay that divides the island into two nearly equal halves and serves as its port (Fig. FOUR-7.01, -7.02).

The massive architectural volume of the Monastery of Saint John the Theologian is, in the words of Lawrence Durrell, "grimly beautiful in a rather reproachful way" (Durrell, *Greek Islands* 164), and sits on a 190-meter

| Fig. FOUR-7.01 Patmos | Fig. FOUR-7.02 Patmos, Monastery, Chora, and Skala, 1971 |

ridge on the southern half of the island, hovering protectively over the successive rings of houses and churches that comprise Chora. Another inspiring variation on the Aegean collective fortification system, Patmos's contribution to an understanding of the vernacular architecture of the archipelago is unique (Fig. FOUR-7.03, -7.04, -7.05, -7.06).

The remoteness and insignificance of Patmos probably prompted the exile there of Saint John the Theologian in 95 A.D.. He wrote the *Book of Revelation* in a cave on the island and, so, put Patmos on the map. Yet it took nearly one thousand years for this important event in ecclesiastical history to be celebrated, by a Byzantine imperial act that allowed for the erection of a monastery on Patmos, "an uninhabited island, at the mercy of piratical raids by the Agarene pirates and the Turks."

A papal bull of 1088 established the Monastery of Cluny, a notable center of French Catholicism from which the First Crusade would be proclaimed a few years later. The year 1088 also saw the issuance of the *chrysobull* ("imperial decree") by the Byzantine Emperor Alexios I Comnenos that gave permission for the Monastery of Saint John the Theologian to be built on Patmos. As Glykatzi-Ahrweiler points out:

> Apart from the coincidence of date, this makes it possible to make common reference to the evolution of the two now rival Christian worlds. Cluny represents the vigour and aggression of the Latins, Patmos the resistance and struggle for survival of Byzantine Orthodoxy. (*Patmos* 11)

Fig. FOUR-7.03 Patmos, Monastery and Chora, 1999

Fig. FOUR-7.04 Patmos, Monastery and Chora, 1999

Fig. FOUR-7.05 Patmos, Monastery and Chora, 1999

Fig. FOUR-7.06 Patmos, Monastery and Chora, 1999

The clash of these competing Christian worlds dominated life and architecture -- formal and vernacular -- in the Aegean archipelago until well after the period of the Ottoman Turkish conquest.

The archives of the Monastery of Saint John the Theologian are a reliable record of the vicissitudes of life on the island as well as a history of the monastery, which is today one of the oldest religious buildings in continuous occupancy in the archipelago. This occupancy was uninterrupted by piracy. "The one place in the Aegean which the Mussulmans never molested was the Monastery of Patmos, whose monks were on the best of terms with them," as Miller pointed out in 1921 (*The Latins* 599). The original imperial chrysobull of 1088 is now exhibited in the monastery's Gallery-Museum (Fig. FOUR-7.07). In this document the Emperor Alexios I Comnenos granted Patmos to the monk Christodoulos, an important figure in the history of Byzantine asceticism, and made him and his successors absolute rulers of the island in perpetuity. Indeed, the promulgation of this and other supporting imperial documents made Patmos in essence a monastic republic in the by-then one hundred-year-old tradition of Ayion Oros. And by a provision with lasting consequences, the monastery was given the right to own ships, a privilege it retained under Turkish rule and which eventually made Patmos a major maritime power in the eastern Mediterranean.

Originally less massive than the building we see today, the first phase of the construction of the monastery was completed in extremely adverse conditions. The strong, chilling north winds characteristic of Patmos, the lack of water at the hilltop location of the site (Fig. FOUR-7.08), and the stone quarries kilometers away made work very arduous. In addition, it was necessary to import all the foodstuffs for the monks, the workmen, and their families, which made building on the scale the monastery required even harder, especially on a hilltop location so exposed to the weather. Moreover, the governing spirit of strict all-male asceticism required that the workmen's wives and children remain at a distance from the monks and the building site, probably in a location vulnerable to a pirate raids. Even so, the monastery walls went up quickly, forming an enclosure to protect its occupants not only from a sinful world but also from the corsairs. But this initial completion only began a 900-year period of demolition, replacement and restoration, and internal carving and external addition -- a process very much in the tradition of Byzantine monastic architecture, whose present-day structures are "evolved" versions of the original edifices.

Systematic research into the architectural evolution of the Patmos monastery began as recently as the 1960s with the publication of several important studies. Yet the necessary scholarly work, particularly in identifying and dating the various segments of the tightly assembled complex, remains to be done, rendering "an understanding and interpretation of the monastery as a whole...unattainable at present" (Bouras, *Patmos* 25).

Some observations on the building can nonetheless safely be made. In its evolution over a 900-year time span, Saint John the Theologian has by and large followed the typical "diagram" of a Greek Orthodox Byzantine monastery. Such a diagram defines a solid, fortress-like enclosure entered

Fig. FOUR-7.07 Patmos, Monastery
archives, imperial chrysobull

through a single well-guarded gate that leads to an open-air courtyard. The monastery church, the *Katholikon*, is normally freestanding and located in that courtyard. Patmos, however, deviates from this typical diagram by attaching its Katholikon to the northeast corner of the enclosure. Besides this unusual arrangement, Patmos also defies the clarity of the diagram, which typically lines up all the rooms with their backs to the exterior wall. Instead, the Saint John Monastery locates cells, chapels, and supporting spaces off a labyrinth of passages and corridors at various levels, articulating a network of spaces very much in the vein of an Aegean island settlement

Fig. FOUR-7.08 Patmos, Monastery and Chora, 1970

(Fig. FOUR-7.09, -7.10, -7.11, -7.12, -7.13, -7.14). A reason for this idiosyncratic plan may be found in the organizational character of the Patmos monastery, which "...from an early date...was an idiorhythmic ["living separately"] rather than a cenobitic ["living in community"] monastery..." (Bouras, *Patmos* 25). The distinctive interpretation of the monastery diagram made by the builders of Saint John is an example of formal and vernacular architecture coexisting in a mutually supportive attitude -- formal, in that the building's intent and concept originated in the imperial capital of Constantinople; vernacular, in that its interpretation on the Patmos site evolved in the local Aegean context and adopted Aegean vernacular practices. True to these practices, the monastery also abounds in recycled architectural parts, the variety of which reinforces the inference that they came from different buildings perhaps at the monastery site, possibly including a temple to Artemis and an early Christian basilica, both of which have predated the monastery at the site. Last but not least, the monastery has terraces which provide places for contemplation that also offer singular and commanding views of most of the island's landscape and of its sea approaches. In times of need, these terraces could be transformed into ramparts and serve as the monastery's outer defenses (Fig. FOUR-7.15, -7.16, -7.17).

The Monastery of Saint John the Theologian stood alone on its site for the first forty-five years of its existence, supporting a monastic life of isolation, contemplation, and prayer. Chora, the secular part of the urban agglomeration on Patmos, did not come into existence until 1132, when the

Fig. FOUR-7.09 Patmos, Monastery, plan

Fig. FOUR-7.10 Patmos, Monastery, interior, 1999

Fig. FOUR-7.11 Patmos, Monastery, interior, 1999

Fig. FOUR-7.12 Patmos, Monastery, interior, 1999

Fig. FOUR-7.13 Patmos, Monastery, interior, 1999

Fig. FOUR-7.14 Patmos, Monastery, interior, 1999

monastery relaxed its ascetic rules and invited the lay population of the island to built quarters in its immediate, protective vicinity: indeed, attached to its massive walls.

The advent of the town of Chora allowed the monks fully to implement the imperial chrysobull, which endowed the monastery with *metohia* -- that is, farmland -- in Crete and on neighboring islands, and which gave the monastery the right to own ships as well. These endowments required farmers and sailors in numbers larger than the monks could themselves provide. Hence, the monastic republic's desire to develop a parallel secular settlement to supply the manpower needed to enhance the value of its endowment. Physical proximity between the Monastery and Chora -- the religious and secular components of life and architecture in Patmos -- was the basis for the development of the settlement, which provided the springboard for a long-lasting, mutually supportive, and beneficial relationship.

Two distinct historical periods define the development of the monastery/Chora urban agglomeration on Patmos. The first and longest lasting, from the erection of the monastery to 1659, was the era of the monastic republic, when the island's governance was in the hands of the abbot. After the devastation of 1659 and its aftermath, which will be discussed shortly, a second period started that lasted from 1720, when the governance of Patmos passed to the citizens of Chora, to 1912, when the Italian administration of Patmos and the Dodecanese Islands began. In both periods there were ups and downs: prosperity followed penury and calamity, and vice versa. But by the beginning of the eighteenth century, Patmos was larger and more populous than ever and boasted 800 houses and 250 churches. Island records show a population of 2,000 people in 1774 during the temporary Russian occupation.

The eminence of the monastery and the protection it afforded attracted refugees and settlers from areas of Ottoman Turkish expansion in the Balkans and elsewhere in the Aegean archipelago. The fall of Constantinople in 1453 brought a group of urban refugees-- a group whose size is in dispute but which was large enough to establish its own neighborhood, *Alloteina*, in the area immediately west of the monastery. The refugees' origin and the urban culture they brought with them enhanced the status of the Chora citizenry and helped to break down the social and educational barriers between monks and workers. In fact, the new arrivals were soon to provide monks and, eventually, abbots for the monastery (Iakovides, *Patmos* 14). Traces of a contemporary "inner Kastro," a fortified perimeter around the new Alloteina neighborhood, are still detectable today.

Suleyman the Magnificent's expulsion of the Knights Hospitaller of Saint John from Rhodes in 1522 and the fall of Candia in Crete in 1669

Fig. FOUR-7.15 Patmos, Monastery, ramparts, 1999

Fig. FOUR-7.16 Patmos, Monastery, terraces and ramparts, 1970

Fig. FOUR-7.17 Patmos, Monastery, terraces and ramparts, 1970

bracket an era of upheaval in the southeastern Aegean, which produced another wave of refugees, some of whom settled on Patmos. Over the one hundred years that followed the fall of Rhodes, these refugees built a number of self-contained compounds -- each sheltering an extended family, perhaps a "clan" -- whose primary task was farming. These new compounds enlarged Chora mostly on the eastern and western sides of the monastery and, eventually, produced an "outer Kastro," a much-enlarged fortified perimeter that oral tradition says included seventeen gates.

These additions to Chora gave the present-day town an urban fabric that exhibits all the characteristics of the vernacular architecture of the Aegean islands: high building density; narrow, labyrinthine streets; adaptation to a

Fig. FOUR-7.18 Patmos, Chora, 1999	Fig. FOUR-7.19 Patmos, Chora, 1999	Fig. FOUR-7.20 Patmos, Chora, 1999

specific site; and upper floors that arch over the streets. Many examples of these four characteristics survive today (Fig. FOUR-7.18, -7.19 -7.20). However, the monochoro dwelling unit characteristic of Sifnos and Kimolos, which defines the substance and geometry of the external defensive walls there, is not clearly present in the Patmos Chora.

The years between 1500 and 1659 were an era of prosperity on Patmos. Neither earthquakes, including a major temblor in 1646, nor the intermittent wars for Aegean supremacy between the Venetians and the Turks seem to have interfered with this prosperity. Indeed, the monastery succeeded so well in its worldly enterprises that the patriarch of Alexandria reprimanded the monks for their worldliness. The reprimand fell on deaf ears, and three decades later, the commercial fleet of Patmos numbered forty ships trading between Italy, the Black Sea, and Egypt.

The port of Skala was created in the early-seventeenth century, establishing what might be described as bipolar settlements. Port and market facilities were concentrated in Skala while the monastery/Chora complex retained its monastic and residential character even as it strengthened its defenses. In an attempt to minimize the chance that raiders might scale its walls, the monastery tore down the dwelling units that had been attached to its defense perimeter from early days. Added escarpments enhanced the visual impact of the edifice.

Late in the seventeenth century an anonymous monk annotated a codex in the monastery archives (Fig. FOUR-7.21) with a brief description of the disaster of 1659 mentioned above:

1659 June 18th, the Venetian armada came and plundered Patmos, it was Saturday, and the Admiral in command Francesco Morosini...may he be cursed.

To defend Venetian Crete from a Turkish invasion, Morosini (Fig. FOUR-7.22) had ventured north to disrupt Ottoman communications. From Patmos he extracted support and supplies. In the hope of distancing itself from the conflict, the monastery secretly communicated its predica-

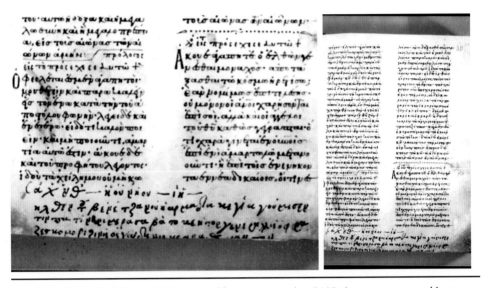

Fig. FOUR-7.21 Patmos Monastery library manuscript #107. Anonymous monk's annotation at the bottom of the page (left, enlargement; right, full page).

ment to the Turks. But the written message fell into Morosini's hands, and he decided to punish the monks for their disloyalty. His revenge was swift and merciless. The Patmian fleet was destroyed; all the ships in Skala were sunk. Chora was plundered. There is no indication that the town was burned or that its buildings were vandalized (Iakovides, *Patmos* 18), but all commercial stores and foodstuffs, including olive oil, grain, and wine, were destroyed. The monastery itself was not touched, a reprieve that allowed our anonymous monk to record his observations, perhaps from the safety of the monastery's ramparts.

Those who would later engage in the rediscovery of Greece with the Acropolis of Athens as the focus should certainly have wished that the Patmian monk's curse had had an immediate effect on Morosini. For it was he who, while leading another Venetian army against the Ottoman Turks, besieged the Acropolis twenty-eight years after the Patmos disaster. Informed by a deserter that the Turks were using the building for ammunition storage, on September 26, 1687, one of Morosini's artillery lieutenants trained his fire on the Parthenon, exploding the stored gunpowder and inflicting maddening damage on this incomparable building, which had survived intact for more than two thousand years (Fig. FOUR-7.22, -7.23).

Morosini's plunder of Patmos illuminates the geopolitical realities of defense on the islands of the archipelago at the time. The Aegean fortifications had been conceived and built to defend against corsair raids. They could not protect against an assault by regular naval forces as formidable as the Venetian fleet. The ease with which Morosini destroyed the goods and commerce of a prosperous community, apparently in a single day -- destruction from which the island would take several decades to recover -- is a grim reminder of the dangers to which all the Aegean islands were exposed and of the fate of the unlucky.

In the context of the Orthodox Church's struggle for survival, the Patmos Monastery of Saint John the Theologian had elicited and received papal protection as early as the thirteenth century. Pope Pius II (1458-64), who never ceased to preach crusades against the Turks, threatened to excommunicate any commander who attacked the monastery. Standing papal orders in later centuries forbade those ecclesiastical dependents of the pope, the Knights Hospitaller of Malta, to attack Christian shipping, a prohibition that was by and large respected. When it was not, that same prohibition provided some protection for Aegean captains who, when their goods were

Fig. FOUR-7.22
Francesco
Morosini
(1618-94)

Fig. FOUR-7.23
The destruction of
the Parthenon,
1687

VEDUTA DEL CAST: D'ACROPOLIS DALLA PARTE DI TRAMONTANA
308

wrongfully seized at sea, could pursue and sometimes win restitution in the courts of Malta. Morosini could invoke military considerations to defend his destruction of the economy of Chora. But given the monastery's papal protection and the threat of excommunication that would have followed a direct attack on it, Morosini apparently thought it politic not to offend the pope by vandalizing the monastery itself.

Patmos took several decades to recover from Morosini's devastation, but the recovery itself has been characterized as Patmos's second renaissance, which lasted from 1720 to 1821, the year the Greek war of independence began. A new regime, the product of a new relationship between the monastery and the secular community of the island, underlay this renaissance. The monastery ceded the northern half of the island to lay ownership, and an enterprising class of ship captains responded by claiming an important stake in Mediterranean trade for Patmos. In 1713 the Patmian School, sometimes called the "university of the archipelago," was established to teach Greek, philosophy, rhetoric, and logic. It attracted students from all over the Hellenic diaspora. From this urban, merchant-class community -- educated, well-traveled, and exposed to liberal European ideas -- emerged Emmanouil Xanthos, who with others formed the *Philiki Etairia* (or, "Friendly Society"), a secret revolutionary organization that laid the groundwork for the liberation of Greece from the Ottoman yoke that culminated in the establishment of the modern Greek state in 1830.

Thus, the people of Patmos were disappointed when they remained outside the borders of the new state and under the benign neglect of the Ottoman empire until 1912. The year before, Italy had declared war on Turkey, and the islanders greeted the invading Italian troops as liberators. But ultimately, they fell victim to Mussolini's dreams of empire. Union with Greece was delayed until Italy's defeat at the end of World War II, when Patmos and the Dodecanese complex, together with all the other Aegean islands, came under a single national and political administration that emphasized development and tourism. New port facilities were built in Skala in the early 1970s to allow ships to dock and to make both Chora and the monastery more accessible to the outside world. So far this new accessibility has not eroded the island's traditional isolation and solitude, and perhaps it portends a third renaissance for Patmos.

The repeated addition of escarpments during the seventeenth century strengthened the monastery's defenses and reinforced the external walls against earthquakes. These escarpments, the final additions to the skin of the monastery building, produced the massive and impressive architectural volume of the building we observe today.

The same massive building and its relationship to the surrounding rings of residential units was charmingly recorded by Vasily Gregorevich Barsky (1701-47), a penniless Russian monk who traveled through Greece motivated by religious devotion and who wrote about his travels. Barsky, better known for his descriptions of life in and drawings of the Ayion Oros monasteries, visited Patmos in 1731 and returned to the island in 1737 for a seven-year stay while he studied at the Patmian School. It is most likely that the drawing shown in figure FOUR-7.24 dates from his second visit.

Barsky had had no formal instruction in drawing, but his unaffected representations and characteristic bird's-eye views provide rare, informative, and unromanticized mid-eighteenth-century documentation of the architecture of the archipelago. The Patmos drawing (Fig. FOUR-7.24) delineates the relationship between monastery and Chora with directness, an intuitive

Fig. FOUR-7.24 Vasily Gregorevich Barsky, drawing, Patmos, Monastery and Chora, c. 1740

understanding of architectural scale and proportion, and a discriminating sense of the detail appropriate to include. The mix of lettering used to identify buildings and orientation in the drawing reminds us that Barsky's ambitions were descriptive rather than artistic.

In the drawing, Barsky observes and records the architecture of the roof of the monastery. Behind the uniform ramparts, the roof of this robust building with its formal Constantinopolitan origins reveals itself as an Aegean vernacular architecture composition with a plethora of volumes at a domestic scale. These volumes, attached to each other, with chapels and domes scattered among them, recall the image of Chora as it appears at the foot of the monastery (Fig. FOUR-7.16, -7.17). Barsky's drawing thus tells us that much of the monastery/Chora composition has not changed appreciably since the 1740s (Fig. FOUR-7.25, -7.26, -7.27, -7.28).

As in other Aegean island towns, neoclassical forms and manners have intruded into the vernacular architecture of Patmos in public buildings like

Fig. FOUR-7.25 Patmos, 1971

Fig. FOUR-7.26 Patmos, 1971

Fig. FOUR-7.27 Patmos, 1971

Fig. FOUR-7.28 Patmos, 1971

the city hall and in ship owners' mansions (Fig. FOUR-7.29, -7.30, -7.31). That this occurred on Patmos, an island that remained under Ottoman Turkish jurisdiction even after the 1830s, suggests that the unity and strength of the nineteenth-century vernacular architecture of the Aegean archipelago transcended national borders.

Built in the early seventeenth century, Skala reveals the growing naval

| Fig. FOUR-7.29 Patmos, Chora, city hall, 1999 | Fig. FOUR-7.30 Patmos, Chora, neoclassical elements, 1999 | Fig. FOUR-7.31 Patmos, Chora, neoclassical elements, 1999 |

strength of Patmos and the islanders' development of sufficient self-confidence to build near the water, despite the continuing pirate infestation of the Aegean Sea. After piracy disappeared, Skala continued to grow well into the twentieth century. Its greatest growth occurred after the 1970s when Patmos's attractions became more accessible with the building of its new port facilities. Despite the functional interdependence between the monastery/Chora complex and the port of Skala, the distance of four and one-half kilometers between them and the nature of the terrain are likely to keep the two from physically merging in the foreseeable future (Fig. FOUR -7.32, -7.33). A similar relationship between a hilltop town and a satellite port exists on Astypalaia between Chora/Kastro and Pera Yialos. There, the physical distance between the two is much shorter and the step-ramp-step formation connecting the hilltop town and the port below creates, at human rather than vehicular scale, a connector, a spine, that constitutes a truly vibrant architectural element. The bipolar development on both Patmos and Astypalaia should be compared with the example of Hydra in Chapter SIX. There, a concave and restricted site forced the original town of Kiafa to cascade downward towards the port when nineteenth-century conditions made the transformation possible.

Fig. FOUR-7.32 Patmos,
Monastery, Chora, Skala,
1970

Fig. FOUR-7.33 Patmos, Monastery, Chora, Skala, 1970

The monastery/Chora complex in Patmos with its clear Byzantine provenance is the oldest of the seven fortified Aegean towns discussed in this chapter, since it dates from the eleventh and twelfth centuries. In this context, Patmos (Fig. FOUR-7.34) also emerges as the preeminent example of formal and vernacular architecture coming together in a mutually informing relationship.

The Sifnos Kastro, built next, in the mid-fourteenth century, testifies to the contemporary importance of the Duchy of the Archipelago and the political fragmentation that prevailed in the Aegean archipelago at the time. Its hilltop site allows it to be read more legibly than the other six examples as an assembly of individual dwelling units built under the collective fortification system of Aegean town organization.

In contrast, the Astypalaia Kastro built fifty years later impresses by the monolithic character of its external wall and reveals its constituent dwelling units only after the visitor has passed beyond its gate.

Built about ten years before the fall of Constantinople in 1453, the flat-sited, geometrically regular, and complete Antiparos Kastro is best understood as crucial to the colonization of the island for the benefit of its Venetian feudal lord.

Kimolos Kastro followed 150 years later. Apparently built by a sea-merchant native to Kimolos to shelter his crews, the Kimolos Kastro marks the end of Venetian rule in the Aegean archipelago and ushers in the naval and commercial ascendancy that the islands achieved under Ottoman rule.

The abandonment of Skaros in Santorini and Kastro in Skiathos bears witness to a dramatic change in the geopolitics of the archipelago after the 1830s in the form of the elimination of piracy, both Christian and Moslem, from the Mediterranean and Aegean Seas. The Sifnos, Antiparos, and Kimolos Kastra still boast residential occupancy and remain precious and refreshing examples of the system of collective fortification that confirm its inherent versatility as well as the unity and variety of its vernacular architecture expression.

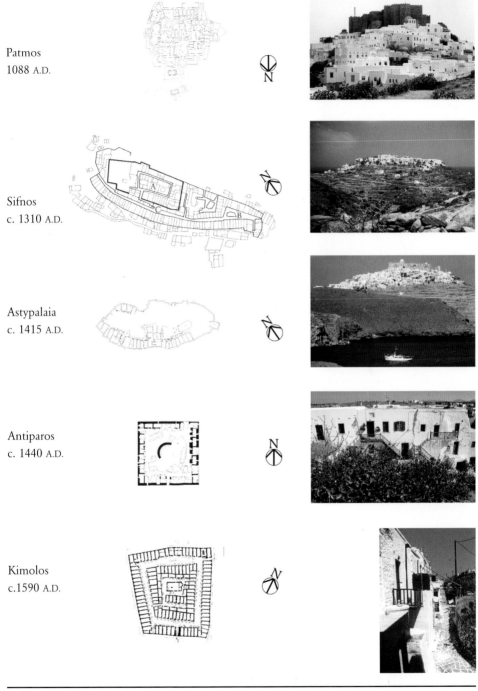

Patmos
1088 A.D.

Sifnos
c. 1310 A.D.

Astypalaia
c. 1415 A.D.

Antiparos
c. 1440 A.D.

Kimolos
c.1590 A.D.

Fig. FOUR-7.34 Patmos, Sifnos, Astypalaia, Antiparos, and Kimolos,
schematic plans at the same scale

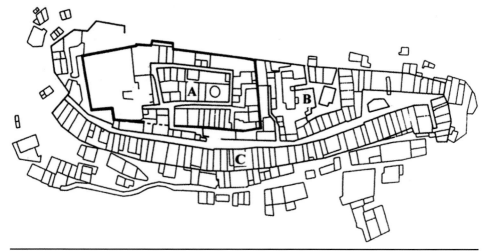

Fig. FOUR-7.35 Sifnos, Kastro, southwest elevation, plan, 1985

Throughout this book, digital technology has been used to produce images, drawings, diagrams, and color photographs and to organize these images within the text. The two concluding pages of Chapter FOUR take additional advantage of this technology to produce an experimental version of the possible appearance of the southwest defense perimeter of the Sifnos Kastro during the middle of the eighteenth century. The images on the left page (Fig. FOUR -7.35) include a color photograph of the Kastro dating from 1985 and a diagram of the plan of the settlement that has been coordinated with the photograph above. The images on the facing page (Fig. FOUR-7.36) have been created by eliminating from the photograph and the diagram all the more recent structures that have been built in front of the arch-like row of dwelling units that constituted the external defense perimeter of earlier days. After erasing the more recent structures, the foreground

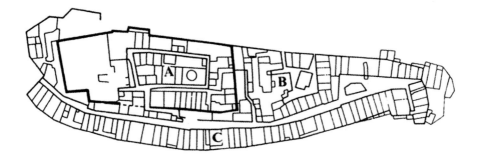

Fig. FOUR-7.36 Sifnos, Kastro, c. 1750

was adjusted to reflect its probable original form. The south end of the arch-like row includes the small number of dwelling units that appear to have been least altered by recent interventions (Fig. FOUR-3.08). For the purposes of this experiment, the elevations of these units have been used as prototypes for the rest of the defensive perimeter of the Kastro. Thus, the elevations that have been altered by the more recent insertions of windows and balconies have been replaced by digital images of these relatively untouched south-end units. Although hardly a restoration, this illustration (Fig. FOUR-7.36) is a reasonable approximation of what the Sifnos Kastro might have looked like in the middle of the eighteenth century.

FIVE

▷◁◁

AEGEAN TOWNS: TYPOLOGY AND MATERIALS

▷◁◁

The collective fortifications of the Aegean islands were a successful response to preserving life and culture in the archipelago when piracy was a constant, daily threat. Later, when the geopolitical environment shifted, the same fortifications were transformed with equal success into springboards for the release of a remarkable and sustained burst of human energy that recaptured control of the Aegean and Mediterranean lanes of commerce for the islanders. The collapse of the feudal system imposed by Latin rule and its replacement by the island self-government the Ottoman Turks allowed offered opportunities eagerly seized by the islanders. What began as small-scale, island-to-island trade, gradually developed in their hands into control of the seaborne trade of the Ottoman empire.

Data about this broadly outlined development is still fragmentary. Near the end of the Napoleonic wars and just before the beginning of the Greek war of independence, Pouqueville, a French visitor to Greece, reported the following numbers for twenty-two Aegean islands: ships owned, 545; tonnage of ships, 140,000; ship's crews, 36,000; ship-borne cannon, 5,500. These figures record the impressive growth of the islands' merchant fleets during the eighteenth century and underscore the shift of their economies from agriculture to seaborne trade.

More significant, perhaps, is the number of cannon carried by this growing commercial fleet, an average of ten per ship, although some of the larger vessels were armed with as many as twenty. Cannon were costly and reduced ships' carrying capacity and speed, but they were also necessary for defense against the corsairs. Acquired with the reluctant permission of the Ottoman authorities, this large number of cannon suggests the willingness of Aegean captains to use them and the islanders' skills and determination to meet the corsairs on equal terms and, eventually, to turn the tables on them. Self-confidence at sea, acquired at considerable human and material cost, found equivalent expression on land as the newly-expanding island towns burst out of their defensive enclosures to house a larger, more enterprising, and more prosperous citizenry.

An inherent characteristic of the palette of vernacular architecture is its limited number of building types, a characteristic that is indeed evident in the Aegean island towns, where, instead of producing new building types, new functions were incorporated into preexisting architectural forms. A limited building palette is, in fact, at the heart of the visual unity of the Aegean settlements. Variety and richness are introduced within this unity by the mutual adaptation of building and site. In addition, a firm architectural attachment to human scale as measured by the ever-present steps and railings; the size and composition of doors and windows, and other, smaller-scale architectural enrichments underscore this variety and richness.

As they have developed during recent centuries, two building types have by and large determined the urban forms of the Aegean island towns: dwelling units and churches and chapels. Rectangular building forms enclose the dwellings; curvilinear forms, the churches and chapels (Fig. FIVE-1.01, -1.02). Thus rectangular forms have come to signify secular functions and curvilinear ones to signify religious functions. (Santorini is a notable exception to this rule, as will be seen in Chapter FOUR.)

Fig. FIVE-1.01 Serifos, Chora, 1973   Fig. FIVE-1.02 Serifos, Chora, 1973

5.1 Dwellings

As defined by internal organization, two dwelling types predominate in Aegean vernacular architecture: the monochoro and the courtyard house. The monochoro (from *mono*, "single," and *choros*, "space"), a single-space dwelling unit, is the typical cell, module, or virtual Lego block that, repeated vertically and horizontally, produces the external defenses as well as the overall high-density, urban character of such settlements as the Sifnos and the Astypalaia Kastra. The courtyard house is a dwelling unit that includes at least one open, uncovered space in its internal organization that is partially or fully surrounded by walls or some other means of indicating property boundaries. The size and relative complexity of the courtyard house precluded its use inside a collective fortification. Later, as more buildings appeared outside the collective fortifications, the courtyard house, on some islands, began to replace the monochoro as the dominant type of dwelling.

| Fig. FIVE-1.03 Patmos, fithes, 1999 | Fig. FIVE-1.04 Serifos, Chora, 1973 |

Local stone and poor-quality wood, mostly the fithes referred to earlier, were the basic building materials of the monochoro. These materials determined its size and form within the larger collective fortification. In nearly all the surviving collective fortification examples, two-foot-thick parallel stone walls form the long sides of the rectangular plan. The spacing of these two long walls depends on the locally available fithes, whose spanning capacity does not ordinarily exceed twelve to fifteen feet (Fig. FIVE-1.03, -1.04). One of the short sides of the rectangle becomes an element of the external defense wall. The entry door located on the remaining short side faces the internal path of the settlement, as is the case, for example, in the Sifnos Kastro (Fig. FIVE-1.05, -1.06).

The typical proportions of the monochoro plan are close to a 1:2 ratio, yielding a 24 x 28 foot depth. The party walls are blind. For defense reasons, the windows on the back wall are as small as possible, but they are nonetheless adequate for cross-ventilation. The entry wall provides natural light and ventilation as well as access (Fig. FIVE-1.07). In the absence of partitions, an elevated platform in the back serves as the unit's sleeping area and suggests

Fig. FIVE-1.05 Sifnos, Kastro, 1997 | Fig. FIVE-1.06 Sifnos, Kastro, 1985

a division of space, with daily functions concentrated in the better-lit front half. The elevated platform also necessitates a ceiling height more generous than the other two dimensions of the monochoro. Other daily and seasonal functions occur within the articulated space of the monochoro, leaving no unused or uncared-for wall or floor space. Folklore studies have extensively documented the inspiring design accomplishment represented by the monochoro, whose thick, solid masonry walls, stuccoed and whitewashed, insulate an internal space that is comfortable both in summer and in winter.

Repeated vertically, the narrow-fronted monochoro dwelling unit produces the high building density characteristic of all the Aegean collective fortifications. Once inside a collective fortification, each monochoro becomes a separate horizontal property with direct access from the street. Solid masonry, multistep, exterior staircases provide access to the upper-level units (Fig. FIVE-1.08). A landing at the entry-door level effectively extends the limited square footage of the dwelling unit and enhances the social life of the street. As active links between the private and the public domains, these solid masonry staircases articulate the street visually and serve as reminders that the long, continuous, external defensive wall was assembled by juxtaposing many individual units.

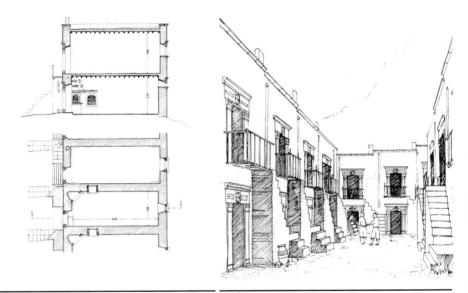

Fig. FIVE-1.07 Kimolos, Kastro, mono-choro units, plans, section

Fig. FIVE-1.08 Kimolos, Kastro, internal path, reconstruction

Solid masonry staircases, indispensable architectural elements in a constricted urban space, provided endless architectural challenges to the vernacular builders' inventiveness. These challenges were met with ingenious responses at human scale that combined unexpected turns and dexterously arranged step placements with narrow treads and steep risers in the ascent from the public street to the private entry (Fig. FIVE-1.09, -1.10, -1.11, -1.12). Above a certain height, the solid masonry steps were replaced by a wooden structure and, often, by latticework, in a visually persuasive combination of materials that underscored a heavier-below, lighter-above architectural relationship (Fig. FIVE-1.13, -1.14). The massively sculpted masonry steps attached to narrow-fronted monochoro dwelling units are distinctive elements of the vernacular architecture of the Aegean island towns. The examples in Sifnos, Mykonos, Antiparos, and Astypalaia are especially noteworthy.

Fig. FIVE-1.09 Sifnos, Kastro, 1997

Fig. FIVE-1.10 Sifnos, Kastro, 1986

Fig. FIVE-1.11 Mykonos, Chora, 1991

Fig. FIVE-1.12 Antiparos, Kastro, 1993

Fig. FIVE-1.13 Antiparos, Kastro, 1993

Fig. FIVE-1.14 Astypalaia, Chora, 1995

Variations in the configuration of the monochoro dwelling unit appear as early as the Antiparos Kastro. There, the units are placed with their long axis parallel rather than perpendicular to the external fortification wall. Extensions of individual property to embrace more than one monochoro bay also occur within some fortified settlements. When the extension is vertical, the limited square footage of each monochoro unit allows, at best, for steep steps under a trap door to facilitate internal communication. But even with this limitation, direct external access to each of the combined monochoro units is almost always retained. Variations occurred most often, of course, when monochoro units began to be built outside the confines of the collective enclosures. Even in these circumstances, the monochoro continued to be an important dwelling unit type in the new towns developing beyond the fortified periphery of Kastra. The current practice of unifying three or four monochoro units into a single property to create the greater square footage expected today bears witness to the architectural versatility of the original building type.

The courtyard house differs from the monochoro by being subdivided into a number of individual spaces, each with a different function. One of these spaces is always left uncovered and open to the sky -- the defining characteristic of this type of unit and the source of the name courtyard house. This building type has evolved over time to meet the changing needs of the Aegean islanders as well as those of the inhabitants of the greater Mediterranean region.

As a distinctive space within a house, a courtyard is similar to other rooms in dimensions and scale. The finishing materials used are the same as those used for enclosed rooms, adjusted to the outdoor functions of the courtyard. Floors are paved with flagstones that allow space for plants, especially vines that when fully grown provide shade and relief from the summer sun. Courtyards serve as sitting or dining rooms and, generally, as spaces for outdoor living rather than as outdoor rooms to be viewed but not inhabited. The mild climate that prevails for most of the year makes the courtyard, with its varied uses, including living and sleeping, one of the most attractive rooms in this type of dwelling. Its presence in the house satisfies the emotional needs of urban dwellers whose ties to the land and the outdoor life have not been severed (Fig. FIVE-1.16).

Fig. FIVE-1.15 Hydra, 1983

Fig. FIVE-1.16 Karpathos, Olympos, 1997

In most instances, the walls of a house define at least two of a courtyard's sides. The other two are subject to individual interpretation. In Hydra, for example, high walls provide an enclosure that visually, and, to a degree, acoustically, separates the court from the public realm (Fig. FIVE-1.15). The entry door in one of these high walls allots to the courtyard behind it a mediating role between the street and the enclosed house. In this role, the courtyard becomes a part of the sequence of architectural spaces that determines the organization of the typical nineteenth-century courtyard house on Hydra, an organization that is discussed in detail in Chapter SIX.

Fig. FIVE-1.17 Santorini, Fira, 1987   Fig. FIVE-1.18 Santorini, Fira, 1973

On Santorini, high walls also enclose courtyards. There, the steeply inclined site expands the courtyard's uses by transforming one of its sides into a balcony with a view of and communication with the area below, which leads to the sea in the caldera (Fig. FIVE-1.17). The site incline in Santorini also allows for a distinctive application of the organizing sequence: public street - private uncovered courtyard - private enclosed space. In this application, the entry to the house is at the highest point of the site. Stairs descend to the courtyard, from which the other rooms of the dwelling can be reached (Fig. FIVE-1.18). As it is repeatedly applied at Santorini's inclined site, the courtyard house allows a rich interplay between public and private space, orchestrating an unprecedented and uniquely rewarding spectacle within the vernacular architecture of the Aegean islands.

The central settlements of Sifnos-Apollonia, Artemon, and so on comprise seven separate but interconnected small towns with a population of about eighteen hundred people. Located in the interior of the island rather than on the coast as the Kastro is, these settlements evolved in the relatively secure conditions of the nineteenth century. It is not surprising, then, that Sifnos developed its own interpretation of the courtyard building type with a more open configuration for the courtyard. Two sides are still defined by the walls of the enclosed part of the house. But architectural elements lower than full-sized walls define the other sides. Despite using different methods of enclosure, the plans of the dwelling units in the central settlements of Sifnos still underscore the primacy of the courtyard within the house (Fig. FIVE-1.19, -1.20). Its dimensions and scale confirm its role in articulating the dwelling unit. And, as elsewhere, the courtyard serves as a mediating space between the public street and the roofed-over parts of the house. Another function characteristic of the courtyard, its use as a central circulation space, has also been retained in the Sifnos plans.

In the vernacular architecture of the Aegean island towns today, outdoor space remains indispensable to the dwelling unit. Where conditions do not permit the presence of a full-sized courtyard, a smaller space, similarly defined, is often attached to the unit, even when its dimensions are minimal

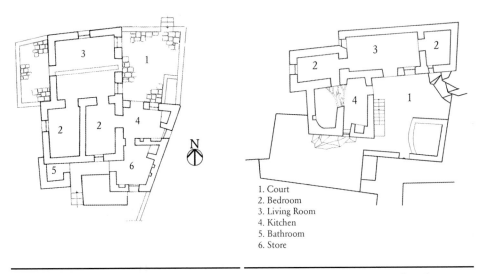

1. Court
2. Bedroom
3. Living Room
4. Kitchen
5. Bathroom
6. Store

Fig. FIVE-1.19 Sifnos, central settlements, courtyard house

Fig. FIVE-1.20 Sifnos, central settlements, courtyard house

and its functional contributions, negligible. Outdoor space in general serves to emphasize the region's climatic possibilities, since mild weather allows such spaces to be used for most of the year; to meet social needs, since courtyards function as outdoor family rooms, and help satisfy aesthetic ambitions, since houses seem incomplete without an outdoor room.

As an architectural expression of privacy, the courtyard dwelling unit is present on all of the Aegean islands and enriches the public realm by including the element that joins the public and the private -- the gate, which is both an entry to the unit and an exit to the street. In this palindromic function, the gate represents a challenging architectural contradiction, since it invites but, at the same time, prohibits access (Fig. FIVE-1.21, -1.22, -1.23, -1.24, -1.25, -1.26).

The gate design also embodies a public message about the personality of the house behind it. Most, if not all, of the islands share a prevailing theme for gate design. As a gate frames a door opening, it is formed by a simple but powerful vernacular interpretation of a formal architectural theme, a pediment flanked by two piers or columns. These borrowed elements originated in the nineteenth-century neoclassical architecture of Athens, the nation's capital, but were subsequently given form and expression by local means. Together with whitewashed stone masonry walls and painted wood plank or panel doors, the neoclassical elements evident in gate design have been assimilated into the vernacular architecture typology of the islands. With as many interpretations as there have been applications, the gate design theme is another reminder of the vitality of the vernacular architecture of the archipelago, which sustains visual unity even as it is enriched by the variations devised by its inventive individual builders (Fig. FIVE-1.27, -1.28, -1.29 -1.30, -1.31, -1.32).

The monochoro and the courtyard house in all of their variations embody the historical evolution of the vernacular architecture of the archipelago. The Kastro, or collective fortification, and the monochoro, the dwelling unit that prevailed when the Kastra were built, established an early and lasting interdependence and a mutually supportive architectural relationship that was crucial to the life and culture of the archipelago for several centuries. As a changing geopolitical environment allowed new building to spill outside the protective walls of the Kastra, the courtyard house gradually reemerged as the prevalent building type in the nineteenth century, a type with historical and environmental roots in antiquity and a strong presence in such towns as Olynthos, Priene, and Delos.

Olynthos, a town planned on a flat site near the Aegean coast of Macedonia, was laid out in about 430 B.C. and was completely built up well before its destruction in 348 B.C. Excavations reveal repeated building blocks incor-

Fig. FIVE-1.21 Amorgos,
Chora, 2000

Fig. FIVE-1.22 Amorgos,
Chora, 2000

Fig. FIVE-1.23 Amorgos,
Chora, 2000

Fig. FIVE-1.24 Kimolos,
Psathi, 1999

Fig. FIVE-1.25 Mykonos,
Chora, 1991

Fig. FIVE-1.26 Paros,
Paroikia, 1973

porated into an orthogonal system of streets, with each block comprising ten dwelling units. Each unit contains a number of rooms dispersed around a court secluded from public view and consistently placed on the south side of the block. The courtyard dwelling unit is thus the typical building cell of the fifth century B.C. town of Olynthos (Fig. FIVE-1.34).

Fig. FIVE-1.27 Paros,
Lefkes, 1993

Fig. FIVE-1.28 Sikinos,
Chorio, 1994

Fig. FIVE-1.29 Santorini,
Fira, 1995

Fig. FIVE-1.30 Sikinos,
Chorio, 1994

Fig. FIVE-1.31 Folegandros,
Chora, 1994

Fig. FIVE-1.32 Symi, 1994

Priene, originally on the Asia Minor coast but now located some miles inland, was also built on the orthogonal street system, but its site is on an incline. The general plan as unearthed by excavations represents the constituent elements of a town: an orthogonal grid, public spaces, and residential areas made up exclusively of courtyard dwelling units. The courtyard

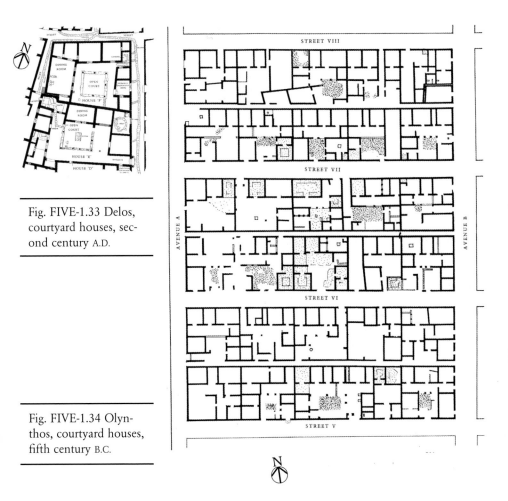

Fig. FIVE-1.33 Delos, courtyard houses, second century A.D.

Fig. FIVE-1.34 Olynthos, courtyard houses, fifth century B.C.

house shown in the illustration Fig. SIX-4.03 is located in the northwest segment of Priene's general layout (Fig. SIX-4.02). As is typical of the courtyard plan, each house is secluded from the public street and encloses a central open-air court to give light and air and space for family activities. Mediating between an orthogonal grid and a sloping site and a detached defense wall encloses the town on its south and west sides and clearly indicates that Priene was more prosperous than the average eighteenth-century Aegean town. The more generous dimensions of the courtyard dwellings of Priene also confirm this prosperity.

With their elegant colonnades and impressive mosaics, the largest and most luxurious versions of the courtyard house from Aegean antiquity are to be found in Delos (Fig. FIVE-1.33). Delos is one of the smaller but better-known islands of the Cyclades group, and, according to mythology, drifted aimlessly in the Aegean until it became the birthplace of Apollo and Artemis. Held in particular esteem by the classical Greek world, Delos continued to flourish as a commercial center in Roman times, when it was declared a free port. The elegant columns, ornate doorways, and exquisite mosaics of the courtyard houses date mostly from this period.

All three of these examples from antiquity attest to the courtyard house's deep historical roots in the islands and the Aegean littoral. Built in geopolitical environments very different from those faced by the later island towns, these houses demonstrate planned urban living in Olynthos and Priene and commercial and cultural prosperity, especially in Delos. Although different circumstances governed the nineteenth-century resurgence of the court-centered dwelling unit, its intimate relationship among house, site, and climate testifies to its continuing social utility and versatility within the archipelago.

5.2 Churches and Chapels

Churches and chapels are equally important components of the vernacular architecture of the Aegean islands. Scattered beyond the boundaries of towns, the numerous chapels -- each island includes hundreds of them – are religious, historical, and physical landmarks in the islands' landscapes. These chapels impress the viewer not only by their ubiquity but also by their diminutive domestic scale, whether incorporated into the urban fabric (Fig. FIVE-2.01, -2.02, -2.03) or freestanding (Fig. FIVE-2.04, -2.05). The great majority originated not as institutionally commissioned buildings but as private chapels erected to fulfill a personal vow. Erecting a chapel and dedicating it to the builder's protector saint gratefully acknowledged a safe return from a perilous sea journey or a cure for a life-threatening illness by divine

Fig. FIVE-2.01 Sifnos, Apollonia, central path, site plan

Fig. FIVE-2.02 Mykonos, 1970   Fig. FIVE-2.03 Kythnos, Chora, 1973

intervention. Most of these private votive chapels have remained private and have been bequeathed, together with family houses, to subsequent generations of the builder's family. The descendants have maintained the chapels and participate in the annual whitewashing that coincides with the feast day of the saint to whom the building is dedicated, an architectural ritual that confirms the chapel's active presence in the post-Byzantine life of the island community.

Enclosed by two-foot-thick heavy masonry walls, the majority of these chapels are constructed on the single-space, single-nave, monochoro principle, adapted to a religious rather than a secular purpose (Fig. FIVE-2.06, -2.08, -2.09, -2.10). The apse attached to one of the narrow sides of the enclosure is always oriented towards the east, as is required by the Byzantine Greek Orthodox tradition. The entry door is located on the opposite, or western, wall of the chapel. No matter how minimally endowed the building is, an iconostasis (a screen separating the chancel from the space open to the laity) always separates the public from the consecrated part of the chapel. A barrel vault spans the width of the chapel, which normally measures between ten and twelve feet and rarely exceeds fifteen. Plan proportions are likely to be 1:2, with one for width and two for length. Open-

Fig. FIVE-2.04 Sifnos,
near Kastro, 1969

Fig. FIVE-2.05 Sifnos,
near Kastro, 1985

Fig. FIVE-2.06 Santorini, near Skaros, 1995

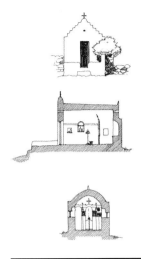
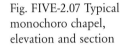

Fig. FIVE-2.07 Typical monochoro chapel, elevation and section

Fig. FIVE-2.08 Astypalaia

Fig. FIVE-2.09 Mykonos, 1991

Fig. FIVE-2.10 Astypalaia, double-apse window, 1971

Fig. FIVE-2.11 Astypalaia, interior, 1971

ings, which are few and moderate in size, allow only a modicum of natural light into the interior so as not to overwhelm the permanent candlelight within (Fig. FIVE-2.07, -2.08, -2.09, -2.10, -2.11).

The architectural scale and the materials that fill the wall openings, including doors and windows, integrate each chapel into the urban fabric of its settlement. The bell tower, a partial extension upward from either the west or the south wall, identifies the chapel and distinguishes it from the secular urban fabric. Aegean bell towers are integral to chapel walls rather than separate, four-sided architectural additions to the building. Infinitely varied in form and execution, bell towers offer a vehicle of personal expression to their builders and an inspiring enrichment to the vernacular architecture of the archipelago. Within their great variety, the careful observer can begin to discern distinctive architectural treatments and themes peculiar to each island's bell towers (Fig. FIVE-2.12, -2.13, -2.14, -2.15, -2.16, -2.17, -2.18).

Two single-nave chapels were frequently joined into one. Two apses at the east end confirm the origins of the building, while, occasionally, a single entrance identifies its new unity. Numerous examples of such double chapels exist on most, if not all, of the Aegean islands (Fig. FIVE-2.19, -2.20, -2.22). The Apollonia Sifnos site plan (Fig. FIVE-2.01) contains two double chapels successfully incorporated into the urban fabric of the town. The Metamorphosis Soteros, or "the Transfiguration of Christ," chapel (Fig. FIVE-2.21) in Apollonia, is a representative example of the double-chapel type. The chapel's physical relationship to the streets on its south and east sides, the open space on its west side, and the house behind it eloquently demonstrate the graceful integration of the building into the urban fabric of the neighborhood. In the past, perhaps, both house and chapel belonged to the same person or family. The vertical section drawing reveals a flat-roofed construction particular to Sifnos rather than the barrel-vaulted type more prevalent in the Cyclades. Some scholars believe that the double-nave, single-chapel building originated during the reign of the Duchy of the Archipelago, when the strong Latin Roman Catholic presence in the islands may have prompted a simultaneous double liturgy designed to meet the religious needs of a mixed community.

In addition to the barrel-vaulted or flat-roofed single-nave chapel, the Aegean islands' church typology also includes single-nave-with-dome chapels, two of which appear in the Apollonia Sifnos site plan (Fig. FIVE-2.01). These chapels are larger in plan and in volume because of their domes, yet their other features, including the heavy stone masonry, the apse projections on the east side, the domestic-scale openings, and the upward extensions of the walls to form bell towers remain the same as those of the barrel-vaulted and flat-roofed types (Fig. FIVE-2.24). In each case the dome sits at the intersection of two barrel vaults: the east-west barrel vault that runs the full length of the building and the north-south barrel vault which, to meet the confines of the rectangular plan, appears atrophic. The plan and

Fig. FIVE-2.12 Sifnos, Ano Petali, 1998

Fig. FIVE-2.13 Sifnos, near Kastro, 1985

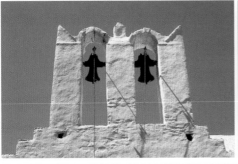

Fig. FIVE-2.14 Sifnos, Apollonia, 1997

Fig. FIVE-2.15 Sifnos, Ano Petali, 1986

Fig. FIVE-2.16 Sifnos, Apollonia, 1997

Fig. FIVE-2.17 Sifnos, Apollonia, 1988

Fig. FIVE-2.18 Sifnos, near Kastro, 1985

Fig. FIVE-2.19 Amorgos, 1977

Fig. FIVE-2.20 Sikinos, Chorio, 1994

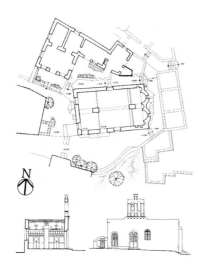

Fig. FIVE-2.21 Sifnos, Apollonia,
Metamorphosis Soteros, plan, section,
elevation

Fig. FIVE-2.22 Sikinos, Chorio, 1994

section of the Timios Stavros, or "Holy Cross," chapel represent one of the
single-nave domed chapels in the Apollonia Sifnos site plan (Fig.FIVE-2.23).
Serving as an anteroom to both the private chapel and to the house at its
southwest corner is a courtyard entered directly from the street. In this
three-part assembly of chapel, court, and dwelling, the scales of public and
private, domestic and religious building, and enclosed and open-roofed
spaces are in gentle harmony with one another. The section drawing indi-

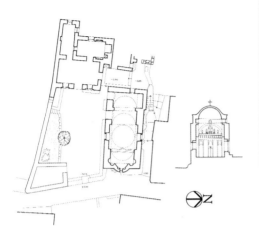

Fig. FIVE-2.23 Sifnos, Apollonia, Timios Stavros, plan, section

Fig. FIVE-2.24 Sifnos, Kastro, 1988

cates a well-appointed iconostasis, which together with the larger-than-average size of the chapel, suggests that its donor was wealthier than the patrons of most of the small barrel-vaulted votive chapels scattered throughout the islands.

A fifth and larger church, Ayios Spyridon, appears at the southeast corner of the Apollonia Sifnos site plan (Fig. FIVE-2.01). A parish church, its plan confirms its Byzantine origin, yet it has absorbed architectural nuances from Athens and, in particular, from the eclectic Metropolis church there, a building completed in 1862.

Six independent, single-nave, barrel-vaulted chapels appear in an assembly in the Astypalaia Chora (Fig. FIVE-2.25). An unusually large number of chapels to be attached to one another, this complex of six appears in the *Karae* neighborhood, 175 feet north of the Querini fortification gate. Well integrated into the site, each of the six chapels has its own distinctive barrel vault, an apse on the east wall, and a door on the west side. Crosses atop or on the door identify the chapel's religious mission (Fig. FIVE-2.25, -2.26, -2.27). Each of the six was built at a different point in the eighteenth century. None of the barrel vaults is identical in its geometry, width, height, or curvature. Average floor plan dimensions are 12 x 18 feet. A small opening above the solid entry door and an even smaller opening in the apse allow in a cautious amount of light. All the whitewashed interiors include an iconos-

Fig. FIVE- 2.25 Astypalaia, Chora, Karae neighborhood, elevation

Fig. FIVE- 2.26 Astypalaia, Chora, Karae neighborhood, 1971

tasis (Fig. FIVE-2.28). The fourth chapel to the north, dedicated to Panayia Leimonetria, or the "Merciful Virgin," encloses a remarkable iconostasis (Fig. FIVE-2.29). Built of wood, the lower part is conventional. But in the upper part, a deeply carved timber with angels and doves has obviously been recycled, probably from a sailing ship. Sailing ship and chapel may once have belonged to the same family, whose two properties were ultimately fused to celebrate its naval enterprise, wealth, and religious dedication.

Centered as it is on an approach path, the west elevation of this chapel can be observed from a greater distance than the other five. At noon, when the rays of the sun run parallel to the surface of the elevation, short shad-

Fig. FIVE-2.27 Astypalaia, Chora, Karae neighborhood, 1995

Fig. FIVE-2.28 Astypalaia, Chora, Karae neighborhood, chapel interior, 1971

Fig. FIVE-2.29 Astypalaia, Chora, Panayia Leimonetria, interior, 1971

ows reveal a wall finished with cut-veneer pieces of marble or stone, apparently recycled from an earlier unidentified building (Fig. FIVE-2.27 and Fig. EIGHT-1.12).

Within easy walking distance of Apollonia, the church of Ayios Konstantinos is detached from the urban fabric of the town of Artemon, another settlement on Sifnos. This church (Fig. FIVE-2.30, -2.31, -2.32) is larger than the chapels just discussed; its plan includes three barrel-vaulted naves. The central nave is wider than the other two. This three-nave plan makes Ayios Konstantinos unique on Sifnos and rare in the Aegean archipelago. The normal building vocabulary of the chapels, including thick walls, bell towers, small openings, and whitewash, is used in Ayios Konstantinos; however, this building offers additional noteworthy features besides.

Certainly not part of the original building, the massive buttresses that support the walls on the north side are reminders of the ever-present threat of earthquakes in the Aegean archipelago. Together with the buttresses, the neoclassical themes of the nineteenth-century frame around the entry door on the western wall point to the continuous evolution and recasting of the building, a distinctive and enriching feature of Aegean vernacular architecture that underscores the diachronic character of its buildings. Flights of exterior steps at the northwest corner provide direct access to the roof and simplify the annual whitewashing. As these irregular steps negotiate their way to the roof, they merge with the architectural volumes of the church and again vividly remind us of the inventiveness and versatility of the ver-

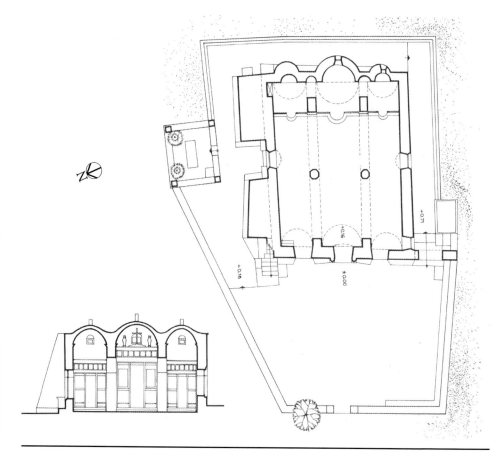

Fig. FIVE- 2.30 Sifnos, Artemon, Ayios Konstantinos, plan, section

Fig. FIVE-2.31 Sifnos, Artemon, Ayios Konstantinos, east side, 1985

Fig. FIVE-2.32 Sifnos, Artemon, Ayios Konstantinos, east side, 1986

nacular architecture builders of the Aegean archipelago.

Photographed and published repeatedly in both scholarly and commercial texts, the church of Paraportiani on the island of Mykonos is perhaps the most familiar and attractive example of Aegean vernacular architecture (Fig. FIVE -2.35, -2.36). Paraportiani is not a single church but a synthesis of five chapels built in vertical and horizontal attachment over a period longer than one lifetime. No one "designed" the complex; rather, time and circumstance worked together to produce an *Acheiropoietos* (or "not-made-by-hand") church that is also an inspiring building and an edifice that vivifies Le Corbusier's definition of architecture as "…the masterly, correct, and magnificent play of masses brought together in light… "(Fig. FIVE-2.33, -2.34).

To understand the Paraportiani complex, it is helpful to think of it in two parts, the western and the eastern (Fig. FIVE-2.37). Three single-space, single-nave, monochoro-type chapels have been attached to form the western half and are dedicated, left to right, to Ayia Anastasia, Ayioi Anargyroi, and Ayios Sozos. A barrel vault covers each of the three chapels, which were

Fig. FIVE-2.33 Mykonos, Paraportiani, morning, 1991

Fig. FIVE-2.34 Mykonos, Paraportiani, afternoon, 1991

Fig. FIVE-2.35 Mykonos, Paraportiani, 1991

Fig. FIVE-2.36 Mykonos, Paraportiani, 1991

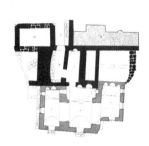

Fig. FIVE-2.38 Mykonos,
Paraportiani, 1991

Fig. FIVE-2.39 Mykonos,
Paraportiani, 1991

Fig. FIVE-2.37 Mykonos,
Paraportiani, lower-level
plan and west elevation

Fig. FIVE-2.40 Mykonos,
Paraportiani, 1991

Fig. FIVE-2.41 Mykonos,
Paraportiani, 1991

apparently built at different times. Since the east end of each of the chapels
is attached to the eastern half of the complex, instead of projecting out, the
apses are absorbed into the wall. The west entry elevations of the same three
chapels employ a familiar Aegean theme. Each wall extends upward and, at
the same time, steps in from both sides to reach a minimal width, crowned

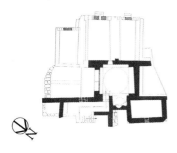

Fig. FIVE-2.43 Mykonos, Paraportiani, 1991

Fig. FIVE-2.42 Mykonos, Paraportiani, upper-level plan, east elevation

Fig. FIVE-2.44 Mykonos, Paraportiani, 1991

by a cross at the top. In the middle chapel, this receding-steps theme becomes a bell tower (Fig. FIVE-2.37, -2.38, -2.39, -2.40, -2.41).

Seen from all four sides, the much taller, two-level eastern half produces the main volumes that constitute the familiar image of the complex (Fig.FIVE-2.42, -2.43, -2.44). Entered from the east side, the lower level is unlit and encloses a small narthex that runs parallel to a similarly sized chapel dedicated to Ayios Stathis. A flat roof of wooden beams serves as the floor for the space above. Essentially space left over from an earlier time which has no known use, the lower level provides a podium on which the dome, the "jewel in the crown," rests. Taller than either of its horizontal dimensions and topped by a dome, the upper-floor chapel encloses a dimly lit space in the Byzantine tradition of an "inscribed cross with a dome" (Fig. FIVE-2.42) and is dedicated to Panayia Paraportiani (or the "Virgin Mary by-the-gate"), the name used to identify the complex (Fig. FIVE-2.45, -2.46). In this particular church, the barrel vaults under the inscribed cross are reduced to the widths of the arches on all four sides. Readable from the outside, a

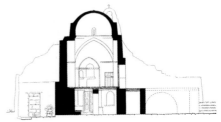

| Fig. FIVE-2.45 Mykonos, Paraportiani, 1991 | Fig. FIVE-2.46 Mykonos, Paraportiani, section |

drum supports the dome, while internally, the drum and the dome merge into a half-sphere. Uncharacteristically, the main space is entered directly through a door next to the off-center apse, which is screened by a wall and reached by two sets of steps and three turns. This complicated access route apparently resulted from unforeseen changes in the life and use of the complex.

The five intact chapels and the parts of the Panayia Paraportiani complex now virtually in ruins contribute powerfully to the present three-dimensional and sculptural form of the complex. In the absence of historical data or a reliable oral tradition, we can only hypothesize that the partially collapsed north-south wall that leads upward to the bell tower formed part of an enclosure that related to the church of Panayia Paraportiani. And we can only guess that the two-level, roofless rectangular building at the northeastern corner of the complex served domestic uses and belonged to a larger set of now-defunct buildings. As for the town of Mykonos, we know from fifteenth- and sixteenth-century travelers that a Kastro enclosed it whose remnants are difficult to locate today (Fig. FIVE-2.47). Indeed, it has been suggested that the Panayia Paraportiani complex was a distinctive part of the periphery of the Mykonos Kastro: the walls of Ayioi Anargyroi, the middle of the three chapels in the western half of the complex, are exceptionally thick (Fig. FIVE-2.37) and might once have served as the base of a tower attached to the defense perimeter that guarded a gate to the town. Ayios Sozos, the northernmost of the three chapels and a later addition to the complex, probably conceals a fortification gate positioned where the apse of the chapel is now located, a location which would help to explain the unusual narthex space of Ayios Stathis. This narthex could previously have been a gate with heavy doors at both its narrow ends, an easily recognizable fortification design that resembles that of the gates of the Sifnos Kastro. The presence of a gate on the spot could also help explain the word *Paraportiani*, a combination of *Para* ("next to") and *portiani* ("of the gate") that produces the name of the complex, the "Virgin Mary by-the-gate."

Panayia Paraportiani is a remarkable assembly of solids and voids; of such architectural parts as walls, buttresses, barrel vaults, and a dome; and of spaces in use or abandoned. Time has eroded some parts and fused others. Benign neglect, together with the removal of some of the building's material for other uses --not to mention the actions of the sun, the wind, and the salt of the sea-- has scored the exterior with marks like wrinkles that age the building. But none of these processes has contributed as much to the building's present form as the annual whitewashing of the complex. Whitewash endlessly applied has created the present monolithic, seamless form so strikingly revealed by the clear sunlight of the Aegean archipelago.

Fig. FIVE-2.47 Mykonos, town and port. Paraportiani appears at the middle right of the illustration, 1991.

Fig. FIVE-2.48 Mykonos, town and port, Paraportiani, 1991

Its size, antiquity, and restoration make the church of Panayia Katapoliani on the island of Paros the most significant early-Christian-era building in the archipelago, comparable in importance to the basilicas of Ayios Dimitrios and the Acheiropoietos (or "not-made-by-hand") church in Thessaloniki. Panayia Katapoliani is not a single building but a complex (Fig. FIVE-2.49). Three discrete but attached buildings emerge as its most important components: the chapel of Ayios Nikolaos at the northeast corner (Fig. FIVE-2.50, -2.51), the larger church of Panayia Katapoliani at the center (Fig. FIVE-2.52, -2.53), and the Baptistry on the south side (Fig. FIVE-2.54, -2.55).

The present-day chapel of Ayios Nikolaos, a basilica with a dome, was built in 326 A.D. when, according to ecclesiastical tradition, Ayia Eleni (or Saint Helena) set out for Jerusalem in search of the Holy Cross and stopped in Paros along the way to visit the chapel. There, she prayed and promised to build a larger church dedicated to the Virgin Mary when she concluded her journey. Her early death meant that the fulfillment of the promise fell to her son, the Emperor Constantine the Great (306–37 A.D.). As a votive offering, the larger church of Panayia Katapoliani was apparently the first in a long line of such churches and chapels built in the Aegean archipelago. The Baptistry, comprising another basilica with a dome, is a rare and evocative building. The cruciform baptismal font for adult baptism indicates that the building dates from before the age of Justinian (527-65 A.D.), when infant baptism was instituted by the Church. The baptismal font also brings human architectural scale to a building filled with abstract symbols.

Early basilicas were roofed with timber trusses whose size determined the width of their naves. But timber roofs were vulnerable to fire and were therefore replaced by barrel vaults and domes in the age of Justinian. The space within the four pillars supporting the dome of Panayia Katapoliani is not the expected square enclosing a circle. Instead, this rectangle's north-south dimension exceeds that of its east-west by about five feet, rendering the base of the dome elliptical rather than circular. Neither earthquakes nor poor workmanship created this odd shape; rather, the elliptical form is evidence of the change from the earlier timber-covered, Constantinian building, which apparently burned down, to the domed, barrel-vaulted basilica built during the reign of Justinian. In the process of rebuilding, the unequal widths of the nave and the transept were fused into the elliptical base of the dome. Panayia Katapoliani was restored to its Justinian form in the early 1960s.

Often called *Hecatontapyliani* ("[the basilica] of one hundred gates") to underscore its extraordinary size within the Aegean context (Fig.FIVE-2.56, -2.57), Panayia Katapoliani is clearly an example of formal rather than ver-

Fig. FIVE-2.49 Paros, Katapoliani, plan

1. Ayios Nikolaos
2. Panayia Katapoliani
3. Baptistry
4. Atrium

Fig. FIVE-2.50 Ayios Nikolaos, 1973

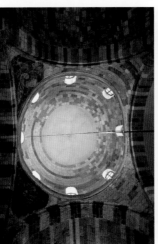

Fig. FIVE-2.52 Panayia, Katapoliani, 1973

Fig. FIVE-2.54 Baptistry, 1973

Fig. FIVE-2.51 Ayios Nikolaos, 1973

Fig. FIVE-2.53 Panayia, Katapoliani, 1973

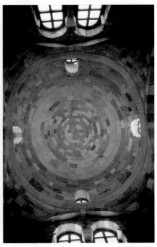

Fig. FIVE-2.55 Baptistry, 1973

nacular building, as is shown by the historical evidence and by its architecture. Its inception, plan, and execution were initiated by the imperial capital of Constantinople and inspired by architectural forms popular there. Over the centuries, the building suffered earthquakes as well as normal wear and tear. In the absence of an imperial Byzantine presence after the fifteenth century, repairs were conducted using local resources, materials, and workmanship. The sizable buttresses, the internal massive reinforcements of walls and columns, the blocking of windows, and the repair of the damage inflicted by the destructive earthquake of 1733 degraded and obscured the building's original formal architectural character. The repair and maintenance work that followed gradually infused it with the manners and techniques of post-Byzantine Aegean vernacular architecture. The application of layers of whitewash to the exterior walls, the erection of three typically Cycladic bell towers on the west wall (Fig. FIVE-2.59), and the introduction of other elements of the Aegean vernacular vocabulary dominated the church's architecture from the eighteenth century. This shift in architectural vocabulary makes Panayia Katapoliani another example of the intimate

Fig. FIVE-2.56 Katapoliani, 1987   Fig. FIVE-2.57 Katapoliani, 1993

Fig. FIVE-2.58 Katapoliani, 1988   Fig. FIVE-2.59 Katapoliani, prior to restoration, 1948

and mutually supportive relationship between formal and vernacular architecture in the Archipelago. The restoration of the Panayia Katapoliani in the early 1960s resembled that of the Acropolis of Athens in the 1830s. Just as the medieval and Tourkokratia buildings were removed to recapture the citadel's fifth century B.C. glory, the Panayia Katapoliani renovation not only secured the church against further damage from earthquakes but also removed the vernacular architecture intrusions, structural and otherwise, to recapture the glory of the Justinian church from the sixth century A.D. (Fig. FIVE-2.57,-2.58).

The political life of the moribund Byzantine Empire came to an abrupt end with the fall of Constantinople in May 1453. The Ottoman Turkish rule that replaced it destroyed the aristocracy that had sponsored the formal culture of the Byzantine Empire but allowed the captive, second-class Christian population to retain its religion and culture and, in certain circumstances, a measure of self-government. (For a discussion of self-government in the Aegean islands, see Chapter TWO.) Of these monumental changes in the region, Speros Vryonis writes, "The effect of Turkish forms on the Byzantine legacy was decapitation on the formal level and isolation on the folk level" ("The Byzantine Legacy" 19). The Aegean archipelago was initially stunned by this combination of "decapitation" with "isolation." But its eventual recovery is eloquently demonstrated by the architecture of the churches and chapels examined in the preceding pages.

After the collapse of Latin rule in the Aegean, the islands' culture continued to be nurtured by the Greek Orthodox Byzantine tradition, as the islanders remained true to their religious rites and the architecture that housed them. In the past, the formal culture that emanated from Constantinople had sponsored such major and innovative buildings as Panayia Katapoliani in Paros and the Monastery of Saint John the Theologian on Patmos. When such state endowments disappeared, Aegean religious building was forced to rely on the islands' own limited means. Materials were restricted to those that could be found locally, and for economic and political reasons, the size and scale of buildings were reduced to the domestic from the monumental. Families expressing their religious devotion by building small chapels were less likely to provoke Turkish rapacity than communities building sizable, richly appointed churches. Left to their own devices, the Aegean island communities adhered to their traditional religious architectural forms and relied on proliferation rather than on innovation.

Aegean island chapels and churches are thus apparently ageless. It is difficult to discern the century in which a particular church or chapel was built, whether the seventeenth, the eighteenth, or the nineteenth, nor does it make much difference, since their spiritual and earthly virtues are diachronic and incorporate traditional post-Byzantine forms that fostered the inventiveness of their vernacular builders. The forms, materials, and details of these chapels and churches yield little archaeological evidence of when they were built, and dendrochronology is unhelpful where door lintels have been created from recycled pieces of marble. Occasionally, a dedicatory inscription dating from the erection or rededication of a chapel will shed some light, although most of these chapels date from the eighteenth century or later, when the Aegean island towns saw a rapid rise in maritime and commercial activity and prosperity. Economic growth meant that a vigorous and enterprising middle class of captains and merchants with money to spend began to develop and to celebrate their culture and religion under the watchful eyes of the Ottoman Turkish authorities.

5.3 Windmills

As noted at the beginning of the chapter, a limited building palette or typology is at the heart of the visual unity of the island towns. Dwelling units and churches and chapels comprise the two major forms within this typology and thus constitute the fundamental determinants of the architecture of the archipelago. But although examples of them are fewer, three other building types add to this limited palette: windmills, dovecotes, and monasteries.

Fig. FIVE-3.01 Amorgos, windmills, 1977

Windmills were built of the same native materials as dwellings and chapels but were configured differently, their massive cylindrical forms having been inspired by their now-superseded function, which has caused their near-demise. Built either as single units or in linear formations, windmills were strategically located on heights and ridges above the towns they served, to harness the power of the ever-present Aegean winds and to provide energy to grind grain for flour (Fig. FIVE-3.02, -3.03, -3.04, -3.05). Since waiting for the grain to be ground created opportunities to gossip, sing, exchange news, find brides, and pass along folklore, windmills were also crucial as communal meeting places.

It is not clear how and where windmills originated, although they may have been inspired by the ancient watermills used to harness the power of the water rather than the wind. The earliest known windmill dates from tenth-century Persia, which supports the conjecture that windmills were brought to Europe by crusaders returning from the Middle East. In Western Europe the earliest references to windmills date from the end of the twelfth

Fig. FIVE-3.02 Amorgos, windmills, 1977

Fig. FIVE-3.03 Mykonos, windmills, 1991

Fig. FIVE-3.04 Ios, windmills, 1973

Fig. FIVE-3.05 Serifos, windmills, 1973

| Fig. FIVE-3.06 Thomas Hope, Hydra, c.1795 | Fig. FIVE-3.07 Santorini, Choiseul-Gouffier, 1770s |

century. In France and the Netherlands, where the windmill found wide application, detailed descriptions and working drawings date from the eighteenth century.

Buondelmonti in the 1420s, Barsky in the 1730s, Choiseul-Gouffier in the 1770s, Thomas Hope in the 1790s, and many subsequent travelers have found the windmills in the Aegean archipelago important enough to include in their drawings (Fig. FIVE-3.06,-3.07). Windmills were, in fact, integral parts of Aegean communities in both form and function. In an extensively researched and documented study, *Windmills of the Cycladic Islands,* Zaphyris Vaos and Stephanos Nomikos state that

> All the necessary conditions for windmill development existed in the Cyclades: scarcity of water, sufficient wind power for over 310 days a year, little rainfall and low humidity, dry conditions which contributed to the upkeep of the sails and wooden mechanism, and finally, the existence of millstones of excellent quality. (387)

Several hundred windmill remnants confirm the widespread presence of windmills throughout the Aegean archipelago. They were valuable pieces of real estate to be maintained, improved, sold, bequeathed, and, at times, vandalized or destroyed by corsair raids and warfare. Built as they were on exposed sites to catch the wind, windmills could also fall victim to its destructive power. By the end of the nineteenth century, with the coming of industrialization and the resulting changes in the islands' economies, windmills were on the decline. Following World War II, they disappeared altogether, as nationwide electrification took their place. More recently, experimental wind turbines have been placed on a number of the islands to generate electricity (Fig. FIVE-3.10), the coming of which had earlier caused

| Fig. FIVE-3.08 Santorini, 1948 | Fig. FIVE-3.09 Amorgos, 1977 | Fig. FIVE-3.10 Paros, wind turbine, 1993 |

the demise of the evocative windmill building type.

Heavy masonry walls, between two feet and four and one-half feet thick, formed the cylindrical body of a windmill (Fig. FIVE-3.11,-3.12). The height of this cylinder averaged about seventeen feet, and the usual exterior diameter was twenty feet. The diameters of the base and the top almost always differed. However, it is difficult to determine standard proportions for these dimensions. A podium provided the base for the cylindrical tower and served as a transitional element from the usually rocky terrain and as a platform from which to operate the windmill's sails. Located on the lee side, an entry door was often the only opening into the massive cylindrical tower. Two and, occasionally, four small openings lit and ventilated the windmill,

Fig. FIVE-3.11 Typical windmill, elevation

Fig. FIVE-3.12 Typical windmill, section

| Fig. FIVE-3.13 Ios, windmill, 1973 | Fig. FIVE-3.14 Mykonos, windmill, 1991 | Fig. FIVE-3.15 Sikinos, Chorio, windmill, 1994 |

whose exterior and interior surfaces were whitewashed annually.

Where islands lacked the proper quality or type of timber, millwrights might travel as far as Mount Athos or Asia Minor to locate, select, and transport the wood appropriate to their commissions. The transportation of the wind shaft, the longest and heaviest part of the windmill mechanism, presented a particular challenge, as it had to be towed by sea and then carried by men and mules to the mill site at a high point on an island. As a specialized structure, the windmill required materials and talents different from those needed to build the more common dwelling unit or chapel.

Transactions with customers and workshop repairs took place on the ground floor of the windmill tower, which also served as temporary storage for grain and flour. Depending on the size and design of the tower, millstone grinding occurred on an upper level or in a mezzanine space. The location, form, and parts of the building all helped to harness the power of the wind to turn the millstone. The millstones, the pivotal parts of any windmill, did not have to be brought from afar; quarries mostly in Melos, but also in the islands of Kimolos and Poliegos, produced millstones for most, if not all, of the archipelago windmills for centuries.

A cone-shaped, thatched roof protected the wood frame of the cap, which housed the windmill mechanism and was the most demanding and time-consuming part of the building to construct (Fig. FIVE-3.14). The need to rotate the cap in the direction of the prevailing wind made the mechanism of a cylindrical windmill relatively complex. The particularly steady

| Fig. FIVE-3.16 Sifnos, near Kastro, "horsehoe" windmill converted to house, 1985 | Fig. FIVE-3.17 Karpathos, Olympos, "horseshoe" windmill, 1987 |

winds that prevailed at a number of island sites, including Sifnos near Kastro, produced an unusual and rare "horseshoe" plan for their windmills. Because such winds made rotating the cap unnecessary, "horseshoe" plan windmills used a fixed wind shaft instead of one that rotated, making for a windmill that was simpler and less expensive to construct and operate (Fig. FIVE-3.16, -3.17). The fixed wind shaft once more suggests that the mutually informing relationship between site and building was a salient feature of the vernacular architecture of the Aegean islands.

Vital to the life and architecture of the archipelago, the power of the wind was harnessed by sail -- sail to move ships and sail to rotate millstones. Although today diesel-powered vessels mark the invisible lanes of the Aegean Sea, the relics of windmills that dot the island ridges are visible witnesses to an earlier time and a different way of life.

5.4 Dovecotes

Although windmills form part of the man-made landscape of every Aegean island, dovecotes or *peristeriones* (from *peristeri* or "dove," "pigeon") exist on only a small number of islands. Nearly twelve hundred of them, a surprisingly large number for a small island, are located on Tenos; neighboring Andros and Mykonos have respectable numbers as well. Sifnos, farther away from Tenos, boasts only a few. Not many dovecotes are in use today. Some have been preserved, but many are in disrepair. But regardless of condition, they all testify to the islands' social and economic history and are unique examples of artistic expression in vernacular architecture.

Fig. FIVE-4.01 Mykonos, dovecote, 1991

Fig. FIVE-4.02 Tenos, dovecote

Fig. FIVE-4.03 Andros, dovecote, 1986

The simple dovecote erected to shelter pigeons is rectangular in plan, with the height always the largest of its three dimensions (Fig. FIVE-4.03). External walls of stone masonry enclose a single interior space without partitions. The lower part of this enclosure has often been used to store agricultural tools and the like, reserving the space above for the pigeons. To protect the birds from the relentless Aegean winds, depending on the orientation of the dovecote, two and, occasionally, three of the external walls are built without openings. The remaining wall provides ledges on which the pigeons can land and perch and openings for them to enter the enclosed space where they build their breeding nests; these nests are incorporated either into the internal surface or into the one-meter-thick walls (Fig. FIVE-4.01).

The materials and methods of construction of these dovecotes are rough and rustic, although an apparent lack of sophistication is compensated for by their extensive and delightful geometric systems of decoration. These decorative systems, which incorporate pigeon ledges, perches, and openings, cover the lee side of every dovecote and offer their vernacular builders nearly infinite opportunities to invent variations on traditional decorative themes (Fig. FIVE-4.02).

Hundreds of small, similarly sized pieces of flat stone are used edgewise to form squares, triangles, diamonds, and circles, shapes abstracted from such typical Aegean vernacular decorative themes as the cypress tree, the sun, and the stars. Repeated in horizontal bands or in vertical formations and executed in a multitude of inventive combinations, these façades render each dovecote unique. Thus, the formal architectural emphasis on unity and variety -- unity in the small number of decorative elements used (triangles, diamonds, and circles) and variety in the numberless ways these elements are assembled -- is once again addressed masterfully and inventively by a plethora of anonymous builders. Occasionally a dovecote's sidewalls are extended, buttress-like, for additional protection and screening from the wind rather than to bolster the structure of the dovecote. Extended across the walls, the geometric decorations enrich the architecture of the peristeriones and provide additional perches for the pigeons.

The sculptures often placed on the flat roofs at the corners of the dovecotes raise the persistent architectural question of how to make a building meet the sky. These exuberant and playful dovecote sculptures seem inspired by the acroteria of classical Greek temples. Some architects, however, see them either as landmarks to guide the birds in their return home or as talismans to ward off birds of prey (Goulandris 25).

Set apart from the high-density building of the island towns, dovecotes were erected in the splendid isolation of cultivated and terraced fields (Fig. FIVE-4.04), where seeds and fruit were immediately available to the pigeons, and their droppings could be recycled as a rich fertilizer for the fields. This link between food and fertilizer thrived on the better-watered islands, which may account for the proliferation of dovecotes on Tenos and Andros, both of which are much greener than most of the other islands in the Cyclades.

Because no systematic research on dovecotes exists, it is difficult to trace the origin and development of this unique building type in the Aegean archipelago. We know that all four "dovecote" islands, Tenos, Andros, Mykonos, and Sifnos, were occupied by the Venetians of the Duchy of the Archipelago that was created just after Constantinople fell to the crusaders in 1204. Tenos, which has the largest number of dovecotes, outlasted the duchy and remained in Venetian hands until 1715, longer than any other Aegean island. The Venetian lords brought the privileges of the medieval European aristocracy to the islands, including the so-called *droit du colombier*, or the right to keep doves, which allowed only fief holders to maintain dovecotes. Since this privilege continued to attach to nobility and wealth and passed to prominent native families after 1715, it is reasonable to assume that the *droit du colombier* produced only a limited number of dove-

Fig. FIVE- 4.04 Tenos, dovecotes, 1988

cotes during the centuries-long Venetian presence on the island of Tenos. The collapse of Venetian rule and the democratization of living conditions in the nineteenth century, however, allowed the common citizens of the island to exercise their new freedom by building dovecotes by the hundreds. This explanation corroborates local testimony that the majority of the dovecotes seen today on Tenos and the other islands were built after the eighteenth century.

Raising pigeons for their meat has a long and widespread history. During the eighteenth and nineteenth centuries, every island farmer dreamed of owning a dovecote. As a result, dovecotes became numerous enough to be included in the Turkish taxation lists together with beehives as "industrial workshops" each liable to annual taxation. Since pigeons were expensive to raise, pigeon meat was not part of the daily diet of the poor. On Tenos and the three other islands, pigeon-raising at first augmented the diet of the aristocracy. Later, pigeons became an export item. In the nineteenth century, pigeons were fed and fattened during the summer to be slaughtered in the fall, pickled in oil and vinegar, and shipped in earthenware jars to the markets in Smyrna and Constantinople as sought-after and expensive delicacies (Goulandris 14).

The social and economic conditions on Tenos enabled the dovecote, a specialized building type, to be built in large numbers. Its existence adds to our understanding of the evolution of the archipelago's island towns within their wider geopolitical context. In the hands of extraordinarily gifted builders, the dovecote, a simple, unassuming edifice not meant for human habitation, became an inspiring example of Aegean vernacular architecture.

5.5 Monasteries

The windmill and the dovecote developed outside the archipelago towns during the years of Venetian and Ottoman domination, between the thirteenth and the nineteenth centuries. The monastery, another building type that enriched the Aegean architectural palette, had, by contrast, a Byzantine provenance. Since monasteries were built well before the thirteenth century, their function, form, and scale underscore the continuity between Byzantine and post-Byzantine life and architecture in the Aegean archipelago.

As Sir Steven Runciman describes it, Byzantine monasticism originated in early Christian Egypt

from the traditions of the Fathers of the Desert, those ascetes who had retired from the world into the wilderness to lead lives of holy

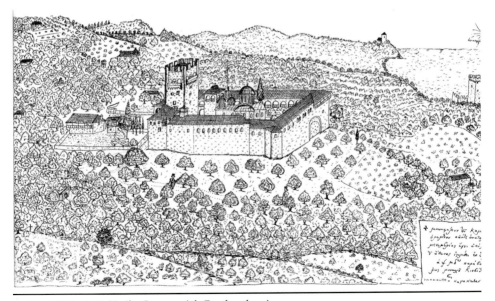

Fig. FIVE- 5.01 Vasily Gregorevich Barsky, drawing, "Ayion Oros, Monastery of Karakalos," 1744

contemplation, in solitude at first, but as time went on gathering together into small groups, so as to give each other a little mutual protection and to perform mutual services and acts of charity. The group formed what came to be called a *Lavra*. (*The Great Church* 38)

During the Christianization of the Roman Empire in the fourth century, Basil the Great (Saint Basil) introduced reforms designed to make monastic life more orderly. He decreed that

the monks, the *monachoi*, or "solitary men," should always be combined into communities, in which they should live lives of perfect communism under the rule of an elected head who should command perfect obedience, and that they should work as well as pray. (Runciman, *The Great Church* 38)

Saint Basil's reforms introduced the *Koinobion*, the common pattern of monastic life, to regulate when and how monks would pray, meditate, work, and eat together in both East and West. Unlike Western monasticism, however, Byzantine monasticism did not develop orders. When it was founded, each monastery established its own constitution and bylaws, or *typicon*, which regulated the rights and duties of the monks. Although subject to the typicon, the abbot, called *higumenos*, or "leader," had virtually absolute control over the monastery's affairs. Such monks as the *bibliophylax*, or librarian, and the *chartophylax*, or registrar, assisted the higumenos in running the monastery. Monks were not necessarily priests, although a priest could become a monk. Women's nunneries were organized along the same lines and were led by elected abbesses, or *higumene*, who exercised the same absolute power that abbots did.

After the Iconoclastic upheavals of the eight century in which reformers opposed the worship of icons, Byzantine monasticism experienced a period of prosperity that extended even into the period after the Latin conquest of Constantinople in 1204. During this period new monasteries were established throughout the Byzantine Empire in rural and urban settings, including Constantinople and Thessaloniki, and in the process, became important centers for learning and public service. Because monasteries encouraged large numbers of ordinary people to renounce the world and enter monastic life, the Koinobion virtually replaced the Lavra, which had been intended for the few. Besides attending services and meditating, the new monks also performed agricultural labor, and their numbers turned the monasteries into "agricultural enterprises" (Mango 109) important to the rural life of the empire.

As they were gradually removed from local episcopal control, many of the monasteries built during this period were privately owned and endowed by rich benefactors and prominent laymen, who could exchange, sell, and bequeath them to their heirs. In turn, monasteries

> often benefited in having a highly placed protector who could invest his resources toward a fuller exploitation of the monastic properties; the beneficiary, for his part, drew the excess profit in addition to having prayers offered up for the salvation of his soul, a place of retirement for himself and his clients and of burial for his family. (Mango 110)

This privatized agricultural enterprise positioned such monasteries at the physical and spiritual centers of the socioeconomic life of the empire.

The Islamic conquest of Egypt, Syria, and, eventually, Asia Minor forced such monastic communities as those in Cappadocia and Bithynia to move to safer places in the Byzantine Empire, including Mount Athos. Hermits had already settled in the peninsula that projected into the waters of the northern Aegean Sea; however, in 963, the first Koinobion monastery was built there under the auspices of the Emperor Nicephoros Phocas. The establishment of this monastery eventually led to Ayion Oros, or "Holy Mountain," a self-governing community of monasteries still in existence. After the tenth century, the history of Greek monasticism, Byzantine and post-Byzantine, is by and large the history of Ayion Oros.

Their proximity and their spiritual preeminence as well as the intimate interplay of landscape and seascape that characterized their design made the Ayion Oros buildings the prototypes for monasteries throughout the Aegean islands and for the later, fortified island towns as well. Certainly, a monastic population in the hundreds meant that the architectural scale and character of an Ayion Oros monastery came to resemble those of an Aegean island town.

The indispensable enclosing defensive wall characteristic of the medieval town was equally indispensable to the monastery. As a way of walling out the secular world and of protecting the inner place of prayer, this massive enclosing wall was the most impressive architectural feature of the monastery (Fig. FIVE-5.02). In a manner that foreshadowed the later building of the Aegean island towns, the living quarters of the monastery, including its cells, refectory, storerooms, and so on were attached to the interior surface of this enclosing wall, a design which insured an economy of materials and gave greater structural strength to this integrated peripheral edifice (Fig. FIVE-5.03)

Fig. FIVE- 5.02 Ayion Oros, Monastery of Xenophontos, 1977

A guarded barrel-vaulted portal on the enclosing wall is the only access to the interior of the monastery and leads to an inner courtyard open to the sky. The courtyard is a platform on which the *Katholikon*, the monastery church, stands free and is visible from all sides.

The diagram in Fig. FIVE-5.03 shows the relationship among the peripheral enclosing wall, the inner courtyard, and the freestanding Katholikon, which together constitute the basic architectural elements of the Byzantine

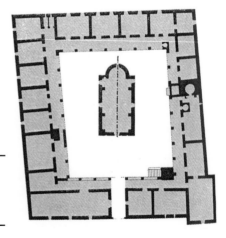

Fig. FIVE- 5.03 Typical monastery diagram: peripheral enclosure, courtyard, Katholikon

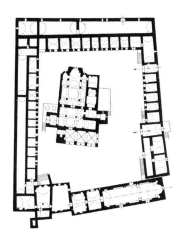

Fig. FIVE- 5.04 Mount Kithairon,
Monastery of Osios Meletios, plan

as well as the post-Byzantine monastery. The varying sizes of these parts, along with their proportional relationships, materials, and details, account for the manifold architectural interpretations of this basic tripartite diagram, and, in turn, confirm the uniqueness of the monastery as a generic building type (Fig. FIVE-5.04, -5.05).

In plan the peripheral enclosing wall is typically quadrilateral, often polygonal, and, occasionally, triangular or rectangular. The topography of the site and the need for defensive advantage largely determined the geometry of a particular monastery plan. As institutions monasteries have had a long life, yet their buildings soon underwent marked physical change. Wear,

Fig. FIVE-5.05
Patmos,
monastery near
Chora

fire, and war all brought damage and destruction. Repairs and replacements were conducted in the spirit of their time, however different from the style of the original building, while still adhering faithfully to the basic diagram described above.

A notable exception to this cycle of destruction and repair is the Katholikon, "the geometric and spiritual center of the monastery" (Orlandos 27), which has remained essentially unchanged and retains its original form and parts today. Because its small size allows it to fit snugly into the tight monastic complex, the cross-in-square church design became the dominant plan for the Katholikon (Fig. FIVE-5.06). The cross-in-square plan with either two or four columns and a dome, originated in the late Byzan-

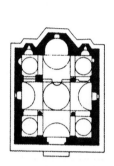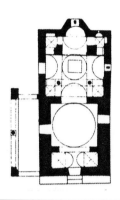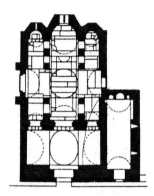

Fig. FIVE- 5.06 Katholikon, variations of cross-in-square plan

tine period between the eleventh and the fourteenth centuries and continued to be used by the post-Byzantine monasteries in the Aegean islands. Freestanding in the courtyard and visible from all sides of the monastery's living quarters, the Katholikon symbolizes the ideal Christian world where God is at the center of the universe. Its detachment from other buildings often prompted an elaborate decorative treatment of a Katholikon's exterior elevations during the Byzantine period that the poorer post-Byzantine monasteries built and maintained on the Aegean islands in less prosperous times found it impossible to emulate.

Access to the Katholikon is provided by the courtyard, which also serves as a communal space for the monks. To accommodate large numbers of pilgrims, a generous part of the courtyard is usually apportioned between the monastery portal and the Katholikon entry. The shared access to the Katholikon through the inner courtyard for monks and pilgrims alike distinguishes Byzantine and post-Byzantine monasteries from their Western equiva-

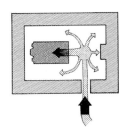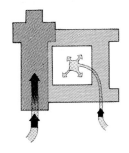

Fig. FIVE- 5.07 Katholikon,
typical access diagram:
(left) Byzantine prototype
(right) Western prototype

lents, whose churches are entered directly from the outside rather than through the cloisters (Fig. FIVE-5.07). Regardless of courtyard articulation, the apse of the Katholikon always firmly faces the east.

Most of the space in the peripheral building is occupied by the monks' cells, which are rectangular, barrel vaulted, and arranged in tiers, with an open portico in front that looks into the courtyard. Its built-in furniture easily identifies a refectory or dining room. Refectories were normally placed near the entry to a Katholikon. A kitchen with an open lantern for ventilation was built adjacent to the refectory, and nearby storerooms were stocked with grain, oil, wine, and pulse, kept in large earthenware jars reminiscent of similar vessels and arrangements in Knossos and Minoan Crete. An infirmary, a bath, a cistern, and other auxiliary spaces supported the communal life of the monastery. A defense and observation tower as well as a *phiale*, or fountain, are regular features of the Ayion Oros monasteries but are absent from the post-Byzantine Aegean examples.

Having lost the often-innovative leadership of the imperial capital after 1453, the post-Byzantine monasteries of the Aegean archipelago continued to reproduce the basic diagram of their Byzantine prototypes. Left to themselves, the islands' monasteries and nunneries maintained the faith and ritual of the Greek Orthodox Church in the traditional setting of the monastic enclosure and the Katholikon, but the sizes, scales, and materials they used reflected the limited local means.

The sites on which they were built -- urban settings, open landscapes, and hilltops -- can be used to categorize the island monasteries architecturally.

The monasteries of Patmos (Saint John the Theologian) and Hydra (Panayia) exist in urban settings. In its location and architectural mass, the Patmos monastery, which predates and physically dominates the surrounding town (see Chapter FOUR, section seven), seems to insist on remaining aloof from it (Fig. FIVE-5.08). The Hydra monastery stood alone on its site when it was founded in the seventeenth century. Two hundred years later,

Fig. FIVE-5.08 Patmos, monastery, 1999   Fig. FIVE-5.09 Hydra, monastery, 1983

the town of Hydra expanded downhill to embrace it. While it still houses hieratic offices, it no longer functions as a monastery, its prominent urban location having made it the perfect building to house the town's city hall and other administrative offices (Fig. FIVE-5.09). As houses and shops crowd around its enclosing wall, the courtyard, which is easily accessible to the public, has become the town square, and the town radiates out from it. (For a more in-depth discussion of Patmos and Hydra, see Chapters FOUR and SIX, respectively.)

Vrissi in Sifnos and Panayia in Poros are both open-landscape monasteries. Built at the top of a deep ravine at 600 feet above sea level, the Vrissi monastery in Sifnos commands an inspiring view of the Kastro below, located slightly more than a mile northeast as the crow flies (Fig. FIVE-5.10). Built after Sifnos passed from Venetian into Turkish hands in the early seventeenth century, the monastery suggests the political and economic conditions within which Aegean vernacular architecture flourished at that period. Given the nominal Turkish presence following the disappearance of the local Venetian lords, native culture and Greek Orthodoxy reasserted themselves in the Aegean, and particularly in Sifnos, where a great number of chapels and monasteries were built: Vrissi is a prime example. Sturdy, whitewashed, stone masonry arches and walls dominate the enclosure. Limited means made it impossible for cell porticos to be built from costly imported timber and mandated a constricted courtyard in which the peripheral buildings and the Katholikon almost touch (Fig. FIVE-5.11, -5.12, -5.13). Layers and layers of whitewash unify the vertical and horizontal planes into a homogenous whole and produce an engaging play of textured white surfaces and gray shadows against the bright blue sky, a visual experience delightfully exemplified by views of the worn-out bell tower, the barrel vaults, and the tiled dome of the Katholikon (Fig. FIVE-5.14, -5.15).

Fig. FIVE-5.10 Sifnos, Vrissi monastery, 1985

Fig. FIVE-5.11 Sifnos, Vrissi monastery, inner courtyard, 1985

Fig. FIVE-5.12 Sifnos, Vrissi monastery, inner courtyard, 1985

Fig. FIVE-5.13 Sifnos, Vrissi monastery, inner courtyard, 1985

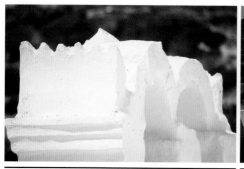 

Fig. FIVE-5.14 Sifnos, Vrissi monastery, Katholikon, bell tower, 1985

Fig. FIVE-5.15 Sifnos, Vrissi monastery, Katholikon, dome, 1985

Separated by a narrow channel from the Peloponnesos, the Saronic Gulf island of Poros is the site of the Panayia Zoodochos-Pigi ("Life-Giving Spring") monastery. Like the Vrissi monastery, the Panayia Zoodochos-Pigi is located in an open landscape away from settled areas (Fig. FIVE-5.16). Built during the first half of the eighteenth century on a hillside covered with pine trees, the monastery, which is still active, rises 150 feet above sea level and affords an unimpeded view of the eastern approach by sea to the town of Poros (Fig. FIVE-5.17). The scale and construction of the quadrilateral enclosure and the freestanding Katholikon in the courtyard (Fig. FIVE-5.18) make Panayia Zoodochos-Pigi an exemplar of the post-Byzantine Aegean monastery (Fig. FIVE-5.18). The portico on the south side enhances this characterization, as a series of robust masonry arches on the lower level and a delicate light-timber structure on the upper tier introduce

Fig. FIVE-5.16 Poros, Zoodochos-Pigi monastery

Fig. FIVE-5.17 Poros, Zoodochos-Pigi monastery, 1985

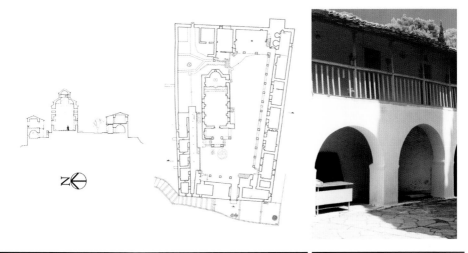

Fig. FIVE-5.18 Poros, Zoodochos-Pigi monastery, section and plan

Fig. FIVE-5.19 Poros, Zoodochos-Pigi monastery, 1985

a gently repetitive measure of human scale appropriate to the contemplative spirit induced by the interior courtyard (Fig. FIVE-5.19).

Representing the hilltop setting, the third and last category, the monastery of the Profitis Elias is closer to heaven than those previously discussed and is the hardest to reach, sitting, as it does, at the 2,300-foot summit of the tallest mountain on Sifnos (Fig. FIVE-5.21). (See Chapter THREE for further discussion of this site.) A two-hour, early morning hike on mule trails through the treeless terrain ends on the windy summit where

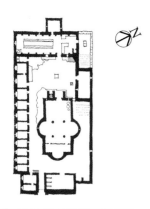

Fig. FIVE-5.20 Sifnos, Profitis Elias monastery, plan

Fig. FIVE-5.21 Sifnos, Profitis Elias, monastery, 1986

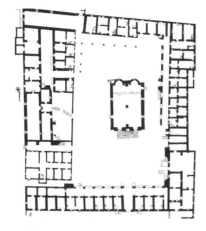

Fig. FIVE-5.22 Crete, Arkadi monastery, plan

Fig. FIVE-5.23 Crete, Arkadi
monastery, Katholikon, elevation

Fig. FIVE-5.24 San Antonio, Alamo,
elevation

the monastery sits. Its remoteness and its difficulty of access both to visitors
and to construction workers and carriers of materials have limited its size to
about one-half that of the monastery in Poros. In accordance with the
diagram of a typical post-Byzantine Aegean monastery, a near-perfect, elongated, rectangular plan encloses a tight courtyard and a Katholikon of about
the same size as the one at Poros (Fig. FIVE-5.20). Besides the characteristic
apse on the east side, the Katholikon has two more apses, one on the north
side and another on the south, that make the plan a trefoil. Although often
used at Ayion Oros, a trefoil plan is extremely rare in the Aegean islands,
and it is puzzling and surprising to encounter one on Sifnos. Stunning views
of the landscape of the island and the surrounding seascape create a unique
sense of place. The fresh whitewash together with the well-kept, if vacant,
cells and refectory made it difficult for a visitor to believe that the
monastery was in fact deserted in 1986.

The fortress-like enclosures designed to defend monastic communities later attracted revolutionaries seeking shelter from their pursuers. As recently as the nineteenth century, the Arkadi monastery in central Crete near Rethymno was the scene of a revolutionary conflict (Fig. FIVE-5.22, -5.23). Arkadi predated the long Venetian rule of the island. Its present architectural form, dating from the second half of the sixteenth century is a remarkable marriage of the characteristic Greek Orthodox monastery plan with Venetian-inspired elevations. The Arkadi Katholikon façade is surprisingly similar in scale, composition, and ornamentation to the Alamo in San Antonio, Texas (Fig. FIVE-5.24). Thirty years after the battle of the Alamo in 1836, during a major revolt against Turkish rule, Cretan revolutionaries found refuge in the Arkadi monastery. As the seventeenth-century enclosing wall gave way to the pounding of modern artillery, Turkish troops forced the gate and rushed into the monastery courtyard. Accompanied by fellow revolutionaries and by monks, women, and children, Gabriel, the monastery higumenos, put a match to the powder magazine. In the enormous explosion that followed, all of the defenders and many of the Turkish troops perished. Widely reported in the European press at the time, this event put Crete on the road to autonomy and eventual union with Greece. Today, the reconstructed Arkadi houses an active monastery as well as a monument to national liberation. Arkadi and its role in the 1866 Cretan revolt is portrayed in Nikos Kazantzakis's *Freedom or Death*.

5.6 Wall Thicknesses, Structural Spans

"To enclose a space is the object of building; when we build we do but detach a convenient quantity of space, seclude it and protect it, and all architecture springs from that necessity." This quotation from Geoffrey Scott's 1914 book on formal architecture *The Architecture of Humanism* helps to illuminate the relationship between building and architecture in the work of the vernacular builders of the Aegean archipelago. Indeed, the monochoro dwelling and the single-nave, barrel-vaulted chapel, key elements in the composition of the Aegean island towns, can be seen as detaching a "quantity of space" appropriate to the islanders' needs. And Scott's reference to "seclusion and protection" finds an equivalent in the threatening geopolitical conditions of the Aegean archipelago after the thirteenth century and in the economic and technical means the islanders mustered to defend against them. Finally, the assembly of monochoro dwelling units and barrel-vaulted chapels into the larger urban edifice of the collective fortification of a Kastro shows an architecture that, in Scott's words, "springs from... necessity," indeed.

An abundance of stone and a limited supply of poor-quality timber constitute the local building materials of the Aegean islands. An intelligent response to both abundance and limitation is characteristic of the ethos of the vernacular architecture builders of the archipelago.

Stone quarried or collected at a short distance from a construction site forms the typical two-foot-thick wall that encloses every building in the Aegean islands. The stone's thickness means that the building of a typical wall does not require special skill (Fig. FIVE-6.02, -6.04). Cut and roughly formed stone is used for both interior and exterior surfaces of the wall, while the space between is filled with rubble, and its interstices, packed with mortar. Stucco placed on the interior and exterior surfaces protects against rain and the elements generally, conceals imperfections, and helps to insulate the wall. Of the four enclosing walls of a dwelling unit, the two longer ones that run parallel serve as load-bearing walls and carry the weight of the roof. The distance between these two walls depends upon the structural capacity of the beams that span it. Where the locally available, poor-quality wood is used essentially in its natural form, these spans cannot exceed twelve to fifteen feet. Roof beams are spaced every twelve to sixteen inches and are adjusted to the shape and dimensions of the available wood, usually from the ever-present fithes, a tree from the juniper family (Fig. FIVE-6.05, -6.06, -6.07). A course of cane tightly bound together forms a continuous skin over the beams and holds above it a thick layer of eight to twelve inches of compacted argillaceous earth. To remain waterproof, this top layer needs to be recompacted annually. To act as a rainwater catchment, the roof is built at an angle that guides the water towards a gutter and a downspout and, eventually, into a cistern where it is stored (Fig. FIVE-6.08, -6.09).

Popular in the islands until after World War II, flat-roof construction and its variants date from antiquity, as is confirmed by the archaeological reconstruction drawing of a middle-Helladic house (Fig. FIVE-6.10). Economic difficulty and emigration from the islands in the 1950s and 1960s caused the maintenance of such roofs to be neglected, resulting in widespread collapse, a phenomenon observable at the time from any high point that overlooked an Aegean town (Fig. FIVE-6.11, -6.12). However, international and, eventually, national tourism have revived the island economies since the 1970s and have prompted reinvestment in building. Looking down from the same high points in the 1990s presents a dramatically altered view, as reinforced concrete slabs have come to replace the compacted earth roofs that had been allowed to collapse. Subsequent generations of the original family or new owners have also converted the old buildings into summer

Fig. FIVE-6.01 Serifos, Chora, 1973

Fig. FIVE-6.02 Serifos, Chora, roof construction, 1973

Fig. FIVE-6.03 Kalymnos, Pothaia, 1971 (left)

Fig. FIVE-6.04 Kalymnos, Pothaia, roof construction, 1971 (right)

Fig. FIVE-6.05 Syros, fithes, 1977

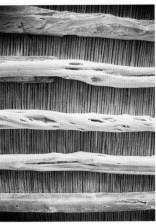

Fig. FIVE-6.06 Sifnos, Kastro, fithes, 1997

Fig. FIVE-6.07 Hydra, fithes, 1998

Fig. FIVE-6.08 Skyros, flat roofs for rainwater catchment, 1971

Fig. FIVE-6.09 Sifnos, Kastro, flat roof and downspout, 1985

Fig. FIVE-6.10
Roof construction,
archaeological
reconstruction
drawing

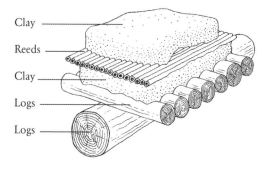

Clay

Reeds

Clay

Logs

Logs

Fig. FIVE-6.11 Serifos, 1988

Fig. FIVE-6.12 Rhodes, Lindos, 1994

houses, and, since hydrofoils, catamarans, and airports have reduced travel time to the islands, even into weekend homes.

Just as reinforced concrete slabs have replaced the old compacted earth roofs, so reinforced concrete frame structures, footings, columns, beams, and slabs have replaced the traditional stone masonry bearing walls. Concrete block or brick now fills in the spaces between posts, as below, to enclose new buildings, a development that has had both positive and negative consequences (Fig. FIVE-6.13, -6.14). On the positive side, the professional design and skilled labor required for reinforced concrete construction

Fig. FIVE-6.13 Santorini, reinforced concrete frame and brick infill, 1995

Fig. FIVE-6.14 Santorini, reinforced concrete frame, 1995

produces structures more resistant to earthquakes and in less need of annual maintenance. On the negative side, walls of concrete block and hollow brick are thinner and less massive than the old masonry walls and provide inadequate thermal and acoustical insulation. The stucco that covers both the reinforced concrete frame and the concrete block and brick walls conceals their functional differences and their imported technology. The whitewash tradition, rigorously followed, together with architectural design sensi-

Fig. FIVE-6.15 Santorini, Fira, new construction, 1982

Fig. FIVE-6.16 Santorini, Fira, 1992

tive to the traditional scale of the settlements, makes it possible to graft new structures onto the old. In a characteristic example from Santorini (Fig. FIVE-6.15, -6.16), a reinforced concrete shell has replaced the traditional barrel-vaulted roof. In addition, the short end of the building has been enclosed with a concrete block wall that incorporates the traditional Santorini elevation -- a skylight above a door flanked by two windows. Stucco and whitewash complete the building, which in size, scale, and the composition of its short elevation (a door and three windows) is indistinguishable from its predecessors.

The abundance of inexpensive local stone and the limited supply of expensive imported wood are reflected in the elevation of a typical dwelling unit. Solid masonry predominates, since openings in the form of doors and windows account for a small percentage of the elevation surface. These small openings detract little from the integrity of the structure or from the thermal insulation provided by a thick stone masonry wall. Smaller openings also require less investment in the expensive carpentry material

Fig. FIVE-6.17 Skyros, 1971

Fig. FIVE-6.18 Ios, 1973

Fig. FIVE- 6.19 Kalymnos, 1971

Fig. FIVE-6.20 Kalymnos, 1971

Fig. FIVE-6.21 Kalymnos, 1971

required to fill them. These building considerations are broadly if not universally observed in Aegean island towns, as examples from Skyros (Fig. FIVE-6.17), Ios (Fig. FIVE-6.18), and Kalymnos (Fig. FIVE-6.19) indicate. The extra ceiling height that results from the barrel-vaulted construction of a typical house on Santorini is elegantly expressed in the elevations by a skylight placed above the door (Fig. FIVE-6.22, -6.23). A semicircular skylight placed immediately above the lintel of the entry door is distinctive to house elevation design on Kalymnos (Fig. FIVE-6.20, -6.21).

Windows provide light, ventilation, and a view. Serving all three of these functions at once, a characteristic type of casement window found on Hydra places the glass panes on the outside and the shutters on the inside

Fig. FIVE-6.22 Santorini, Oia, 1992

Fig. FIVE-6.23 Santorini, Oia, 1992

(Fig. FIVE-6.24, -6.25, -6.26). This arrangement allows the residents to exclude the intense summer sunlight by adjusting the inside shutters; when the glass panes remain shut, draughts are avoided. In addition, security bars shaped to allow the occupants to lean outside the window to observe or converse with others across the street are common in the older houses on

Fig. FIVE-6.24 Hydra, 1983

Fig. FIVE-6.25 Hydra, 1995

Fig. FIVE-6.26 Hydra, 1995

Fig. FIVE-6.27 Hydra, 1997   Fig. FIVE-6.28 Santorini, 1992   Fig. FIVE-6.29 Hydra, 1997

Hydra and Santorini (Fig. FIVE-6.27, -6.28, -6.29). Stone-carved or colored frames on three, or even all four, sides of a window signify a family's social status and improve the aesthetic quality of an elevation (Fig. FIVE-6.30, -6.31). Relief arches above the window protect the structural integrity of the lintel.

Fig. FIVE-6.30 Kalymnos, 1971   Fig. FIVE-6.31 Kalymnos, 1971

| Fig. FIVE-6.32 Amorgos, Chora, 1977 | Fig. FIVE-6.33 Amorgos, Chora, 2000 (same portal as in Fig. FIVE-6.32 twenty-three years later) |

Stone masonry is also the basic material of the typical Aegean vernacular interpretation of a neoclassical house portal. In an example from Amorgos (Fig. FIVE-6.32, -6.33), a pediment with a base as wide as the door opening below and two robust, square, masonry posts, one on either side of the portal, are all placed on the front wall and frame the entry door. A thin stone ledge separates the sculptural exuberance of the upper parts from the functional mission of the lower parts of the portal. Oil-based color on the wooden door and whitewash on the masonry underscore the differences in hardness and texture between the two materials that compose the portal. Steps ascending to the door and the presence of a knocker make both materials conform to the discipline of human scale.

The profusion of carpentry work -- the brightly colored handrails of the stairs, entry landings, and the balconies that overlook its narrow streets -- distinguishes Mykonos from other Aegean island towns (Fig. FIVE-6.34, -6.35). Unsurprisingly, its inventive vernacular builders have also produced a unique interpretation of the house portal that uses no masonry (Fig. FIVE-6.36). Mounted on the lower steps that lead to an upper-level dwelling, a door whose wooden frame is attached to the wall on one side and to the

| Fig. FIVE-6.34 Mykonos, 1991 | Fig. FIVE-6.35 Mykonos, 1991 | Fig. FIVE-6.36 Mykonos, 1991 |

handrail behind it on the other creates a physical, but not a visual, separation between the public and private domains. The neoclassical pediment is also still present. But the door's attachment to the wall allows only one decorative element to project from the door's free side. Its paneled structure and its round bronze handles suggest urban sophistication, but the outward-opening door without a landing would give any fire marshal in the United States apoplexy.

Entry doors receive special attention in Patmos and Hydra, where heavy-duty cloth is stretched in front of painted wooden doors to protect them

| Fig. FIVE-6.37 Serifos, 1970 | Fig. FIVE-6.38 Patmos, 1990 | Fig. FIVE-6.39 Hydra, 1988 |

Fig. FIVE-6.40 Hydra, 1960   Fig. FIVE-6.41 Hydra, 1993   Fig. FIVE-6.42 Kimolos, 1999

from the hot rays of the afternoon sun (Fig. FIVE-6.38, -6.39), a strategy that cats seem to pursue intuitively. (Fig. FIVE-6.37).

Stone masonry walls sitting comfortably on massive rocks demonstrate the directness with which vernacular builders addressed the problem of relating a building to its site. Happily, vernacular builders lacked the technology to clear the rock from a site and were forced instead to attach and adjust the house (Fig. FIVE-6.40, -6.41) or the chapel (Fig. FIVE-6.42) to the top of the rock, thus creating a lasting and impressive architectural relation-

Fig. FIVE-6.43 Hydra, 1983   Fig. FIVE-6.44 Serifos, 1973   Fig. FIVE-6.45 Sifnos, 1997

ship between rock and building. Thick masonry walls that absorb forty-five-degree corner cuts to accommodate street traffic demonstrate a similarly imaginative and uninhibited attitude towards building (Fig. FIVE-6.43, -6.44, -6.45). Miles of dry stone walls outline properties throughout the island landscape. Large, flat, stone slabs, available mostly in Andros and nearby Kythnos, are placed in an unusual upright position within a dry stone wall and are a distinctive feature of the vernacular architecture of the island of Andros (Fig. FIVE-6.46, -6.47, -6.48, -6.50).

In Hydra preparations for new construction to be built over ruins in the upper part of the town revealed an indispensable but usually invisible feature of the traditional house -- a cistern with interior walls treated with a regionally devised form of hydraulic cement (Fig. FIVE- 6.51, -6.52).

Fig. FIVE-6.46 Andros, 1986

Fig. FIVE-6.47 Andros, 1986

Fig. FIVE-6.48 Andros, 1986

Fig. FIVE-6.49 Kythnos, 1973

Fig. FIVE-6.50 Andros, 1986

Fig. FIVE-6.51 Hydra, 1983   Fig. FIVE-6.52 Hydra, 1983

The whitewash that is the most distinctive feature of the vernacular architecture of the Aegean archipelago is of uncertain historical origin. Some scholars believe that the exterior elevations of early settlements were built of exposed stone without stucco and whitewash so that they might blend more easily into the natural environment and conceal the buildings from potential raiders. The buildings of Anavatos (Fig. FIVE-6.53), a settlement on the island of Chios uninhabited since the nineteenth century, support this theory, which holds that the application of whitewash is a recent practice. Scholars who disagree point to the reliable descriptions by such travelers as Thevenot, a Frenchman who visited thirteen Aegean islands in

Fig. FIVE-6.53 Chios, Anavatos, 1992

Fig. FIVE-6.54 Astypalaia, 1971

Fig. FIVE-6.55 Poros, cemetery, 1999

1655; of Skaros in Santorini he wrote, "the houses are well built, all white of round shape surrounded by high walls so they cannot be seen at all, and you think you are in front of fortifications." To reconcile these views one might speculate that whitewashing in the Aegean began inside the densely populated Kastra of the seventeenth century and only later, during the eighteenth century, came into widespread and exterior use.

Possibly whitewash was used initially as a disinfectant, given that hygienic conditions within the fortified settlements were hardly ideal. The absence of sewers with street drainage only, in a high-building-density environment that also housed pack animals, posed a constant threat to public health.

Fig. FIVE-6.56 Hydra, 1993

Thus, whitewash may have been applied as a disinfectant in an attempt to reduce the threat. Whitewashing for hygiene goes on today, as is illustrated by an example from Astypalaia (Fig. FIVE-6.54) in which the narrow and irregular whitewashed line on the ground (that begins in the shaded part of the house at the center and fades out at the lower left-hand side of the picture) marks the path of a kitchen drain, and has been applied to prevent food bacteria from developing in it. A second illustration is from a cemetery on the island of Poros (Fig. FIVE-6.55). In most island public spaces and in cemeteries like that on Poros, tree trunks are whitewashed up to a (human) height of six feet to ensure public health, cleanliness, and good maintenance in general.

Repeated applications of whitewash over stuccoed masonry or stone and mortar (Fig. FIVE-6.62, -6.63) protect the exterior walls of buildings from

Fig. FIVE-6.57 Hydra, 1995

Fig. FIVE-6.58 Astypalaia, 1971

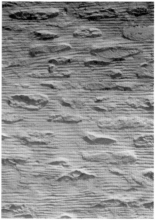

Fig. FIVE-6.59 Andros, 1986

Fig. FIVE-6.60 Spetses, 1991

Fig. FIVE-6.61 Hydra, 1971

natural wear and tear and from the harmful effects of salt from the nearby sea. A fresh and bright layer of whitewash also impressively increases the heat-reflective capacity of the exterior surfaces of the walls, as can easily be confirmed by a visitor who crosses from a cool, dark interior to a sun-drenched, hot summer day outdoors (Fig. FIVE-6.56, -6.57, -6.58, -6.59, -6.60, -6.61).

Before electricity and public street lighting were introduced, whitewash was also applied to street surfaces for the night glow it gave to mark steps and edges and to facilitate night walking, an application that continues today, as two relatively recent examples from Astypalaia (Fig. FIVE-6.64) and Serifos (Fig. FIVE-6.65) confirm.

These functional uses of whitewash continue, but social and aesthetic considerations are also prominent today. A fresh layer of house whitewash,

Fig. FIVE-6.63 Mykonos, 1991

Fig. FIVE-6.62 Mykonos, 1970

Fig. FIVE-6.64 Astypalaia, 1971

Fig. FIVE-6.65 Serifos, 1973

Fig. FIVE-6.66 Serifos, Chora, 1973

Fig. FIVE-6.67 Folegandros, 1994

often extended to the joints of the street pavement in front (Fig. FIVE-6.66), expresses family pride and, perhaps, some competition with the neighbors. When the schoolchildren of Folegandros (Fig FIVE-6.67) whitewashed the pavement and step joints that lead to the entrance of their school as they prepared to observe the 28 October national holiday (the anniversary of Mussolini's failed invasion of Greece), they engaged in an act of civic and national pride. Last but not least, drawings of flowers, fish, and other traditional motifs done in whitewash on poured concrete street surfaces express

Fig. FIVE-6.68 Paros, Paroikia, 1993

Fig. FIVE-6.69 Sikinos, Chorio, 1994

Fig. FIVE-6.70 Sifnos, Apollonia, 1997	Fig. FIVE-6.71 Kythnos, Chora, 1973	Fig. FIVE-6.72 Kythnos, Chora, 1973

Fig. FIVE-6.73 Sifnos, Apollonia, 1997	Fig. FIVE-6.74 Sifnos, Artemon, 1986

some residents' dismay at the loss of the human and architectural scales of the old cobbled streets (Fig. FIVE-6.73, -6.74). At the same time, these drawings represent a fresh and ingenious attempt to make good this loss (Fig. FIVE-6.70, -6.71, -6.72).

Successive layers of whitewash unify surfaces, whether vertical or horizontal, heavily textured or smooth, stuccoed or not, and create a plastic continuity that enhances the engaging qualities of the islands' vernacular architecture by creating a continually changing play of light and shadow.

Fig. FIVE-6.75 Hydra, 1998

Fig. FIVE-6.76 Hydra, 1997

Fig. FIVE-6.77 Hydra, 1998

Fig. FIVE-6.78 Hydra, 1998

This plastic continuity of form together with the changing light of the Aegean archipelago brings to mind again Le Corbusier and his poetic definition of architecture as "the masterly, correct and magnificent play of masses brought together in light…"(Fig. FIVE-6.68, -6.69).

Construction materials, including sand, gravel, cement, brick, and concrete block must be imported to the islands from production centers on the mainland. The illustrations from Hydra show an assembly site for building materials that have been brought in by sea (Fig. FIVE-6.75, -6.76) and their transportation to a construction site by mule (Fig. FIVE-6.77, -6.78). Hydra's terrain and its local regulations prohibit the use of automobiles. High building density and narrow footpaths make assembling materials near a construction site a slow and significant event in the daily life of a neighborhood (Fig. FIVE-6.79, -6.80, -6.81). On most of the other islands, Toyotas have replaced mules, although the last leg of the journey to the site, over inclined and stepped paths, frequently still requires the muscle power of donkeys and mules to negotiate. Either way, the demanding process of transporting, loading, and unloading building materials adds considerably to the cost of construction.

Fig. FIVE-6.79 Hydra, 1997   Fig. FIVE-6.80 Hydra, 1998   Fig. FIVE-6.81 Hydra, 1998

But for the most part, hard-surfaced roads have replaced the old mule tracks and have made almost all of the islands' terrain accessible. On Skyros, a new, wider road has carved a deeper mark into the landscape than the old road (Fig. FIVE-6.82, -6.83,) and inevitably attracts building to it and away from the old settlement with its core that is difficult to reach by automobile.

A terrain that once necessitated the merger of building and rock (Fig. FIVE-6.40, -6.41, -6.42) has also been inhospitable to the building of elec-

Fig. FIVE-6.82 Skyros, 1971   Fig. FIVE-6.83 Skyros, 1993 (same view as in Fig. FIVE-6.82 twenty-two years later)

| Fig. FIVE-6.84 Hydra, 1990 | Fig. FIVE-6.85 Hydra, 1993 |

tricity or telephone service trenches. Thus, new construction and the upgrading of old buildings have relied on a less expensive and more visible network of wires supported by electricity poles and punctuated by a forest of television antennas to obtain these services. An offensive visual intrusion, this "wirescape" was as unimaginable four decades ago as the present-day accessibility and economic prosperity of the islands would have been.

Life in the traditional settlements of the archipelago produced little refuse, and the little trash that was produced was easily discarded. But late-twentieth-century society and the tourists it has brought have produced an excessive amount of refuse that the old settlements were not designed to manage. During the summer months in particular, waste collection overtaxes municipal services. As signs urging citizens to comply with the rules for waste disposal and collection proliferate, it appears that the problem has come to the fore but remains unresolved (Fig. FIVE-6.84, -6.85).

SIX

▷ ◁

HYDRA REVISITED

▷ ◁

6.1 An Island and a Town

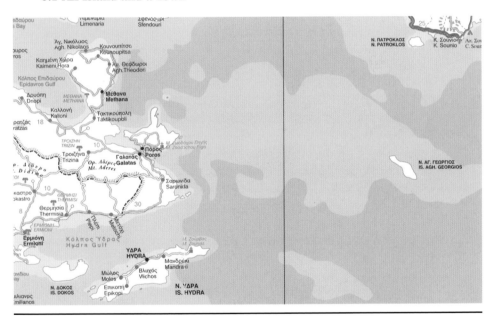

Fig. SIX-1.01 Hydra

Hydra shares many characteristics with the majority of islands in the Aegean archipelago, but is set apart both by its absence from the long list of islands whose history has been documented since early antiquity and by its proximity to the mainland (Fig. SIX-1.01, -1.04). Apparently, settlement on the island did not begin before comparatively recent times, but its proximity to the Peloponnesos helps to explain the development of the present town after the sixteenth century.

Fig. SIX-1.02 Hydra and Peloponnesos, 1963

Fig. SIX-1.03 Hydra, northeast coast, 1990

In early days Hydra seems to have served repeatedly as a temporary shelter for refugees from the Peloponnesos fleeing invaders from the north. Prolonged wars over Peloponnesos in the sixteenth and seventeenth centuries between the Ottoman Empire and the Republic of Venice created the necessary conditions for a permanent settlement to be built on the island.

The island's poor soil (Fig. SIX-1.02, -1.03) and its limited pasture land caused the first settlers, who had been shepherds and farmers, to turn to the sea, first, as a source of subsistence, and later, as an avenue for commerce with the outside world. This transformation of shepherds and farmers into fishermen and sailors took place over a number of generations and eventually brought the island to seafaring prominence in the eighteenth century.

Besides the island's limited resources and the islanders' enterprising spirit, other factors led to the emergence of Hydra's merchant marine. By the middle of the eighteenth century, despite its small size, Hydra found itself affected by the major events of contemporary Mediterranean and European history and with an important role to play in the internal life of the Ottoman Empire as well.

After the Turkish conquest in 1715 of the remaining Venetian possessions in southern Greece and the Aegean Sea, Hydra and the other islands of the archipelago were placed under the jurisdiction of the *Kapudan Pasha,* the commander-in-chief of the Ottoman fleet. This administrative arrangement, together with the Turkish taxation that required the islanders to serve in the imperial fleet, made Hydra and the other islands of the archipelago into prime recruiting arenas for the Ottoman navy. Both sides gained as a result. The Sultan recompensed the island for losses suffered by crews from Hydra in Turkish war service by allowing the island to collect its own taxes, which spared it the rapacity and corruption of the Ottoman system of government, and gave it a degree of independence that was important to its future commercial and physical development.

Fig. SIX-1.04 Hydra, island and port from Peloponnesos

To protect against corsairs, the captains of Hydra were also given permission to arm their ships. Yet the Sultan, foreseeing the events of the Greek revolution of the 1820s, limited their tonnage, lest their size and number become a serious threat to Ottoman authority.

Russia's eighteenth-century elevation to the status of a major European power prompted her to try to expand towards the Mediterranean Sea. The immediate obstacle to that expansion was the Ottoman Empire, which controlled both the Black Sea littoral and egress to the Mediterranean. In her efforts to defeat the Ottoman Turks, Catherine the Great (1729-96) understood the important role that the Christian subjects of the Ottoman Empire and, particularly the Greeks, might play in implementing her strategies. By that time the Greeks themselves had come to realize that should they attempt to shake off Ottoman rule, they could count on little assistance from the West. Impressed by Russia's geopolitical achievements and attracted by the religious affinity they shared (since the Russians, too, were Orthodox), the Greeks began to look to Saint Petersburg as a possible source of help.

In 1768, Russia and Turkey went to war. As the war progressed, the Russian Baltic Sea fleet sailed around Western Europe to enter Mediterranean and Aegean waters for the first time. When the Russians arrived, most of the islands in the Aegean archipelago revolted against Ottoman rule and were

Fig. SIX-1.05 Thomas Hope, sepia drawing, "Town and Harbor of Hydra," c. 1795

taken over as operational headquarters by the Russian forces. Indeed, the bay of Naoussa on the northern shore of the island of Paros became the Russian fleet's winter anchorage for the duration of the war.

Russian successes on both sea and land resulted in the conclusion of the war by the treaty of Kuchuk-Kainardji signed in July 1774, which was "historically far more important than the war which preceded it" (Palmer 45) for the Ottoman Empire and its captive Christian Orthodox population. Supplemented by a commercial convention in 1783, the treaty gave the seafaring Aegean islanders the privilege of trading under the protection of the Russian flag. With the added protection against Turkish interference and the corsairs that affiliation with Russia gave, the merchant fleets of Hydra and the other islands grew rapidly and extensively. Napoleon did not fail to note this extraordinary growth. In his continuous search for short-lived strategic alliances, in the summer of 1806, he sent General Horace-Francois Sebastiani, another soldier-diplomat, as ambassador to the *Sublime Porte*. Sebastiani's instructions, which Napoleon personally dictated, included the following:

My unswerving objective in policy is to make a triple alliance between myself, the Porte, and Persia, aimed directly or indirectly against Russia.... . All our negotiations must seek these points: (i) closure of the Bosphorous against the Russians...; (ii) forbidding Greeks from sailing under the Russian flag; (iii) arming every fortification against the Russians; (iv) subduing anti-Ottoman rebels in Georgia and re-asserting the Porte's absolute rule over Moldavia and Wallachia. I do not want to partition the empire of Constantinople; even were I offered three-quarters of it, I should refuse to do so. I wish to strengthen and consolidate this great empire and to use it, as it stands, against Russia. (Palmer 65)

The impressive development of the merchant fleets of the Aegean islands was aided by the decline and, in some instances, the complete disappearance of other flags from Mediterranean waters. For example, an eventually fatal blow was dealt to Venetian naval and commercial power when Bartholomeu Dias, the Portuguese navigator, rounded the Cape of Good Hope in 1488. After that, Venetian possessions in the eastern Mediterranean and the Aegean Seas were lost one by one to the Turks, and the republic's importance as a naval power steadily declined. Napoleon's invasion of northern Italy and the Treaty of Campo Formio, which concluded his campaign in October 1797, ended the independent existence of the Republic of Venice. By this treaty, Austria acquired sovereignty over Venice and recognized French sovereignty over the Ionian Islands of western Greece.

The French merchant marine had been an important player in Mediterranean commerce during the eighteenth century. But the French Revolution and its aftermath diminished its importance. When the Venetian republic disappeared, much of French and Venetian commerce fell to the Aegean islanders.

The Napoleonic wars themselves benefited Hydra. By breaking the British blockade of French-controlled ports, the island's captains amassed sizable fortunes. The island's archives show extraordinary yearly profits from 1810 to 1815, followed by a sharp decline immediately after the Napoleonic wars ended.

But breaking the British blockade also involved great risks. Ships from Hydra were often captured and confiscated by the British, as can also be seen in the archives, which contain correspondence about the capture of several of Hydra's ships. One letter is addressed to the admiral of the Turkish fleet, asking for his mediation to secure the release of a captured vessel. Another letter about the same ship is addressed directly to Admiral Nelson. Both documents illustrate Hydra's autonomy and the islanders' self-confi-

Fig. SIX-1.06 oil on canvas, "*Athena*," brig of Captain Tsamados, 1871
(Note town and port of Hydra at lower right.)

dence in addressing geopolitical as well as marine problems. Other documents from the same archive contain evidence that ships designed for speed were specially built to run the blockade.

Thus, exceptional opportunities for commercial expansion opened up at the end of the eighteenth century and the beginning of the nineteenth for Hydra and the other islands of the Aegean archipelago. These opportunities were enhanced by a series of fortuitous events, as when Ukrainian wheat was brought to the Black Sea after the Russian conquest of its northern shore, and when the treaty of Kuchuk-Kainardji opened the Straits of Bosporus, the Sea of Marmara, and the Dardanelles to free passage by merchant ships sailing under the Russian flag. Since Aegean captains could now fly that flag, both their ships and their owners were immune from the capriciousness of Turkish rule.

With the other major merchant fleets unable for their own reasons to take advantage of these newly open seas, the transportation of wheat from the granaries of the Ukraine to western Mediterranean ports and markets fell into the hands of the captains of Hydra. Finally, the Napoleonic wars and the British blockade of French ports offered the venturesome islanders rare opportunities for unprecedented profits.

Fig.SIX-1.07 Thomas Hope, sepia drawing, "Hydriotes" (men and women of Hydra), c.1795

As the Napoleonic wars ended, normal life resumed in Europe. The Western European merchant fleets began to recover their prewar importance in Mediterranean commerce. This renewed competition brought Hydra difficult times. Many of its ships were moored, and its sailors, unemployed. But the Greek revolution of 1821 and the long war of independence that followed radically changed Hydra's destiny and fortunes as, together with the other Aegean islands, it enlisted its navy in the cause of the revolution. The wealth accumulated by the community and its prominent seafaring families was generously committed to the revolutionary struggle. In the late 1820s, at the end of the war, Hydra found itself part of an independent Greece, its privileged autonomy under Turkish rule exchanged for the fulfillment of its national identity.

Although Hydra's prominent families continued to play an important role in the political affairs of the new nation, the island never again saw the prosperity it had enjoyed at the turn of the nineteenth century. Indeed, as other commercial centers grew, Hydra's population declined. Unemployment increased, and the islanders began to move to Piraeus and Athens. By the end of the nineteenth century, the displacement of sail by steamship had devastated the economy of the island. Sponge diving offered a brief but modest economic revival during the first half of the twentieth century.

Fig. SIX-1.08 Nikos Hadjikyriakos-Ghikas, oil on canvas, "Grand Composition of Hydra," 1948

But a period of new prosperity was ushered in during the 1950s, when international tourism "discovered" Hydra, transformed the island's economy for the next half century, and caused dramatic physical and social change, as it did in most of the Aegean island towns and in Greece as a whole.

My earlier study of the architecture and urban form of the town of Hydra (1967) hypothesized that the island's architectural character was less the outcome of localized and isolated incidents than the result of a vision, of an overall form -- an impressive, perceptible, and consistent architectural form.

Two early nineteenth century visitors registered the town's impressiveness as follows:

> Hydra itself is a barren rock. But on turning the eastern points of the principal harbor, the town opens like an enchantment. It is the only town on the island, contains nearly 13,000 native inhabitants, and the white houses, thickly set and out-topping one another as they ascend from the water high up the rocky hill, are together an exhibition of surprising beauty. A nearer view increases the traveler's surprise -- at the dimensions of the houses, their structure, their furniture, their elegance. (Anderson 143-44)

| Fig. SIX-1.09 William Linton, "The Scenery of Greece and its Islands," 1842 | Fig. SIX-1.10 Henri Belle, "Trois Années en Grèce," 1881 |

Enter its little harbour, and cast your eye upward, and you are aston-ished and delighted at the amphitheatrical spectacle of snow-white dwellings, rising in succession above one another, from the water's edge up towards the crest of the rock. When gazing on this rock-built city in the stillness of the evening, it appeared to me one of the most striking objects on which my eye ever rested. (Hartley 169)

The perceptible form of the town is akin to the simple shape of a classi-cal theater. This shape clearly delineates where the town begins and ends, and where its center is. And it provides the visitor with a physical means of orientation within the town fabric. Finally, the form of the town is consis-tent because its structuring concept is present in nearly every detail and at all possible scales.

My previous book *Hydra: A Greek Island Town, Its Growth and Form* treats these issues of impressiveness, perceptibility, and consistency by examining the physical development and the various components of the town. Sum-maries of these themes follow under the headings "Urban Development" and "Town Components." A third section, "Continuity and Change, 1963-1998," presents and discusses developments since the original study was begun in the summer of 1963.

6.2 Urban Development

Hydra (pronounced "ee-dra"), a craggy, almost treeless ridge of an island, is eleven miles long, between two and four miles wide, and about four miles off the southeastern coast of Argolis, the province of Peloponnesos west of Hydra (Fig. SIX-2.01). Formed of stony, precipitous hills crowned by the

Fig. SIX-2.01 Hydra, with topographic contour lines

Fig. SIX-2.02 Hydra, port and town site, contour lines at five-meter intervals

Fig. SIX-2.03 Hydra, rainwa- ter collection system, 1963

Fig. SIX-2.04 Hydra, rainwa- ter collection system, 1998

Fig. SIX-2.05 Hydra, water tanker, 1997

two-thousand-foot Mount Ere, the island's eighteen and one-half square miles offer a few hundred acres of arable land and a rocky coastline with a few sandy beaches. Hydra has the dry and moderate climate typical of the Aegean region, with temperatures ranging from one hundred degrees Fahrenheit in the summer to thirty-two degrees Fahrenheit in the winter. It is the only sizable settlement on the island.

In the 1820s, during the Greek war of independence, Hydra boasted twenty-eight thousand people, an historic high. Since the 1960s, the town has had a stable year-round population of about twenty-five hundred; at the height of the summer tourist season, this number triples or even quadruples.

The island is nearly waterless, and in the past, settlers relied on cisterns and rainwater collection systems like those found in the Aegean islands gen- erally (Fig. SIX-2.03, -2.04). More recently, local development and tourism have necessitated the construction of a public water distribution system and the importation of water from the mainland by tanker (Fig. SIX-2.05).

Probably the early settlers of Hydra never abandoned the hope of return- ing to their lands of origin. In their minds' eyes, the sea was a link with their old homes, and it was important to them both symbolically and physically that their new settlement be near the shore.

A topographic map of the island reveals a rocky, precipitous, and exposed southern shore that does not lend itself to a port settlement. The northern side provides a number of alternatives, none ideal.

The choice of the site for the present town was influenced by its loca- tion on the island, its geographic features, and its specific topography. But it was also reinforced by the location of a monastery built in the 1640s on the coast at the deepest point of the natural port, a building whose existence would have drawn attention to its site (Fig.SIX-2.02). No record remains to explain why the monastery was built at this location, although it is known that a nun from the nearby island of Kythnos founded it. Given the strength of the corso then, building by the water's edge would have been risky, which suggests Hydra's insignificance and isolation at the time.

The site chosen had an additional and important advantage over other possible sites -- its proximity to the top of Mount Ere. There, a guard scanning the approaches to the island could quickly report any suspicious activity at sea within a radius of several miles. As on Serifos, discussed in Chapter FOUR, the gradual slope of the terrain as it ascended from the bay offered a protective distance from the shore as well as a defensive height. Both considerations were a sine qua non for the survival of any Aegean settlement during the seventeenth and eighteenth centuries. The disadvantages of the site created by the port's northern exposure were apparently disregarded in favor of the advantages of high elevation and a commanding view of the sea approaches. In the light of later developments in Hydra and the Aegean archipelago, this choice seems eminently justified.

According to George D. Kriezis, a nineteenth-century historian of the island, Kiafa, as the original settlement was named, consisted of 370 houses in about 1680. Given five persons per family and one family per house, the town's population would have been about eighteen hundred fifty. Kiafa was almost deserted by the early 1960s, as the town was gradually moved to the lower parts of the larger site. But the foundation walls and other ruins of Kiafa correspond to eighteenth- and nineteenth-century descriptions and illustrations: this old part of the town of Hydra shared features common to other contemporary settlements in the Aegean archipelago -- party walls, flat roofs, a limited number of openings in the outside walls of houses, and controlled entrances to the town, all of which underscore the defensive character of the settlement.

The path that connects Kiafa with the port follows the principle of minimum effort. It descends the hill where the slope is most gradual, and as it reaches the land saddle southwest of the port, it turns east, again following the most gradual slope, towards the west wall, the traditional location of the entrance to the monastery.

Another important path originates at the water source below the eastern edge of Kiafa and leads down to the east side of the monastery; this path was apparently used to carry water to supply the ships there (Fig. SIX-2.06).

The paths run parallel to the east and west sides of the monastery and converge in the area north of the building to form an important space where ships loaded and unloaded, and commercial transactions took place. Since

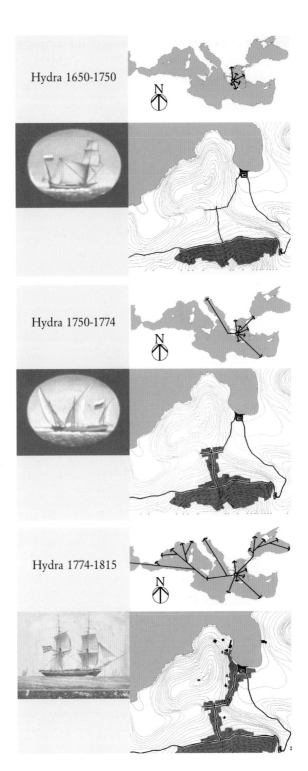

Fig. SIX-2.06, -2.07, -2.08
The diagrams outline successive stages of Hydra's development, indicating the spread of travel, the predominant type of vessel used, and the probable extent of the town during the period in question.

Fig. SIX-2.09 Hydra, town and port, 1971

this space adjoined the most important public building in the town, it naturally became the nucleus of the town's future civic center.

Wars in the Peloponnesos brought successive waves of refugees to the island during the first half of the eighteenth century. Around 1750, the population of the town consisted of 604 families or about 3,000 persons. By this time, the original farmers and shepherds had become a community of seafarers.

The settlement's development now took a different direction. To accommodate the increase in population, the town had to expand. At the same time, the presence of more men to man more ships led to the expansion of Hydra's sea power. This combination of circumstances inevitably led to the dilution of the original, primarily defensive character of the settlement (Fig.SIX-2.07). A town of 3,000 with a prospering and powerful navy is not likely to fall easy prey to a corsair raid. A newly acquired sense of confidence and relative security allowed the town to expand beyond its original protective enclosure. As more and more of the town's life took place near the port as a consequence of its increasing commercial activities, the old settlement itself expanded towards the port.

The last decades of the eighteenth century in Hydra witnessed the rise of prominent sea-captain families, the beneficiares of many profitable sea-

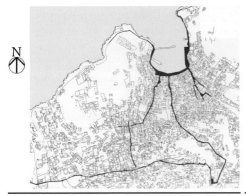

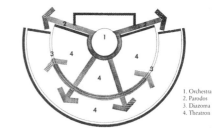

Fig. SIX-2.10 Hydra, town and port, plan

Fig. SIX-2.11 Epidauros, theater, diagram

Fig. SIX-2.12 Hydra, town and port,
1963

Fig. SIX-2.13 Epidauros, theater, 1963

faring ventures. Wealthy families built *archontica*, large private residences that required larger sites than the densely built Kiafa could provide. A large number of these archontica were built in an area just west of the port where an elevated but rocky site reflected and enhanced these families' prominence in the town's life.

The population of the town in 1765 was 667 families, and in 1770, 706 families or about 3,500 persons. The census of 1794, which reflected the large influx of refugees from the Russo-Turkish War of 1768-74, showed 2,235 houses and a population of more than 11,000.

Hydra's great economic boom occurred during the forty-one-year period between 1774, when the treaty of Kuchuk-Kainardji was signed, and 1815, the year the Napoleonic wars ended. The prosperity of these years essentially produced the town's present perceptible form (Fig.SIX-2.08).

Two other important changes occurred, however, before the consolidation of Hydra's town form as it appeared during the second half of the twentieth century. First, there was the partial development of the area known as Kaminia, west of the town over a saddle path, probably the result of a population overspill during the 1820s, the years of the Greek war of independence when another influx of refugees swelled the population of the town to its high of 28,500. Second, there was the near-abandonment of Kiafa for lower elevations closer to the port. This relocation occurred as the need for defense from a high point diminished, and the population of the town declined. In a remarkable reversal, however, Hydra's current prosperity and the related physical changes of recent decades have brought substantial building activity back to the previously abandoned site of Kiafa.

Diagrams of Hydra's growth over time indicate that the developments described earlier -- the building of the monastery near the port, the choice of Kiafa as the original site, and the network of paths created by the interrelationship between of these two centers of activity -- produced a skeleton, an armature, or a structuring frame that the growing town followed faithfully as it filled in the areas delineated above. The result of this filling in is the present form of the town (Fig. SIX-2.09, -2.10, -2.12), with its strong resemblance to the form of the classical Greek theater (Fig. SIX-2.11, -2.13).

At first, this association between the plan of Hydra and the plan of a classical theater might seem to stem from a formalist and superficial perspective. But a more careful examination suggests that it does not. Why? Because, of all the building types of antiquity, the Greek theater was the one best adapted to its site conditions. The Greek temple, by comparison, was clearly designed to separate the natural landscape from its man-made architecture. But the very form of the theater evolved from site considerations. Originally, religious rites required a flat place for dancing, with a slope that rose above it to accommodate onlookers. Yet the final form of the Greek theater as we know it, with its geometric articulation, stepped seats, proscenium, and so forth resulted from a secularization of the building's content that occurred even as its form continued to respond to site conditions.

Similarly, site considerations were paramount from the beginning in Hydra. The present form of the town developed as its society underwent a period of economic and social transformation, but this form is as much the result of site considerations as the original had been.

The similarities between the Greek theater and the town form of Hydra are intriguing. The orchestra in the theater (Fig. SIX-2.11, -2.13) and the port in the town (Fig. SIX-2.10, -2.12) symbolically and physically control the entry to their respective complexes. And the orchestra is the focus of the theater as the port is the center of life in the town. Furthermore, access to the town from the port area of Hydra resembles both the parodos and the up-and-down aisle pattern used in the design of the theater. The diazoma is equivalent to the collector path at the foot of Kiafa, and the stepped seats of the theatron proper are like the clusters of houses that compose the town.

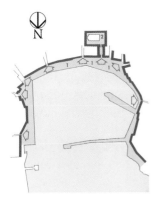

| Fig. SIX-2.14 Hydra, port and quay:
1. Commercial-social center
2. Governmental-religious center | Fig. SIX-2.15 Hydra, port, quay, and town, 1971 | Fig. SIX-2.16 Hydra, quay, 1983 |

| Fig. SIX-2.17 Hydra, port and quay, 1960 | Fig. SIX-2.18 Hydra, quay, afternoon, 1971 | Fig. SIX-2.19 Hydra, quay, morning, 1983 |

However, this is not to suggest that the town developed according to a predetermined design. Indeed, Hydra grew naturally. The point is that the character of the site had a determining role in producing the form of the town, just as the sites of the Greek theaters had in producing theirs. Like the Greek theater's, the form of the town of Hydra is perceptible both visually and structurally, as is recognized and understood intuitively by its citizens. Every step taken over the years to build the town conformed to the basic theme and contributed to the overall image. Indeed, the crucial architectural process of adjusting the building to the site and the site to the building has been a preeminent form-giving device not only for the town of Hydra but also for all the island towns of the Aegean archipelago.

The sea dominated life in the town of Hydra at all stages of its development, Hydra has always been a port town but one that never served an inland region, and, so, did not develop as an industrial, manufacturing, or transportation center. Neither did it develop such features of a typical port town as warehouses, inland communications, and so on, the absence of which allowed its society to continue more or less unchanged through the drama of the booming last decades of the eighteenth century and the first decades of the nineteenth. Few ships from elsewhere used the port, which meant that it served as a dormitory, a recruitment and retirement center for local crews, and a site for shipbuilding, maintenance, and repairs to Hydra's fleet. Its shipyards filled orders only for Hydra's entrepreneurs; its manufacturing facilities produced food supplies, ropes, sails, and so forth only for Hydra's ships.

Today, the austere, continuous, semicircular façade wall that still encompasses the port and its activities (Fig. SIX-2.14, -2.15) also serves physically to separate two distinct functions, the public on one side of the wall, and the private on the other. The quay is the town's center of activity and serves several functions. Early in the day, it is a commercial center; later it becomes a social center. On holidays and other days of public celebration, it becomes a formal civic center. The absence of motorized traffic on each side of the façade wall gives both public and private functions a tranquility that characterizes all aspects of urban life in Hydra (Fig. SIX-2.16, -2.17, -2.18, -2.19).

A limited number of narrow openings penetrate the continuous façade wall and lead to the town's residential sectors. Beyond these openings, the scale and character of the built environment change dramatically. Narrow, stepped streets carry pedestrian traffic and link the town's center of activity with the fabric of the residential areas and the individual dwelling units.

At the widest part of the quay, an opening that leads to the monastery's internal court and its church physically connects the commercial space on its north side with the monastery, now the governmental and religious center of town, and confirms an eloquent and articulate continuity between the two.

Hydra owed its rise to fame and importance to the extraordinary historical circumstances described at the beginning of this chapter. When these circumstances changed, the island lost its prominence in Mediterranean life but retained its dignified form. This form has survived, sustaining and sustained by an extremely successful tourist industry that has been built on Hydra's attractiveness as an example of urban scale and human use.

Most architects today would endorse the Modernist dictum that architectural form follows function, or more precisely, that form and function interact. The town of Hydra supports the notion that a strong and dignified form can remain so even when its original functions have given way to new ones.

6.3 Town Components

Hydra's impressive urban form is sustained by the quality of its component parts. Indeed, the form of the town emerges as the sum of its complementary parts: the structuring armature is informed by the organization of the typical house, the interrelation of clusters of houses, the formation of streets and paths, the generation and containment of public spaces, and the way in which streets are paved, windows framed, stones laid, doors painted, color used, and so on. In other words, Hydra is an organic whole none of whose parts could be removed without diminishing the whole.

Fig. SIX-3.01 Hydra, town components

The town of Hydra, then, evolved within a physical frame of reference well understood by its citizens. Within this frame of reference, the individual builder, guided as he was by the parameters of the vernacular architecture traditions of the Aegean archipelago, also had room to respond intuitively to the challenges of a given building task.

The following pages rely heavily on my book on Hydra (1967), which has been out of print for several years. They present in detail the important components of the town of Hydra and comment on their status, whether unaltered or evolved. The locations of six of these component parts are circled in the town plan reproduced here from my original study (Fig. SIX-3.01). Two represent clusters of houses -- one resting on a relatively flat, the other, on an inclined site (*Clusters of Houses,* areas A and B on the town plan, respectively). A typical street and its auxiliaries follow (*Street Study,* area C) before a discussion of a space of architectural and social importance (*Twin Wells,* area D). A representative archontico, the house of a prominent sea captain (*Voulgaris House,* area E) and a building with historic as well as urban design significance (*The Monastery,* area F) will also be discussed.

Save for some small differences, areas C, D, E, and F have remained basically unaltered and are discussed first. Area B, with its inclined site, provides visual evidence that such a site can induce the disintegration of a contained cluster like the one in area A, and for brevity's sake, will be omitted. The substantial changes that have occurred in area A, on a flat site that I have studied during repeated visits over the last four decades, are presented last, in a section titled "Continuity and Change, 1963-1998."

Street Study (area C, Fig. SIX-3.01)

The variety of pedestrian street forms in Hydra has resulted from the site's topography. Over time streets considered "void" space have become as important compositionally as the "solid" parts of the town.

The streets of Hydra fall into two types: those that run parallel to its topographic contours and those that run perpendicular to them. The ramp type is the most prevalent among the parallel streets. The ramp-step-ramp sequence familiar from other islands is widely encountered (Fig. SIX-3.02). A steps-landing-steps assembly is most common among those streets that run perpendicular to the contours. A long succession of steps without a ramp normally addresses the problems posed by abrupt changes in elevation (Fig. SIX-3.03), but the ramp-step-ramp sequence is also used for that purpose.

Fig. SIX-3.02 Hydra, street, 1963

Fig. SIX-3.03 Hydra, street, 1963

Fig. SIX-3.04 Hydra, street, 1983

Fig. SIX-3.05 Hydra, street, 1983

Fig. SIX-3.06 Hydra, street, 1983

Fig. SIX-3.07 Hydra, street, 1983

Most streets in Hydra developed first as paths from one point to another, after which houses were built along their sides. Streets were further defined by such adjustments between houses and paths as the forty-five-degree corner cuts we have seen before that allow ampler turns by pedestrian and beast-of-burden traffic (Fig. SIX-3.04), a technique with wide application in the vernacular architecture of the Aegean archipelago.

The town's main arteries are wide enough for two basket-carrying mules to pass in opposite directions (Fig. SIX-3.05). Secondary streets allow room

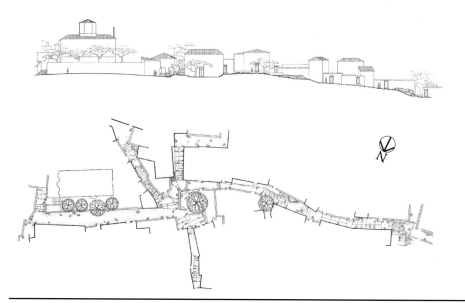

Fig. SIX-3.08 Hydra, *Street Study* (area C), plan and section

for only one. Streets just wide enough for one person are not uncommon (Fig. SIX-3.07). Only one street in the entire town is wide enough, long enough, and surfaced to allow automobile traffic, which continues to be restricted by local ordinance. But the narrowness of most streets and their stepped formation in fact provide the best defense against four-wheeled intruders (Fig. SIX-3.03). Along these narrow streets, mules and donkeys rule unchallenged as they transport people, heavy equipment, refrigerators, furniture, and such building materials as sand, gravel, bricks, concrete blocks, steel reinforcing bars, and so on.

Like other settlements in the Aegean archipelago, Hydra is densely built, reflecting the defense considerations of its early years. Narrow streets and arched-over street segments (Fig. SIX-3.06) minimize the extent of the built-up area and limit the length of the town perimeter to be defended, again confirming the primacy of defense in the urban development of Aegean towns.

In the street study presented in Figure SIX-3.08, the main pedestrian traffic axis runs east-west parallel to the topographic contours. Secondary streets run perpendicular to these contours. The intersection where these streets converge is acknowledged by a large space, which is also a place of social importance. Contributing to its identity are the sizable tree in its midst, the church on its eastern side, and the general store on its southern side. I recorded the presence of this store in the 1960s. It survived into the 1970s but disappeared in the 1980s, perhaps when its owner retired. After that it remained closed for years until, in the summer of 1997, it reopened, probably under new management.

Twin Wells (area D, Fig. SIX-3.01)

As a source of water, the Twin Wells have been extremely important to the town. Although no historical reference to them exists, it seems probable that water was tapped here during the early stages of the settlement's development. Indeed this assumption underlies the diagrams that show the early and staged developments of Kiafa (Fig. SIX-2.02, -2.06, -2.07, -2.08). Again, like any other Aegean island town, Hydra has suffered chronically from a limited water supply. Elaborate rainwater collection systems that led to cisterns for storage (Fig. SIX-2.03, -2.04) were traditional well into the 1960s. The twin wells provided an additional and, by Hydra's standards, plentiful public source of water. Donkeys and mules laden with metal containers

Fig. SIX-3.09 Hydra, *Twin Wells*, 1983

Fig. SIX-3.10 Hydra, *Twin Wells*, 1983

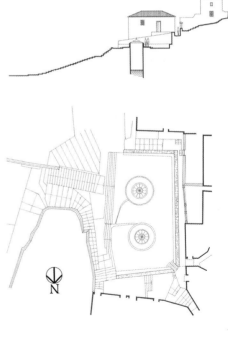

Fig. SIX-3.11 Hydra, *Twin Wells* (area D), plan and section

Fig. SIX-3.12 Hydra, *Twin Wells* (area D), plan and section

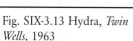

Fig. SIX-3.13 Hydra, *Twin Wells*, 1963

Fig. SIX-3.14 Hydra, *Twin Wells*, 1963

Fig. SIX-3.15 Hydra, *Twin Wells*, 1983

lined up for water, while their owners traded news, stories, and gossip with their neighbors, an activity that did much to establish the architectural and urban character of the Twin Wells.

Delineating the main area of activity around the wells is a podium, an elevated platform that organizes the area's elements, including the tops of the wells, the trees that provide shade, and the seating facilities along the base of the retaining wall. The borders of the podium are determined by a set of monumental steps on its open side and retaining walls in the foreground (Fig. SIX-3.09, -3.10, -3.11). The unbroken series of house façades in the background determines the area's borders on its other three sides. A break in these façades occurs at the northwest corner of the platform, where a path opens to Kiafa (Fig. SIX-3.12, -3.13, -3.14, -3.15).

Windows and doors have been punched through the houses' façades in irregular patterns. The sizes and locations of the openings meet the traditional requirement for a continuous and monolithic façade and enhance the concept of the delineated architectural space. The primary colors used on these doors and windows are consistent with the restrained character of the environment and help distinguish among the properties.

Finally, the three-dimensional organization of the Twin Wells appears to echo the perceptible form of the town and, so, to reinforce its kinship with the shape of the Greek theater.

The demand for water increased exponentially when international tourism discovered Hydra. To meet this increased demand, a tanker ferries in water from a source on Peloponnesos, several miles away by sea (Fig. SIX-2.05). After the water is pumped to a concealed reservoir built at a high point in the area of the abandoned original settlement of Kiafa, the water is distributed by gravity for residential and institutional use. Although the twin wells survived the early stages of water importation, the completion of the distribution system made them redundant. While the metal covers of the wells still operated during the summer of 1995, not a single neighbor appeared to draw water or to trade news and gossip during a long period of observation.

Voulgaris House (area E, Fig. SIX-3.01)

Fig. SIX-3.16 Hydra, *Voulgaris House* (area E), 1983

Archontica, the houses of prominent families and virtual palaces, are distinguished from ordinary houses by a number of features. In size they tower over neighboring structures. In form they are always rectangular, and approximate a cube in volume. Their rigorous architectural character is determined by their exposed, gray, cut stone masonry laid in regular coursing and by the direct, self-restrained, and unpretentious treatment of their façades (Fig. SIX-3.16).

These façades act as architectural screens to separate life within the building from that outside, and as such, they are strictly two-dimensional. The roof eaves protrude very little. The window frames are placed on the same plane as the masonry surface. Three-dimensional embellishment is nearly absent. A reluctant departure from this restrained treatment appears in the whitewashing of window outlines and relieving arches above, which can be painted by reaching out a window, rendering exterior scaffolding unnecessary (Fig. SIX-3.17, -3.18).

Voulgaris's house, built in the early nineteenth century for Francesco Voulgaris, the brother of the island's governor, is representative of the archontica genre in many ways. Yet the relationship of the house to the port and the town, underscored by an elevated courtyard, gives the building a strong, unique, urban character.

The two segments of the plan for the main level of the house -- that is, the elongated part at the north end (the original house) and the rectangular principal house at the south end (a later addition) -- reveal an evolving attitude to the articulation and composition of residential architectural space that expresses a shift from an informal composition, in which one room is attached to the next, to a biaxial, formal arrangement. The Voulgaris family's increasing wealth and status and the changed worldview that resulted from commercial contacts with the Western European world are evident in this design shift and reflect the change experienced by the citizens of Hydra

Fig. SIX-3.17 Hydra, *Voulgaris House,* windows, 1963

Fig. SIX-3.18 Hydra, *Voulgaris House,* windows, 1983

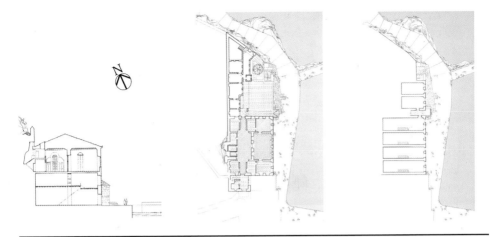

Fig. SIX-3.19 Hydra, *Voulgaris House* (area E), section and plan

generally during this period (Fig. SIX-3.19).

The sophistication and formality of the new principal house plan suggest the possibility that foreign builders (perhaps from northern Italy) were employed for the construction of the Voulgaris archontico and other buildings of its type. For example, the mezzanine orchestra balcony shown in the section drawing indicates that the house was expected to be the setting for a more elaborate social life than was possible in a traditional house on Hydra.

Despite this substantial change in design, however, the traditional spatial sequence leading to the house has been retained. The first crossing from the public street occurs at the foot of the entry stairs. At the top of the stairs, a visitor arrives at a private, uncovered space -- a roof terrace in this instance -- before entering the principal house itself.

Fig. SIX-3.20 Hydra, *Voulgaris House*, 1983

Fig. SIX-3.21 Hydra, *Voulgaris House*, 1983

It is likely that a desire to match the floor level of the old part of the house brought the main level of the new principal house to its present considerable height above the quay and created the high-ceilinged spaces below (Fig. SIX-3.20, -3.21).

The relatively large front openings at street level indicate that these spaces were used as storage and repair shops for small craft.

The two-level mezzanine floor built from the heavy logs used in shipbuilding, the skylights over the stairs, and the orchestra booth all demonstrate an   inventive attitude towards architectural problems. The substantial thickness of the wall -- about three feet -- is mainly structural, although it also provides proper thermal insulation for the house. The slanted window sides, designed to maximize light and minimize exposure to the weather, also demonstrate a creative understanding of environmental control (Fig. SIX-3.19).

The Monastery (area F, Fig. SIX-3.01)

The monastery of Hydra, dedicated to Panayia, has occupied the same site since the 1640s. But most of the present-day buildings were built between 1774 and 1776 to replace those destroyed by an earthquake in 1769. Parts were added later, including the narthex of the church in 1870. Not much information about the monastery survives for the period from the 1640s to 1769, but it seems certain that the buildings the earthquake destroyed were not parts of the original monastery.

Monasteries were built to provide for a life detached from worldly affairs. In Hydra, however, the location of the monastery in what is now the center of town made it indispensable to town life (Fig. SIX-3.22). The monastery church was originally used as a parish church and eventually became the cathedral; non-clerical representatives from the town helped to administer the monastery's affairs. Numerous individual donations confirm the loyalty and affection the citizens of Hydra felt for the monastery over the years.

During the Greek war of independence, the monastery's refectory was used as a meeting room by the sea captains and town leaders who planned revolutionary strategy. Today, the same room is used for the meetings of the town council, while the rooms and cells immediately adjacent serve as the city hall's offices. Other cells house a variety of community and ecclesiastical offices. This double identity of the monastery building today as both the religious and the governmental center of the island should also be understood within the context of the traditionally close relationship between church and state in Greece and throughout the archipelago.

Fig. SIX-3.22 Hydra, *Monastery*, 1983

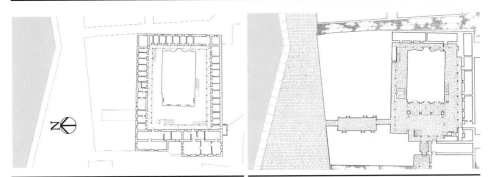

Fig. SIX-3.23 Hydra, *Monastery* (area F), upper-level plan

Fig. SIX-3.24 Hydra, *Monastery* (area F), lower-level plan

Organized according to the traditional diagram discussed earlier, the monastery encloses a paved court where the Katholikon, the monastery church, stands free (Fig. SIX-3.23, -3.24). This court is enclosed on all four sides by two tiers of cells. The old entry to the court on the west wall is still in use, while the newer entry through the north side is a late-nineteenth-century concession to the daily uses of the quay. This newer second entry establishes continuity between the various spaces of the town's civic center in a sequence: large space/small space -- quay -- monastery entry -- monastery court -- church narthex -- church proper. A drawing showing a longitudinal section through the monastery illustrates the physical relationship of the

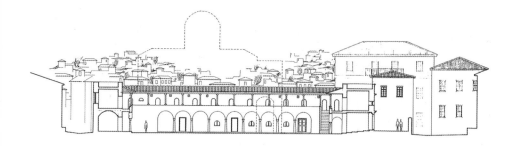

Fig. SIX-3.25 Hydra, *Monastery* (area F), section

Fig. SIX-3.26 Hydra, *Monastery*, 1990

Fig. SIX-3.27 Hydra, *Monastery*, 1990

court to the rest of the town (Fig. SIX-3.25).

Since it turns inward towards the court, the monastery complex lacks an
exterior façade. The two-story arcade in front of the cells is a time-honored
architectural element gracefully executed (Fig. SIX-3.26, -3.27). With prototypes that can be traced back to Greek antiquity, this arcade serves as a transition space between the small and dimly lit cells and the large and brightly lit open court and effectively bridges the difference between their levels
of light. The heavy masonry arches at the ground level of the arcade are elegantly related to the light wooden structure at the level above. The direct
and unpretentious manner that governs the locations of the massive staircases in various parts of the court is matched by the equally unpretentious
placement of the marble columns in both the lower and upper arcades. The
similarities between the architectural treatment of this arcade and that of the
Poros monastery discussed in Chapter FIVE can be explained by the geographic proximity of the islands.

The more than thirty-five years of observation I have conducted since I

Fig. SIX-3.28 Hydra, *Monastery*, 1963   Fig. SIX-3.29 Hydra, *Monastery*, 1983

researched my original study have confirmed that the monastery building has been lovingly preserved for both daily and festive uses. Repair work, whitewashing, painting, the replacement of worn and damaged parts, and restoration work to the ground floor (Fig. SIX-3.28, -3.29) have all been accomplished with sensitivity and a respect for the architectural character and quality of the building and its public spaces. Today, the monastery reflects the essential character of the town on a smaller scale and presents the visitor with a strong and dignified architectural form

6.4 Continuity and Change, 1963-1998

Formed during the last stage of Hydra's development in the nineteenth century, the cluster of houses discussed in this section occupies a nearly flat site (area A, Fig. SIX-3.01). The cluster exemplifies a typical residential block better than any other in this part of town: four streets in roughly rectilinear relationship to one another delineate and contain the cluster.

At approximately 145 x 165 feet, the cluster of houses covers about twenty-four thousand square feet. Its sixteen residential units represent a density of twenty-nine families per acre. The two-level building type prevalent in the cluster is typical of houses to be found throughout the town, although single-level houses are also present in the cluster. Three-level houses, found where the topography of an inclined site dictates, are absent (Fig. SIX-4.01).

Hydra grew naturally and was never regulated by a master plan or by building codes. An oral tradition representing community interests, family privacy, and tacitly understood construction rules made formal codes unnecessary. The builder of a new house -- in many cases, the owner, too – needed first to make sure that the proposed building would not interfere with an established public domain. Once that provision was satisfied, the builder, guided by the vernacular architecture traditions of the island and, indeed, of the Aegean archipelago, enjoyed as much design freedom as the particular features of the site allowed. For example, orientation, although important, was secondary to the need to adjust the house to the site and the site to the house. Indeed the lack of officially established building lines also made for streets with irregular widths and edges.

Each house in the cluster represented one family -- that is, a set of parents and their unmarried children. When a son or daughter was married, a new house was built, often within a vacant part of the parental lot. But that house was treated as a separate unit and given direct entry from the street. This custom gave rise to oddly shaped lots and dead ends, including the L-shaped lot off the west side of the cluster. Horizontal ownership, a practice in which different families own floors of the same house, also exists in the cluster, as elsewhere in Hydra, and results from a similar practice.

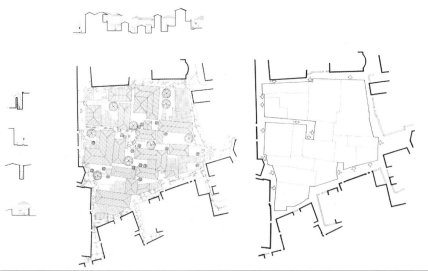

Fig. SIX-4.01 Hydra, cluster of houses (area A), sections and plans

Common materials and methods of construction -- stone masonry walls, timber roofs and floors, and so on – help define the typical house in the cluster and suggest an urban life closer to the sophistication of the capital at Athens than to life on the other Aegean islands. Another important form-giving and morphologically unifying element in the cluster seen elsewhere in Hydra is the spatial organization of the house itself, which generally follows the sequence: public street - threshold - private uncovered space (courtyard) - threshold - private enclosed space (house proper), as illustrated in the adjacent diagram (Fig. SIX-4.04). All but two of the sixteen residential units apply this organizational sequence (also discussed under the heading "Dwellings" in Chapter FIVE). Indeed, this form of house organization is common in the vernacular architecture of practically every Aegean island town and has deep roots in the region, with historical prototypes dating from the fifth century B.C. town of Olynthos on the northern Aegean coast and the second century B.C. town of Priene on the eastern Aegean coast (Fig. SIX-4.02, -4.03), also discussed in Chapter FIVE.

The house whose plans are shown in Fig. SIX-4.05 is characteristic of Hydra and adheres to the principles of spatial sequence and organization just discussed. Planned on two levels, the house offers direct access from the court to rooms on both floors. The original house was probably built as a simple rectangle with a north-south axis and later expanded into an L-shaped building. However, rather than following the customary assign-

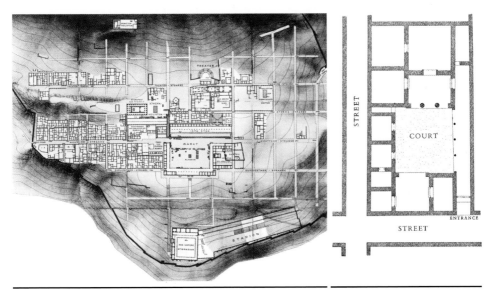

Fig. SIX-4.02 Priene, general plan. The house in SIX-4.03 is located in the upper left row of urban blocks.

Fig. SIX-4.03 Priene, house plan, historical prototype

ment of upper-floor spaces to private use and lower-floor spaces to public use, the individual areas in this house follow a topographic assignment: the kitchen is downstairs and is served by a cistern and a well, while the living room is upstairs where it takes advantage of three different exposures (south, west and north) and overlooks the street and the house court. Bedrooms are located on both floors. Openings on the south wall overlook the entry court of another property that was perhaps originally one with the house and was divided from it after a marriage in the family.

To the thousands of travelers and tourists who visit the island each year, Hydra seems an untouched nineteenth-century town, frozen in time, characterized by its perfect, unadulterated vernacular architecture. But a careful analysis performed block-by-block, building-by-building, and door-by-door reveals the inaccuracy of this stereotype.

The casual observer, for example, might easily overlook the changes in building density, vegetation, color, the utility wirescape, and other elements that only a systematic scrutiny and the use of archival records reveals. A detailed comparison of color slides from 1963 with those from 1998 shows that although Hydra's vernacular architecture has been widely assumed to be fixed and unchanging, in fact, it has undergone a significant evolution

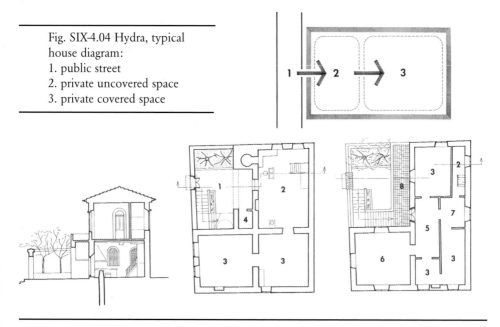

Fig. SIX-4.04 Hydra, typical
house diagram:
1. public street
2. private uncovered space
3. private covered space

Fig. SIX-4.05 Hydra, typical house location in cluster of houses in Fig. SIX-4.01, section and plans: 1. entry court 2. kitchen (with oven, cistern, and well) 3. bedrooms 4. toilet 5. entry hall 6. living room 7. family room 8. balcony

during this thirty-two-year period. But since the evolution has occurred by and large in sympathy with the established fabric and scale of the town, the man-made landscape of Hydra appears to have remained unchanged.

When it became part of Greece in the 1830s, Hydra, like the other Aegean island towns, naturally surrendered some of its distinctiveness to the emerging national culture and the ideology of the new Greek state. Neo-classical architectural forms that originated in the capital at Athens (see Chapter TWO, section six) began to enter the vocabulary of the vernacular architecture of Hydra and of many other towns on the mainland and in the islands. Apparently, the role played by prominent Hydra families in the struggle for national liberation and these families' equally important role in the politics of the new state made Hydra's nineteenth-century adoption of neoclassical forms more intense and widespread than that of any other Aegean island. The town's proximity to the port of Piraeus and to Athens itself was probably also a factor.

Since the early 1960s, new and powerful intrusions into Hydra's vernac-ular manners and forms have occurred as the result of national and inter-national tourism and related economic development. The result has been dramatic social change on the island, as elsewhere in Greece. Hydra's status has become international, a tranformation paralleled in other areas of life, including patterns of employment, gender relationships, and education. While the island's year-round population has remained steady at about twenty-five hundred, seasonal waves of temporary visitors bring it to many times that number. Ironically, during this period of great change, Hydra has been recognized as an architectural treasure and has come under a strict national preservation law.

The architectural changes that have accompanied these developments are noted in twelve photographs taken in 1963 of the periphery of the clus-ter of houses described earlier, paired with a set of photographs of the same locations from 1998. (See Fig. SIX-4.06 for locations.)

The pairs of photographs allow the reader to see the changes that have occurred along streets that define the cluster over a period of thirty-five years. The juxtapositions reveal the impact of affluence upon the vernacu-lar architecture of Hydra as expressed in new construction and new building methods and materials. The observations that follow identify and summa-rize these changes.

Antennas, wires, and electricity poles

The increasing use of electricity, telephones, and televisions since 1963 has profoundly affected Hydra's skyline, particularly since the rocky terrain

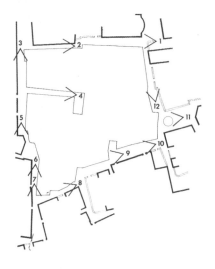

Fig. SIX-4.06 Hydra, cluster of houses, photo location diagram

Fig. SIX-4.07 Location 1, 1963

Fig. SIX-4.08 Location 1, 1998

Fig. SIX-4.09 Location 2, 1963

Fig. SIX-4.10 Location 2, 1998

Fig. SIX-4.11 Location 3, 1963

Fig. SIX-4.12 Location 3, 1998

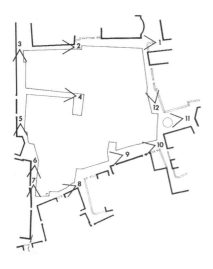

Fig. SIX-4.06 Hydra, cluster of houses,
photo location diagram

Fig. SIX-4.13 Location 4, 1963

Fig. SIX-4.14 Location 4, 1998

Fig. SIX-4.15 Location 5, 1963   Fig. SIX-4.16 Location 5, 1998

Fig. SIX-4.17 Location 6, 1963   Fig. SIX-4.18 Location 6, 1998

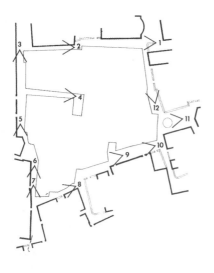

Fig. SIX-4.06 Hydra, cluster of houses,
photo location diagram

Fig. SIX-4.19 Location 7, 1963

Fig. SIX-4.20 Location 7, 1998

Fig. SIX-4.21 Location 8, 1963

Fig. SIX-4.22 Location 8, 1998

Fig. SIX-4.23 Location 9, 1963

Fig. SIX-4.24 Location 9, 1998

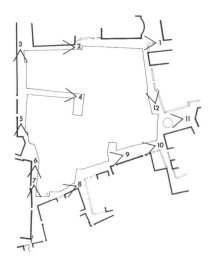

Fig. SIX-4.06 Hydra, cluster of houses,
photo location diagram

Fig. SIX-4.25 Location 10, 1963

Fig. SIX-4.26 Location 10, 1998

Fig. SIX-4.27 Location 11, 1963

Fig. SIX-4.28 Location 11, 1998

Fig. SIX-4.29 Location 12, 1963

Fig. SIX-4.30 Location 12, 1998

of the town's site makes subterranean conduits prohibitively expensive. The resulting proliferation of antennas, electricity poles, and overhead wires has a startling visual impact, particularly on an observer who knew Hydra before their appearance. The photographs of locations 1, 4, 6, 8, 9, and 10 make clear the difference. Electricity poles, in particular, appear to have been installed erratically with no concern for how they might affect the architecture of the area.

Density, massing, and architectural scale

Building density has increased greatly during the period from 1963 to 1998. Vacant buildings have been reoccupied, remodeled, or enlarged. Empty lots have been built on. In the process, traditional architectural materials have usually been replaced by industrially produced ones. In general, however, the building activity has been kept within the traditionally established scale of the town, and happily, no multistory hotel has pierced the skyline of Hydra. Buildings with reinforced concrete frames and hollow brick infill walls seem to imitate, or at least to interpret, the vernacular architecture forms of the past with their massive stone masonry walls. The massing and architectural scale of recent construction thus merge comfortably with those of the past, as seen in the before-and-after photographs of locations 2, 3, 4, and 11.

Architectural elements and materials

The new construction's sympathetic use of scale and massing, of architectural elements such as windows and doors, and of building materials such as roof tiles and stucco have contributed to a sense of continuity with the traditional forms of Hydra's vernacular past. The recent introduction of certain nineteenth-century features that were found in other parts of Greece but not in Hydra should also be noted. These include the shutters shown in the photographs of locations 3, 5, and 12, and the light fixtures in the photographs of locations 6 and 7. Such elements, although foreign to the island vernacular, have been allowed by the regulatory authorities as being in keeping with the town's architectural character.

Views

Some of the distant views that were visible from the meandering alleys of the cluster in 1963 have been blocked by increased building density, as is confirmed by the paired photographs of locations 2, 3, and 4. The sense of enclosure pedestrian experiences is thus enhanced, but the eclipse of well-known landmarks decreases the walker's sense of orientation.

Vegetation

One of the most surprising and welcome changes in Hydra during the last three decades has been the extensive increase in vegetation shown in the pairs of photographs of locations 9, 10, 11, and 12. Water has always been a precious commodity in Hydra. But the importation of water and the building of a water distribution system have had a profound effect on vegetation. Trees, climbing vines, and flower beds and pots are present in much greater abundance now, softening the outlines of buildings and providing shade from the harsh sun and relief from the blinding glare of the whitewash. Where water is concerned, another transformation can be observed in the photographs of location 10, which show a well in the foreground. In 1963, the well contained brackish, nonpotable water for domestic use. By 1998, the movable well cover of 1963 had been replaced by a concrete slab to prevent the use of the now polluted water.

Color

The photographs on these pages also document another important change -- the increased presence of color in the cluster and, indeed, throughout the town of Hydra. The traditional custom of whitewashing is still widely followed, as it is associated with status, cleanliness, maintenance, and disinfection. But color added to the whitewash is now widely used to enliven the exterior, public aspects of houses and, more recently, to celebrate the newfound prosperity of the island. By contrast, I remember visiting Hydra in the late 1940s when the only color available to the islanders was war-surplus battleship gray. Applied everywhere, it suited the mood of a town emerging from the ravages of World War II and a vicious foreign occupation.

The vernacular architecture of the Aegean archipelago has evolved continuously in response to local considerations and distant influences from the capital and beyond. Developments in Hydra between 1963 and 1998 illustrate this evolution. The changes described above occurred over a thirty-five-year period that parallels the era of Hydra's spectacular growth between 1774 and 1815. But the changes that have been made more recently, although perhaps equally extensive, have been controlled by laws and regulations that originated outside Hydra and have been meant to preserve the island's vernacular architecture and character. As a result, the changes of the last three decades have been less detrimental to the overall architectural character of the town than those made in other, less protected areas of Greece. The wider use of color in Hydra and the growth of trees, vines, and flowers made possible by the greater availability of water have enriched the traditional architecture of the town in many ways. To a degree, both have acted to soften the unwelcome impact of television antennas, electricity poles, and overhead wires.

Important aspects of the architectural character of Hydra maintain a distinct sense of continuity. The overall scale and the size and proportions of new buildings remain compatible with past structures, despite the introduction of such nontraditional materials as reinforced concrete and hollow-core brick in place of the massive stone masonry walls of the past.

The profusion of overhead wires and antennas is the innovation most dissonant with the vernacular architectural forms of the town. Granted, the cost of burying cables underground is prohibitive, but even so, electricity poles have been placed haphazardly, with disappointingly little respect for the architectural qualities of the town (Fig. SIX-4.31, -4.32, -4.33).

Another subtle but important shift has been the incorporation of nineteenth-century architectural elements foreign to the island into the town's preservation regulations. This practice is currently innocuous, but if applied too widely, it will tend to erode the very sense of authenticity that characterizes the town and constitutes its greatest attraction. These injurious changes are additional evidence that what appears to the casual observer an unchanged environment is in truth subtly fluid, and, as a consequence, vulnerable. While the architecture and urban forms of Hydra seem to have

Fig. SIX-4.31 Hydra, 1993   Fig. SIX-4.32 Hydra, 1998   Fig. SIX-4.33 Hydra, 1999

Fig. SIX-4.34 Thomas Hope, watercolor, "Town and Harbour of Hydra," c.1795

absorbed the assault of the tourist trade with dignity so far, concerns for the course of future development persist.

Unsurprisingly, a developer's proposal to build a deluxe resort on the island produced an intense public debate during the first half of 1997. The local authorities and the business community strongly supported the proposal as, potentially, a financial blessing for the island. But the intellectuals and preservationists who saw the proposal as a first step towards the destruction of the island's tranquility, landscape, and distinctive architecture were adamantly opposed to it. To be located in a valley near the town, the proposed one hundred-bed resort was reportedly designed to be sensitive to Hydra's vernacular architecture and its natural landscape. The proposed resort would have included solar power and desalination plants and would have used traditional nonvehicular means of transportation. When the Athens-based Central Archaeological Council charged with the protection of historical sites recommended that the Ministry of Culture reject the proposal, the rejection ironically transformed the conflict into a debate between the local community and a national authority, just the sort of conflict that two hundred years earlier in a different geopolitical context had produced Hydra's greatest days.

SEVEN

SANTORINI OBSERVED

Fig. SEVEN-1.01 Santorini, caldera, Fira, 1995

Architects use plans to communicate ideas about buildings. Architectural plans speak of building outlines, circulation patterns, room sizes, structural concepts, and related issues. But most architects find vertical sections more exciting to their minds' eyes. Together with two-dimensional plans, a vertical section exposes the third dimension of a building and thus reveals architecture in the most appropriate light. The magnificent natural section through the caldera on Santorini sets the island apart from all other Aegean islands (Fig. SEVEN-1.01). Its awe-inspiring site, the product of prehistoric volcanic activity, appears today as a colossal cut, or vertical section, that slices through both the land and the sea. An immense incision whose extraordinary physical dimensions far exceed the limits of any architectural section, this vertical rift (on a scale similar to the Grand Canyon's) dramatically fuses Aegean geology and Aegean history at the unique site of Santorini.

A corruption of "Santa Irene," the name "Santorini" derives from the era of the Duchy of the Archipelago. Officially, the island is known as "Thera," a name that originated in Greek antiquity. But from the perspective of the Aegean crucible that is the subject of this book, "Santorini," rather than "Thera," has been chosen as the title and the subject of this chapter.

Fig. SEVEN-1.02 Santorini

The largest of three islands located in close proximity and including Therasia and Aspronisi, Santorini is at the southeastern periphery of the Cyclades Islands and lies about one hundred twenty kilometers north of Irakleion in Crete, a location with historic, or better, prehistoric significance for both Santorini and Crete (Fig. SEVEN-1.02). The island is of average size within the Cyclades group and comprises seventy-six square kilometers compared with Sifnos's seventy-three. According to the 1991 census, Santorini was home to 9,360 people, the same number of inhabitants as in 1940, the island having lost population after the destructive earthquake of 1956. As Santorini emerged as a major tourist attraction in the 1970s, it gradually regained its pre-1956 population. Currently, for several weeks during the summer tourist season, Santorini's population more or less doubles.

Santorini's history spans three major periods of development -- the prehistoric, the Greek-Hellenistic, and the contemporary, which dates from the era of the Duchy of the Archipelago. Extensive prehistoric volcanic activity produced Santorini's unique site and will be discussed below. The significant remains from the Greek-Hellenistic period that are located in Mesa

Vouno in the southeastern part of the island fall outside the scope of this book. The contemporary period that dates from the era of the duchy produced a number of fortified settlements, including Skaros, which was discussed in Chapter TWO and Chapter FOUR. Today, these two periods, the prehistoric and the contemporary, merge physically as Fira, Merovigli (Fig. SEVEN-1.03), and Oia, the present-day descendants of the fortified settlements of the past, seem to form white eyebrows over the polychrome face of the caldera cliffs when seen from the sea below (as noted in the Prologue).

Fig. SEVEN-1.03 Santorini, Merovigli, 1992

Herodotus called Santorini *Strongyle*, or "the circular island." Sixteen kilometers in diameter, the Strongyle he knew had a centrally located summit of perhaps sixteen hundred meters and a circumference that included all three existing islands (Fig. SEVEN-1.06). Although the original circular outline is still traceable, it was ruptured, and three fragments -- Santorini, Aspronisi, and Therasia - replaced what was once one island.

The largest fragment, which is crescent-shaped, is today's Santorini, or Thera. Therasia is a smaller fragment that has two small settlements and lies to the northwest of Santorini. Aspronisi, "the white island," much smaller than the

Fig. SEVEN-1.04 Santorini, caldera, Fira, 1973

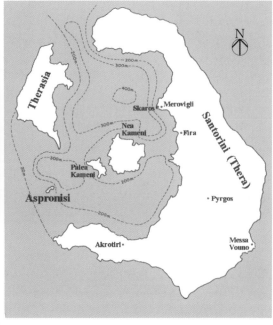

Fig. SEVEN-1.05 Santorini, caldera, Skaros, 1995

Fig. SEVEN-1.06 Santorini, schematic map and section

other two, is uninhabited (Fig. SEVEN-1.06). All three islands are covered in layers of white ash and pumice as thick as fifty-five meters and encircle a crater filled by a large body of water, or a caldera. With depths reaching four hundred meters, the caldera marks the location of the collapsed Strongyle summit.

A great volcanic eruption or, more likely, a series of eruptions, demolished Strongyle during the Late Bronze Age, either between 1500 and 1470 B.C. or after 1628 B.C., as more recent research suggests. Beginning in the second century B.C. and continuing to expand as late as the 1950 eruption, two distinct island masses emerged above sea level in the center of the caldera.

| Fig. SEVEN-1.07 Santorini, Nea Kameni, 1973 | Fig. SEVEN-1.08 Santorini, Nea Kameni, 1995 |

These islands, Palea Kameni and Nea Kameni, "the burnt islands," constitute the dome of the volcano (Fig. SEVEN-1.07, -1.08).

When the Suez Canal was built in the 1860s, pozzolana, a material used to make hydraulic cement, was in great demand. It was available in quantity in Santorini's layers of volcanic ash. Quarrying pozzolana from Santorini for the canal brought to light buried prehistoric buildings more than three millennia old. After World War II, the work of the Greek Archaeological Society in Akrotiri also uncovered a thriving city with strong Minoan-Cretan features in the utensils of everyday life found there and in its architecture, pottery, and wall painting. The two- and three-story houses in Akrotiri parallel Santorini's present-day settlements in planning and in scale and underscore the continuity of human habitation on the island through the millennia. The walls of these houses are reinforced with wooden tie beams that serve as seismic protection and that show an impressive early understanding of the relationship between building and site. Stone staircases lead from floor to floor (Fig. SEVEN-1.10). Wall paintings of remarkable sophistication in theme and execution are the earliest known large-scale paintings in Greece (Fig. SEVEN-1.09).

Fig. SEVEN-1.09 Santorini, Akrotiri

Fig. SEVEN-1.10 Santorini, Akrotiri, 1982

In recent decades, the excavations at Akrotiri, other archaeological evidence, and the work of geologists, volcanologists, and oceanographers from all over the world have begun to suggest what might have happened to the inhabitants of Strongyle and their prehistoric city during the great, Late-Bronze-Age, volcanic eruption.

The first outburst of the volcano must have produced a fall of pumice large enough to prompt the citizens of Akrotiri to evacuate: "So few skeletons and valuables have yet been found that it seems as if the inhabitants had enough warning to collect some of their belongings and make a getaway" (Luce 69). A period of relative calm followed. Later came the major blast, here described in all its devastating detail:

> Huge earthquakes, a dense gas plume charged with pumice and ash rose as much as 36 km into the stratosphere, warm pumice rained down everywhere accumulating as rapidly as 3 cm/minute. That triggered quick evacuation of anyone remaining on the island... . Roofs collapsed from loading of pumice and buildings were buried up to their second and third floors: the entire Late Bronze Age landscape was gently covered. Then it got nasty. The entire center of the island collapsed... . And then there were the volcanic bombs -- huge lithic [stone] boulders blasted out from the vent that were deeply buried upon impact with the tephra [ash]. More destruction of buried buildings occurred. An eruption of such magnitude...must have caused great havoc in the region. Ash fell from the Nile Delta to the Black Sea with [the] thickest accumulations towards the east of almost a meter on Rhodes and Kos... . Tsunami, dozens of them, radiated out in all directions... . Rafts of pumice floated throughout the Aegean and eastern Mediterranean Seas for years, providing a source of material for tools and construction material." (McCoy)

Silence then reigned for centuries (Fig. SEVEN-1.11 to 1.16).

Plato's legend of Atlantis (c. 400 B.C.) describes a great ancient civilization that "disappeared in one terrible day and night." Recent scholarship has led to a growing belief that Minoan Crete was Plato's Atlantis and that the extremely violent eruption of the volcano at Thera/Santorini, a Minoan outpost, destroyed Cretan thalassocracy, or maritime supremacy, and led to the transfer of power in the Aegean from the Minoans to the Mycenaean Greeks. A detailed discussion of Plato's legend of Atlantis and its current interpretations is beyond the scope of this book. Suffice it to say that more than two thousand books have been written on the subject over the last one

Fig. SEVEN-1.11 Santorini, caldera cliffs, 1995

Fig. SEVEN-1.12 Santorini, caldera cliffs, 2000

Fig. SEVEN-1.13 Santorini, caldera cliffs, 1995

Fig. SEVEN-1.14 Santorini, caldera cliffs, 2000

Fig. SEVEN-1.15 Santorini, caldera cliffs, 2000

Fig. SEVEN-1.16 Santorini, caldera cliffs, 2000

hundred fifty years; J.V. Luce's *The End of Atlantis* is perhaps the best.

The inhabitants of Greek-Hellenistic settlements on Santorini at Mesa Vouno were apparently unaware of the earlier existence of the nearby Late-Bronze-Age Akrotiri. Save for brief references in Homer, the rest of classical Greece had also forgotten the Minoan thalassocracy. But memories of the Thera/Santorini eruption persist in Greek mythology and in Plato's Atlantis legend, which came to him from Egyptian sources. From the rich spectrum of Greek mythology come two other myths about the landscape/seascape of the area that are particularly poignant, the stories of Delos, the floating island, and of Talos of Crete, the bronze giant. Both resonate in our time.

Pumice blown from the mouth of the Thera/Santorini volcano floated throughout the Aegean and eastern Mediterranean Seas for months, and perhaps years, after the eruption. Aegean sailors saw these island-sized floating concentrations of pumice as unexplained visual phenomena that interfered with their familiar navigational routes. Their search for an explanation for them may be responsible for Delos's mythical beginning as the island that drifted through the Aegean Sea until Apollo was born there, when it put down roots and became Delos, the "clear island" (Luce 169).

As for Talos, his story derives from the Argonaut saga, which probably represents an attempt to rationalize the early Greek voyages of exploration in the Aegean, the Black, and the Mediterranean Seas. In the saga the Argonauts were confronted by the solid bronze giant Talos, who prevented them from landing on Crete by throwing boulders at them. Talos had been given to Europa by Zeus and made the guardian of the island. Talos moved quickly on his legs of brass, patrolling the island. The Argonauts, terrified by his rock throwing, were fast retreating when Talos, preparing to hurl another of his boulders, scratched his ankle, his one weak spot, on a pointed rock. "Then the ichor flowed out like molten lead." Losing strength rapidly, Talos fell from his rocky crag "with a terrible crash." Perhaps as Luce suggests, the Talos story embodies a residual memory of the Thera/Santorini volcanic eruption:

> Thera "guards" the northern approaches to Crete which would have been used by the early Mycenaean sailors. His frame of "unbreakable bronze" represents the wall of the newly formed crater on the mountain peak of Thera as it then was. The rocks which he throws are the "bombs" shot from the vent of the volcano. [Talos's] "heel" is a subsidiary volcano on the coast of the island, like Cape Kolumbo or Cape Mavrorachidi. He collapses and becomes quiescent when all his ichor has flowed out like "molten lead"-- a reminiscence of the cooling off of lava streams after the end of an eruption. (149)

These two legends offer a glimpse of the important physical and meta-physical roles the Thera/Santorini eruption played in the formation of Greek culture and consciousness. The Atlantis myth suggests that the catastrophic eruption destroyed the infrastructure of Minoan Crete and allowed the Mycenaean Greeks from the mainland to extend their power to Crete, which led to a remarkable interpenetration of the two cultures:

Minoan religion left a lasting impress on Greek polytheism. Perhaps

the most potent symbol of the cultural conquest is still to be seen in the great relief over the Lion Gate at Mycenae. There the royal lions of the house of Atreus support themselves against a Minoan pillar standing on a Minoan altar base. (Luce 175 and Fig. SEVEN-1.17)

The Santorini we see today lies atop tens of meters of volcanic ash

Fig. SEVEN-1.17 Mycenae, Lion Gate, 1999

and pumice 250 meters above the water surface of the caldera and dates from the days of the Duchy of the Archipelago. (See Chapter TWO for the Venetian conquest of the Cyclades Islands in the early thirteenth century and the survival of the duchy for the next three hundred and fifty years until it was conquered by the Ottoman Turks.)

Santorini's history during the duchy's flourishing resembled that of the other Aegean islands it controlled. Marco Sanudo, the first duke, kept a number of islands besides Naxos for himself and gave others to his comrades-in-arms as subfiefs. Santorini was granted to a Barozzi. Soon after, the island reverted to Byzantine rule but was regained by the Barozzi family at the end of the thirteenth century. Two other Latin families, the Pisani and the Crispi, possessed the island in whole or in part during the duchy period. (Late in the fifteenth century the two families were involved in a dispute over the seat of the Santorini lordship in the Kastro of Skaros. For more on this dispute see Chapter FOUR.)

In the seventeenth century, when we get our first complete picture of the island, mention is made of five *Kastelia*, or fortified settlements (Philippides, *Santorini* 10). *Kasteli*, another term for Kastro, is used exclusively on Santorini as far as I know. Skaros Kastro, located in the upper third of the island, is one of the five Kastelia (the plural of Kasteli). Another Kasteli, Oia (the present-day name of Saint Nicholas), is at the northern tip, while the remaining three, Pyrgos, Emporio, and Akrotiri, are located in the southern half of the island. The *Goulas* or *Goulades* (plural) found on Santorini are fortified buildings located either inside a Kasteli or freestanding and are unique to the island, dating from the era of the duchy. The Kastelia and Goulades were reserved for the Latin overlords until the duchy collapsed, when they became the residences of prominent Greek families. The peasantry, by contrast, lived in dugout houses in the countryside -- houses also unique to Santorini and made possible by the island's layers of volcanic ash that could easily be excavated and carved out to provide habitable, connected living spaces (Fig. SEVEN-1.35).

The development of Santorini's economy was fostered by the religious and administrative autonomy permitted by the *millet* system that operated during Tourkokratia and was discussed in Chapter TWO. The existence of local products for export, primarily prized wines, and the availability of shipyards led Santorini to develop its inter-Aegean trade early. Eventually, the commercial opportunities opened up by the Ottoman Empire led the islanders to develop a substantial merchant fleet that traded in most Mediterranean ports. Commercial activity in Santorini was so extensive by the mid-seventeenth century that France opened a consulate there in 1650. England followed suit in 1706. Russia, Holland, Austria, and Sweden eventually did likewise. By the outbreak of Greece's war of independence in 1821, Santorini's merchant fleet was the third largest in the islands, exceeded in size only by Hydra's and Spetsai's.

Santorini's fleet continued to flourish after the island became part of the newly established Greek state. In the 1840s, the islanders owned more than one hundred fifty vessels of various types and sizes, manned by more than fifteen hundred sailors. The introduction of steamships marked the beginning of a decline, although shipping continued to employ a substantial majority of the island's population even after the beginning of World War II. A number of island families eventually came to own merchant fleets that now operate on an international scale.

As if to remind Santorini's inhabitants of the island's volcanic origins, a catastrophic earthquake struck in 1956, destroying substantial parts of the island's settlements. This earthquake dealt such a severe blow to the island's

Fig. SEVEN-1.18 Santorini, Merovigli, Skaros, and Fira, 1995

traditional economy that the population declined precipitously at first. But recovery and regeneration occured relatively quickly. Less than two decades after the volcano's devastation, the islanders' entrepreneurial instincts and hard work, together with the island's natural attractions and its vernacular architecture had placed it on the road to recovery and transformed it into a major Aegean and Mediterranean tourist destination.

Skaros, Santorini's preeminent Kasteli, is discussed at length in Chapter FOUR in the context of Papadiamantis's story *Ftochos Ayios*. Skaros and Skiathos, where *Ftochos Ayios* is set, are examples of Aegean collective fortification that were deserted in the nineteenth century after piracy declined. A mid-seventeenth-century visitor to Santorini described Skaros thus:

> There are five citadels at Santorini. The first is called Kastro. This is where the Dukes and the governors of the island lived prior to Tourkokratia. The Ducal palace was also located there. Today Kastro is the seat of the Latin bishop. Kastro is at a high location and it takes half an hour to reach its external walls. The gates were shut when an enemy invasion was feared. A huge rock rises in the middle of it where two hundred houses had been built. Now they have been deserted and are slowly collapsing.

Before Thomas Hope visited Santorini at the end of the eighteenth cen-

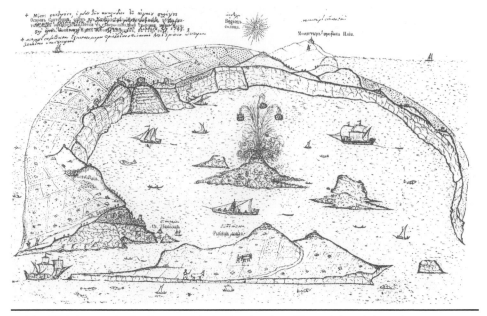

Fig. SEVEN-1.19 Vasily Gregorevich Barsky, drawing, "Santorini and the Volcano," 1745

tury and acquired the pencil drawing discussed in Chapter FOUR, there were apparently two fortifications on Skaros. The older one *Epano Kastro* ("upper citadel"), or *Roka*, was built on the flat space atop the massive rock; the newer and larger one *Kato Kastro* ("lower citadel") was built at the base of the same rock, where it faced the hazard of rocks falling from above.

Vasily Gregorevich Barsky (1701-47), the Russian monk whose drawing of the Patmos monastery appears in Chapter FOUR, also drew the island of Santorini. Dated 1745, the drawing was rendered from Barsky's characteristic bird's-eye perspective and was executed in his typical "see-think-record" manner. It identifies the promontory and the Kastro on top of Skaros and a Goulas farther south. Barsky labeled the site of today's settlement "Fyra" and indicated vineyards and related structures that supported the production of wine. Barsky's intentions were more descriptive than artistic and in general, he was quite accurate in drawing what he saw. We can therefore assume with reasonable certainty that Skaros's citizens had not begun to move their permanent residences to Fira by 1745 and would not do so until several decades later (Fig. SEVEN-1.19).

Not bound by the constraints of a collective fortification and for reasons of topography, Fira developed during the nineteenth and twentieth centuries as a linear settlement along the edge of the volcanic cliffs; its residents had breathtaking views of the caldera. Some of the citizens of Skaros

Fig. SEVEN-1.20 Santorini, Fira, 1982

Fig. SEVEN-1.21 Santorini, Fira, 1982

Fig. SEVEN-1.22 Santorini, Fira, aerial photograph, 1939

Fig. SEVEN-1.23 Santorini, Fira, 1995

Fig. SEVEN-1.24 Santorini, Fira, 1995

Fig. SEVEN-1.25 Santorini, Fira, 1992

moved to Merovigli instead, another linear settlement located next to Skaros (Fig.SEVEN-1.03) and apparently contemporary with Fira. Today, Fira, whose northern edges touch Merovigli, is the major population center, and, in effect, the capital of the island. From its poorly recorded early days as a collective fortification, Oia, at the northern tip of Santorini, developed according to a linear pattern for the same reasons that Fira did.

Starting from about the middle of the length of Fira, a path led to the bay below, where sailing ships were loaded with the island's major export, wine, the trade in which apparently attracted residents to Fira and which in turn, led to its current prominence. Another distinct and remarkable feature of the vernacular architecture of Santorini, the long downward path from Fira to the sea, comprises a series of nearly six hundred steps and ramps that zigzag, hug, embrace, negotiate, and adjust gracefully to the sloping cliffs of the caldera (Fig. SEVEN-1.20 to -1.25 and -1.39). The path, a simple linear architectural form, descends the 250 meters of the caldera cliff to engage its immediate site in an architectural conversation of indisputable fluency and elegance.

Pyrgos in the interior is another of the five Kastelia on the island. A schematic plan of the town drawn from a 1950s aerial photograph shows a collective fortification built on a hill, probably in two stages, reminiscent of the staged building of the Sifnos Kastro. The first stage of Pyrgos consists of a core made up of houses and two churches, one of which replaced a central defense tower torn down circa 1735. The second stage is composed of monochoro units attached to form a ring around the original core that

Fig. SEVEN-1.26 Santorini, Pyrgos, gate, 1992

Fig. SEVEN-1.27 Santorini, Pyrgos, 1992

Fig. SEVEN-1.28 Santorini, Pyrgos, 1973

Fig. SEVEN-1.29 Santorini, Pyrgos, gate, 1973

Fig. SEVEN-1.30 Santorini, Pyrgos, schematic plan

Fig. SEVEN-1.31 Santorini, Pyrgos, 1973

Fig. SEVEN-1.32 Santorini, Fira from Pyrgos, 1973

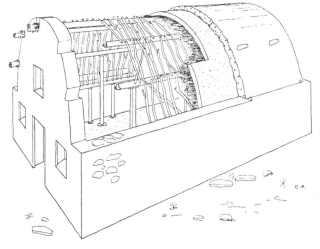

Fig. SEVEN-1.33 Santorini, typical barrel-vault construction

Fig. SEVEN-1.34 Santorini, remnants of barrel vault, 1995

allows for a single gated access on the west side. Behind the gate a narrow footpath concentric with the core provides direct access to each of the monochoro units in the external wall. Pyrgos's roughly triangular plan and curved walls respond to the hill at the site of the original collective fortification. A small chapel incorporated into the external wall and a part of the second stage of Pyrgos's development apparently dates from the fourteenth century and provides a possible reference point for dating the rest of the settlement.

Repeating the general pattern of eighteenth- and nineteenth-century development in the Aegean archipelago, and on Santorini in particular, Pyrgos expanded westward and northward beyond the confines of the original collective fortification. In the 1956 earthquake, the town was severely damaged. But enough remains and has been repaired to allow us to see Pyrgos as a fine application of the principles of Aegean collective fortification and as reminiscent of the Antiparos, Sifnos, Astypalaia, and Kimolos Kastra discussed in Chapter FOUR.

The systematic extraction and export of volcanic ash containing pozzolana, locally known as "Theran earth," began during the second half of the nineteenth century and became an important part of Santorini's economy. But the degradation of the island's landscape that the mining caused was incompatible with the emergence of tourism as the island's major industry in the 1970s. This incompatibility made the demise of the mining industry inevitable, and the last quarry closed at the end of 1989.

As established in Chapter FIVE, two building types have determined the urban forms of the Aegean island towns: dwelling units and churches and chapels. It will be remembered that rectangular building forms normally enclose dwelling units, and curvilinear forms enclose churches and chapels. However, Santorini is a notable exception to this rule, since curvilinear forms are used there to cover both dwelling units and religious structures. A pivotal reason for this difference is the local abundance of pozzolana and volcanic ash. "Easily quarried, with exceptional hydraulic qualities" (Philip-pides, *Santorini* 17), this "Theran earth," intelligently used, has generated the typical Santorini barrel vault, a structural element distinctive to the vernac-ular architecture forms of the island. Mixed with other building materials, pozzolana forms a particularly strong concrete that, when poured over formwork, can span upwards of twelve to fourteen feet without requiring steel reinforcing (Fig. SEVEN-1.33, -1.34).

The structural qualities of this "Theran earth" have produced another

Fig. SEVEN-1.35 Santorini, Messaria

Fig. SEVEN-1.36 Santorini, fog in September, a source of moisture for a dry island, 1995

Fig. SEVEN-1.37 Santorini, fog in September, a source of moisture for a dry island, 1995

architectural form found only on Santorini, the dugout mentioned earlier. Dugout rooms at the scale of the monochoro tunnel into the vertical face of the pozzolana layers, their upper parts forming barrel vaults. A regular façade wall, including a door and three windows, controls access to the dugout's interior. The barrel-vaulted geometry of the dugout and of an "above-the-earth" building provides extra ceiling height at the center of the room and creates an elegant elevation on the short side of the monochoro, where two windows flank a door with a third over it in the form of a skylight. Combinations of barrel-vaulted dugouts and "above-the-earth" buildings comprise larger houses and even whole neighborhoods, as the drawing from Messaria, another settlement on Santorini, indicates (Fig. SEVEN-1.35). Interestingly, as a seventeenth-century visitor noted, the citizens of the island cleverly turned a dugout into a church to avoid breaking the Sultan's prohibition on building new Christian churches in the Ottoman empire.

As they did throughout the archipelago, neoclassical architectural elements made inroads into nineteenth-century Santorini. Rows of pilasters, pairs of columns, and crowning pediments combined with surfaces of local red volcanic stone were used in the impressive façades of captain's houses and reflected the prosperity and sophistication of the island's inhabitants and its vernacular builders. Philippides explains the factors responsible for Santorini's flourishing economy:

> The spread of viniculture on Santorini began in the eighteenth century and reached its peak in the last quarter of the nineteenth. The island's sweet red wine traveled well and so the sizeable mercantile fleet of sailing vessels was born, supplying markets in Greece and

Fig. SEVEN-1.38 Santorini, drawing by the author, 1951

Fig. SEVEN-1.39 Santorini, caldera cliffs, steps and ramps

abroad. The ship-owners-skippers *(kapetanaioi)* were usually vine-growers and wine producers, as well as merchants who acquired wine from other producers and promoted it in the market. The organization of viniculture was adapted to the island's peculiarities. A cottage-industrial system prevailed, covering the needs of the family and generating a surplus for trade. The small farmers formed coalitions with large producers in order to supply the merchants with this surplus. The sailing ships docked in the sheltered coves inside the caldera, and the muleteers brought the wine down to them in wine-skins, from which it was emptied into barrels. (Philippides, "Kanaves," 384)

Collecting wine from across the island at a single location established Fira as the commercial capital of Santorini. The use of mules to transport the wine from Fira down to the sailing ships below demonstrated the need for the town's long sequence of steps and ramps, a construction wonderfully adapted to its spectacular site. Today, with wine production at a minimum, the step-and-ramp system has become superannuated: a cable car runs beside it, and there is a new port farther south in the caldera where car ferries land. Only those fun-loving tourists willing to risk a mule ride now brave the once-indispensable steps and ramps.

EIGHT

▷ ◁

THE URBAN FABRIC

▷ ◁

Fig. EIGHT-1.01 The urban fabric, 1960-94

Defense needs, inclined sites, mild climate, and native materials combined to produce the larger-scale architectural forms of the island towns of the Aegean archipelago examined in the preceding pages. An infinite variety of detail -- flat roofs and roof tiles, recycled columns and temple parts, steps and corner cuts, apses and bell towers, color and whitewash, doors and windows, boats and domes -- makes up an evolving smaller-scale urban fabric that humanizes the harsh living conditions on these "nests of seagulls," and continues to impress and delight us today with its inventiveness. In the pages that follow, a selection of such images represents this distinctly Aegean urban fabric.

Fig. EIGHT-1.02 Mykonos, 1960

Mykonos, Panayia Paraportiani: The illustration of the chapel of Parapor-tiani above is among the oldest photographic "notes" in this book. Its chief interest lies in the juxtaposition of the chapel with the boat being built in front of it, especially since chapel and boat stand for different approaches to the art of building, the <u>monolithic</u> and the <u>analytical</u>. The chapel's years of wear, collapse, and repair together with its multiple layers of whitewash have caused its walls, buttresses, drums, and domes to lose their individual archi-tectural identities and merge into a single, continuous <u>monolithic</u> shell. The boat, on the other hand, is the product of an <u>analytical</u> vision, in which the keel, the ribs, and the planks retain their identities even when, together, they constitute the completed vessel. The two approaches, the <u>monolithic</u> and the <u>analytical</u>, are mutually informing and have produced, respectively, the fortified citadels and the sailing ships that together constituted the major accomplishments of Aegean society in the eighteenth and nineteenth centuries.

Fig. EIGHT-1.03 Kythnos, 1973

Kythnos, Chora, House: Closer to Athens than most of the Cyclades Islands, Kythnos readily embraced the neoclassical forms that came from the culture of the capital in the nineteenth century. Stylistic vocabulary aside, the house above is admirable for its display of responsibility towards the larger community to which it belongs. As paths fork to the right and left in front of the house, the familiar forty-five-degree corner cut at each end of the front wall acknowledges the public domain with its pedestrian traffic. The five masonry steps under the front door represent an even more impressive display of responsibility to the community. As they descend and diminish in width, the steps gently touch the street, interfering minimally with its public uses and its pedestrian function. Once more, the link between the private domain and the public is illuminated by a unique architectural element, the five steps, inventively designed to respond to their particular circumstances.

| Fig. EIGHT-1.04 Serifos, 1973 | Fig. EIGHT-1.05 Serifos, 1973 |

Serifos, Chora, City Hall: Such government buildings as schools and city halls first brought nineteenth-century neoclassical architecture "intruders" into the vernacular architecture of the Aegean archipelago. The Serifos City Hall (ΔΗΜΑΡΧΕΙΟΝ in the illustration), located as it is next to a church that represents the island's vernacular tradition, is a measure of such intrusions. Given the composition, proportions, and details of the city hall building, it is apparent that a formally trained architect designed it (Fig. EIGHT-1.04, -1.05). But it is also important to note that its neoclassical intrusions do not overwhelm the vernacular architecture of the forms of the church. Instead, as in the house in Kythnos, Chora (Fig. EIGHT-1.03), neoclassical architectural elements have been selectively borrowed and incorporated into the vernacular forms of the island. A plethora of examples taken from throughout the islands confirms the vernacular builders' openness and adaptability to forms and messages that originated far from home.

Fig. EIGHT-1.06 Paros, Paroikia, 1988

Fig. EIGHT-1.07 Paros, Marpissa, 1993

Fig. EIGHT-1.08 Amorgos, Chora, 1977

House Portals: In these three illustrations, the typical archipelagic theme of house entry -- that is, a robust square post on each side of a door with a pediment above it -- merges neoclassical inspiration with challenges created by the local context. The Paroikia house portal from Paros has admirable Doric proportions (Fig. EIGHT-1.06) that prevail in a scene of whitewashed walls and steps. Sadly, since this picture was taken, a handrail has been added to the steps on the right, perhaps to conform to current notions of safety. The house portal in Marpissa on Paros (Fig. EIGHT-1.07) preserves its identity despite the large volumes on both sides that threaten to appropriate it. The funerary plaque and the horizontal architectural element in the photograph from Chora, Amorgos, both recycled from a nearby cemetery dating from antiquity, have been correctly incorporated into the house portal theme; the human figures on the plaque allude convincingly to the sculptural content of a Greek temple pediment (Fig. EIGHT-1.08).

Fig. EIGHT-1.09 Paros, Paroikia, 1988

Paros, Paroikia: The figure above shows the lower half of the entry door of a house located just outside the medieval wall enclosure in Paroikia, the major port town on Paros. The white object near the threshold is a cooking utensil known locally as a *foufou*. Fish are placed on the metal grill that is heated from below. The eight-inch-tall, coal-burning foufou, likely a product of the ceramic workshops on nearby Sifnos, has an autonomous and time-tested shape traceable to Aegean antiquity (Fig. EIGHT-1.09). In wide use before the arrival of electricity, the foufou testifies to the millennia of continuity that inform the daily life of the archipelago. In the illustration, the foufou stands just outside the threshold to the house's entry door. As the breeze from the street ignites the coals, the private realm of the house, in this case, its kitchen, extends temporarily into the communal realm of the street. This spatial extension is permissible, perhaps, because the house's owner has whitewashed the street's surface and so, already demonstrated an assumption of responsibility and control over this segment of the street.

Fig. EIGHT-1.10 Paros, Paroikia, 1973

Paros, Paroikia, Thirteenth-Century Tower: The recycling of building parts has been widely practiced throughout the Mediterranean littoral and, indeed, throughout the Aegean archipelago. Buildings constructed in antiquity from solid marble blocks mechanically rather than chemically bonded were obvious and accessible quarries for later centuries. With its high quality marble, Paros represents a rare example of the dismemberment of archaic and classical temples and their reassembly nearby as fortification walls and a citadel tower in the era of the Duchy of the Archipelago. The remains of a sixth century B.C. marble temple that once stood on the site that corresponds to the central part of today's town of Paroikia survive in recognizable form even after their reassembly into the thirteenth-century tower of the Paros Kastro (Fig. EIGHT-1.10). Column drums and segments of the architrave, the stylobate, and the cornice are easy to identify, so that, in theory, the tower could be pulled apart, and its parts reassembled in their original sixth-century positions. In addition, as the medieval fortification wall that extends from the south side of the tower absorbs chapels and dwellings built on and around it, its curving shape remains legible within the urban fabric of Paroikia.

Fig. EIGHT-1.11 Patmos, Monastery, 1999   Fig. EIGHT-1.12 Paros, Paroikia, 1973

Conceptually and visually, this thirteenth-century recycling of building materials from antiquity into a defense tower on Paros is unique in the archipelago. There are, however, abundant smaller-scale examples of recycling scattered throughout the Aegean islands. Four randomly selected illustrations of recycled architectural fragments illustrate this time-honored practice.

Patmos, Chora, Monastery: The gray stone bell tower pictured in figure EIGHT-1.11 is inside the eleventh-century Monastery of Saint John the Theologian. A marble Ionic capital of unknown provenance, probably from a building from the island's little-known past, has been placed correctly both with regard to its original purpose and to the architectural composition of the bell tower itself (Fig. EIGHT-1.11).

Paros, Paroikia, Ayios Konstantinos: Coming from different, unknown quarries, three columns unequal in height (Fig. EIGHT-1.12) have been recycled into the south porch of the chapel of Ayios Konstantinos. Since the

Fig. EIGHT-1.13 Astypalaia, Chora, 1995   Fig. EIGHT-1.14 Amorgos, Chora, 1977

tops of the three columns must provide a common, structurally sound spring line for the arches above, their bases have been variably built up to compensate for their differences in height. The delightful result exemplifies the direct, uninhibited attitudes of the anonymous Aegean builders who produced architecture not dependent on learned preconceptions.

Astypalaia, Chora, Chapel Elevation: Each day, the vertical rays of the noon sun briefly reveal a pattern of joints on the west elevation of a small, room-sized, barrel-vaulted chapel -- one of the six adjacent chapels in the Karae neighborhood of the Astypalaia Chora that were discussed in Chapter FIVE. Despite the building's many layers of whitewash, the joints suggest that recycled stone slabs from an unknown quarry were applied as a veneer to an otherwise typical Aegean masonry wall (Fig. EIGHT-1.13).

Amorgos, Chora: An elaborately carved architectural fragment recycled as a window lintel competes for attention with a more recently installed electricity meter (Fig. EIGHT-1.14).

| Fig. EIGHT-1.15 Serifos, 1973 | Fig. EIGHT-1.16 Symi, 1994 |

Steps: In the architecture of a Greek temple, a stylobate mediates between the irregular, natural site below and the precisely cut parts of the man-made building above. Ever-present in an Aegean town, steps perform a function similar to the stylobate's as they mediate between irregular town

Fig. EIGHT-1.17 Sifnos, Apollonia, 1997   Fig. EIGHT-1.18 Sifnos, Vathi, 1986

sites and the buildings above them. Steps lead to an observation point in
Serifos (Fig. EIGHT-1.15), to three different and unknown destinations in
Symi (Fig. EIGHT-1.16), and to flat roofs in Sifnos, Apollonia (Fig. EIGHT-
1.17) and Sifnos, Vathi (Fig. EIGHT-1.18).

Fig. EIGHT-1.19 Paros, Paroikia, 1988   Fig. EIGHT-1.20 Sifnos, Ano Petali, 1986

Bell Towers: The bell towers of the Aegean islands emerge as partial upward extensions of a chapel's south or west wall. As such, they resemble their cultural and geometric precursors, the *stelae* (*stele*, singular), the upright, narrow marble slabs that formed funerary monuments in Greek antiquity. The typical bell-tower façade is treated in minimal relief with little depth, the dimensions of height and width prevailing, a treatment that accords with the two-dimensional character of Byzantine iconography. Indeed, all four bell towers shown here share delicate horizontal stone ledges that articulate their upward thrust.

A stepped base leads to a single-bell arch (the bell is missing) topped by two pairs of acroteria in the Paros, Paroikia example (Fig. EIGHT-1.19).

Its double arches, elegantly slender proportions, and a touch of dovecote geometry at the top distinguish this bell tower in Ano Petali, a settlement in central Sifnos (Fig. EIGHT-1.20).

The bell tower of the church of Theologos inside Sifnos Kastro is the only external indication of the building's religious mission in a neighbor-

Fig. EIGHT-1.21 Sifnos, Kastro, 1997 | Fig. EIGHT-1.22 Sikinos, Kastro, 1994

hood crowded with monochoro dwelling units of similar size. Two acroteria on top and the sturdy proportions that separate the thin ledges above from the five small arches below, as they assert their firm grip on the south wall, are the main architectural features of this bell tower (Fig. EIGHT-1.21).

The multiple arches and bells that have been added to the original tower support the exuberant mini-cupolas crowned with crosses atop the bell tower inside the Sikinos Kastro. The palm trees in front of the tower are a reminder that the islands of the Cyclades lie in the same latitude as the northern coasts of Algeria and Tunis (Fig. EIGHT-1.22).

The hundreds of bell towers on chapels throughout the archipelago demonstrate the islanders' deep religious feelings and express the talent and inventiveness of their builders as they enhance the engaging qualities of the vernacular architecture of the archipelago.

Fig. EIGHT-1.23 Kalymnos, Pothaia, 1970   Fig. EIGHT-1.24 Kalymnos, Pothaia, 1971

Kalymnos --Color and Whitewash: Four pairs of photographs from Kalymnos date from visits to the island in 1970 and 1971. An uneasy sense that the buildings had changed prompted me to rerecord them during the second visit. Only when the pairs of slides were projected onto a screen in tandem did it become apparent that the change involved color, subtle in some cases, more intense in others (Fig. EIGHT-1.23, -1.24). Perhaps unique to Kalymnos, change in color is a variation on the annual whitewashing, produced by adding powdered paint to the whitewash. The change is subtle and often difficult to detect.

In figure EIGHT-1.25, subtlety governs the color change made in the entire house façade (Fig. EIGHT-1.25). In (Fig. EIGHT-1.26), the new layer of color can be seen only at the edge of the new application at the vertical property line on the left side of the elevation.

Fig. EIGHT-1.25 Kalymnos, Chorio, 1970

Fig. EIGHT-1.26 Kalymnos, Chorio, 1971

Fig. EIGHT-1.27 Kalymnos, Chorio, 1970   Fig. EIGHT-1.28 Kalymnos, Chorio, 1971

The elimination of the two strong, blue horizontal lines makes the change in the above examples lucid and immediately apparent (Fig. EIGHT-1.27, -1.28). In the fourth pair, a family argument might have been responsible for dampening the exuberance of 1970 and replacing it with the placid color scheme of 1971 (Fig. EIGHT-1.29, -1.30).

Fig. EIGHT-1.29 Kalymnos, 1970

Fig. EIGHT-1.30 Kalymnos, 1971

Fig. EIGHT-1.31 Sifnos, Kastro cemetery, 1969

Sifnos, Kastro Cemetery: These two illustrations of the Kastro cemetery date, respectively, from 1969 and 1997, that is, twenty-eight years apart (Fig. EIGHT-1.31, -1.32). Here, a stone wall possessively encloses two chapels, along with retaining walls, graves, and trees, as it adjusts continuously to its inclined site. This enclosure, which allows only a single entry into the cemetery -- indicated by the long axis of the pedestrian bridge over the brook that metaphorically separates the world of the living from that of the dead -- makes for an engagingly symbolic site plan. No essential features have been altered during the twenty-eight-year period covered by the paired photographs. But patient observation registers subtle changes even so. For

Fig. EIGHT-1.32 Sifnos, Kastro cemetery, 1997

example, the whitewashing has been expanded over the vertical surfaces of the enclosing and retaining walls. The saddles of the peripheral walls have been rebuilt. Blue paint underscores the architectural and religious importance of the chapel's two domes. And the trees appear better trimmed and cared for. A close-up would probably reveal additional improvements. The old wall, where whitewash was applied with restraint to underscore such important architectural features as the saddle of the enclosing stone wall and the sides of the single-entry door, may have been more appealing, but the changes undeniably show a more prosperous society that is using its surplus wealth to enhance its communal property.

Fig. EIGHT-1.33 Paros, Paroikia, 1973

Paros, Paroikia: Narrow side streets that break out of the compact core of an Aegean island town are infrequent but exciting urban surprises. The length of such streets, pointing as they do towards a horizon of infinite vanishing points, offers visual escape and relief, and, where there is shade, a cooling breeze.

Fig. EIGHT-1.34 Paros, Naoussa, 1973

Paros, Naoussa: Here, buildings, colors, light and shade, and an opening to the shared Aegean horizon compose a theme that might have inspired Giorgio de Chirico.

Fig. EIGHT-1.35 Folegandros, 1994

Folegandros, Chora: In this illustration, the rocky terrain, the macchia vegetation, the precipitous drop of more than six hundred feet to the sea on the left, the stabilizing Aegean horizon, and the Chora of Folegandros all speak of the relationship between the man-made forms and the natural landscape and seascape of the archipelago. The retaining walls close to the settlement in the lower left sector of the Folegandros illustration above have prevented erosion and allowed the cultivation of the land for generations. Appropriately whitewashed, the Chora includes an undignified but temporary reinforced concrete building skeleton, while it ingeniously conceals the existence at its core of the still-inhabited Kastro that compares favorably with Antiparos's. The whitewashed path behind the Chora leads to the church of Panayia, where the citizens of Folegandros celebrate important religious and national holidays. The man-made elements of this impressive composition -- the retaining walls below, the fortified town at mid-level, the religious center above -- engage with the natural landscape in a manner that respects its character and spirit, which is always of the essence in the vernacular architecture of the Aegean archipelago.

▷ ◁ ▷ ◁

EPILOGUE

▷ ◁ ▷ ◁

This account of the *The Aegean Crucible* has offered a journey through the spectacular natural and man-made world of the Aegean archipelago. To conclude, it might be enough to quote Constantine P. Cavafy's admonition in his poem "Ithaca" that "Ithaca gave you the marvelous journey," and say no more. But a few final comments are in order.

The architecture of the Kastro, the collective fortification characteristic of the Aegean archipelago, succinctly conveys the conditions that governed life in the post-Byzantine Aegean region. The Kastro brings into an enviable architectural balance its citizens' need for security with the islands' limited economic resources and building materials and their natural assets of site and climate. This fine balance also depends on the unique Aegean shoreline as it defines the intricate relations between landscape and seascape that distinguish the region.

The Kastro, inspired in form and scale by imported and local prototypes, thus constitutes an urban container that has allowed such common elements of vernacular architecture to survive as Kastro's characteristic high building density; the ubiquitous monochoro; the labyrinthine, narrow pedestrian paths; the massive masonry walls; the small and scanty openings into buildings; and the near universality of whitewashing.

As Sifnos, Antiparos, and Kimolos confirm, the Aegean Kastro has been continuously occupied for several centuries -- rare among buildings in daily, secular use and nearly unique in the Greek cultural space with its turbulent geopolitical history. Clearly, though, occupancy raises challenging questions about continuity in the future.

As we have seen, the vernacular architecture of the islands was significantly transformed after Greece was liberated from Ottoman Turkish rule in the 1830s, first, as piracy was eradicated from the Mediterranean, which allowed settlements to expand beyond the protective peripheries of the Kastra walls, and second, as neoclassical forms intruded into and eventually merged with the visual character of the vernacular. Such "intrusions" were easily absorbed into a vernacular architecture already enriched by the effective recycling and enwalling, structural and otherwise, of fragments from Greek antiquity and later times. The hundreds of neoclassical house portals throughout the islands testify vibrantly to the vernacular's ability to appropriate and absorb architectural forms from elsewhere in time and space. This ability to absorb and reinterpret is of the utmost importance and promise today, when the Aegean island settlements have come under intense pressure from Athenian, European, and other international sources to develop and recast their traditional forms.

This book traces the history of vernacular architecture by using two time scales: a long scale that spans the period from the thirteenth-century Fourth Crusade to today and a short scale that covers the years from 1963 to 1998, the period during which I observed the changes that occurred in a single neighborhood of the town of Hydra. Changes that happened across the long scale would have been imperceptible to a single generation of islanders. But the short time scale has made it possible to detect and record changes across a mere thirty-five years. In the 1960s and 1970s, it was common to observe abandoned properties and collapsed roofs from any high point in an Aegean town. But as regional and international tourism have become economically important to the islands, properties have been reclaimed, and roofs repaired and replaced. Prosperity has also brought new buildings into being, though often with mixed results.

The dialectic between continuity and change is an important theme in both vernacular and formal architecture. The vernacular architecture builders of the Aegean archipelago have managed that dialectic skillfully -- an accomplishment that offers both hope and promise for the future.

GAZETTEER

Note: The alphabetical list below has been prepared to ease the difficulty of transliterating from Greek the names of islands, island towns, geographic groups of islands, and the related locations that are mentioned in the pages of *The Aegean Crucible*. Each line contains four entries: the first entry spells the name of a place as it appears in the book. If an alternate spelling is in frequent use elsewhere, it appears as a second entry. The next major entry is the Greek spelling of the place name, in capital letters. The geographic location of each entry is given last, in italics.

Acropolis, Akropolis, ΑΚΡΟΠΟΛΙΣ, *Athens*
Aegean, ΑΙΓΑΙΟΝ, *Aegean Sea*
Aegina, Aigina, ΑΙΓΙΝΑ, *Saronic Gulf*
Amorgos, ΑΜΟΡΓΟΣ, *Cyclades Islands*
Andros, ΑΝΔΡΟΣ, *Cyclades Islands*
Antiparos, Andiparos, ΑΝΤΙΠΑΡΟΣ, *Cyclades Islands*
Aspronisi, Aspronesi, ΑΣΠΡΟΝΗΣΙ, *Santorini, Cyclades Islands*
Astypalaia, Astipalea, ΑΣΤΥΠΑΛΑΙΑ, *Dodecanese Islands*
Ayion Oros, Aghion Oros, ΑΓΙΟΝ ΟΡΟΣ, *northern Greece*
Chalki, Halki, ΧΑΛΚΗ, *Dodecanese Islands*
Chios, Hios, ΧΙΟΣ, *northern Aegean Sea*
Chora, Hora, ΧΩΡΑ, *most islands*
Corfu, ΚΕΡΚΥΡΑ, *Ionian Islands*
Crete, Kriti, ΚΡΗΤΗ, *southern Aegean Sea*
Cyclades, Kyklades, ΚΥΚΛΑΔΕΣ, *central Aegean Sea*
Delos, Dilos, ΔΗΛΟΣ, *Cyclades Islands*
Dodecanese, Dodekanisos, ΔΩΔΕΚΑΝΗΣΑ, *Dodecanese Islands*
Fira, Phira, ΦΗΡΑ, *Santorini, Cyclades Islands*

Folegandros, Pholegandros, ΦΟΛΕΓΑΝΔΡΟΣ, *Cyclades Islands*
Hydra, Ydra, ΥΔΡΑ, *northeast Peloponnesos*
Ios, ΙΟΣ, *Cyclades Islands*
Irakleion, ΗΡΑΚΛΕΙΟΝ, Crete, *southern Aegean Sea*
Ithaca, Ithaki, ΙΘΑΚΗ, *Ionian Islands*
Kalymnos, Kalimnos, ΚΑΛΥΜΝΟΣ, *Dodecanese Islands*
Kameni, ΚΑΜΕΝΗ, Santorini, *Cyclades Islands*
Kastellorizo, Kastelorizo, ΚΑΣΤΕΛΟΡΙΖΟ, *Dodecanese Islands*
Kastro, ΚΑΣΤΡΟ, *most islands*
Kimolos, ΚΙΜΩΛΟΣ, *Cyclades Islands*
Kos, Cos, ΚΩΣ, *Dodecanese Islands*
Kythera, Kythira, ΚΥΘΗΡΑ, *southwestern Aegean Sea*
Kythnos, Kithnos, ΚΥΘΝΟΣ, *Cyclades Islands*
Lemnos, Limnos, ΛΗΜΝΟΣ, *northern Aegean Sea*
Lepanto, Nafpaktos, ΝΑΥΠΑΚΤΟΣ, *Corinthian Gulf*
Leros, ΛΕΡΟΣ, *Dodecanese Islands*
Melos, Milos, ΜΗΛΟΣ, *Cyclades Islands*
Merovigli, ΜΕΡΟΒΙΓΛΙ, Santorini, *Cyclades Islands*
Mykonos, Mikonos, ΜΥΚΟΝΟΣ, *Cyclades Islands*
Naxos, ΝΑΞΟΣ, *Cyclades Islands*
Oia, Ia, ΟΙΑ, *Cyclades Islands*
Paros, ΠΑΡΟΣ, *Cyclades Islands*
Paroikia, Parikia, ΠΑΡΟΙΚΙΑ, Paros, *Cyclades Islands*
Patmos, ΠΑΤΜΟΣ, *Dodecanese Islands*
Poros, ΠΟΡΟΣ, *Saronic Gulf*
Psathi, ΨΑΘΗ, Kimolos, *Cyclades Islands*
Rhodes, Rodos, ΡΟΔΟΣ, *Dodecanese Islands*
Santorini, ΣΑΝΤΟΡΙΝΗ, *Cyclades Islands*
Serifos, Seriphos, ΣΕΡΙΦΟΣ, *Cyclades Islands*
Sifnos, Siphnos, ΣΙΦΝΟΣ, *Cyclades Islands*
Sikinos, ΣΙΚΙΝΟΣ, *Cyclades Islands*
Skaros, ΣΚΑΡΟΣ, Santorini, *Cyclades Islands*
Skiathos, ΣΚΙΑΘΟΣ, *northern Aegean Sea*
Skopelos, ΣΚΟΠΕΛΟΣ, *northern Aegean Sea*
Skyros, ΣΚΥΡΟΣ, *northern Aegean Sea*
Symi, Syme, ΣΥΜΗ, *Dodecanese Islands*
Syros, ΣΥΡΟΣ, *Cyclades Islands*
Telos, Tilos, ΤΗΛΟΣ, *Dodecanese Islands*
Tenos, Tinos, ΤΗΝΟΣ, *Cyclades Islands*
Thera, Thira, ΘΗΡΑ, *Cyclades Islands*
Therasia, Thirasia, ΘΗΡΑΣΙΑ, Santorini, *Cyclades Islands*

▷ ◁

BIBLIOGRAPHY

▷ ◁

Allen, Edward. *Stone Shelters*. Cambridge: MIT Press, 1969.

Allison, Robert J. *The Crescent Obscured: The United States and the Muslim World, 1776-1815*. New York: Oxford University Press, 1995.

Anderson, Rufus. *Observations upon the Peloponnesos and Greek Islands Made in 1829*. Boston: Crocker and Brewster, 1830.

Architectural Association. *Dimitris Pikionis, Architect, 1887–1968: A Sentimental Topography*. London: Architectural Association, [1989].

Arnaoutoglou, Chrysavgi K. *Hydra*. Translated by Philip Ramp. Athens: "Melissa" Publishing House, 1986.

Asdrahas, Spyros, Anna Avramea, and Vasilis Sphyroeras. *Maps and Map-Makers of the Aegean*. Translated by G. Cox and J. Solman. Athens: Olkos, 1985.

Augustinos, Olga. *French Odysseys: Greece in French Travel Literature from the Renaissance to the Romantic Era*. Baltimore: Johns Hopkins University Press, 1994.

Baltoyianni, Chr. *Limania Ke Karavia Sto Vyzantino Mouseio*. Athens: Ministry of Culture, 1997.

Bat, Ye'or. *The Decline of Eastern Christianity under Islam: From Jihad to Dhimmitude, Seventh-Twentieth Century*. Translated by Miriam Kochan and David Littman. Madison, N. J.: Fairleigh Dickinson University Press, 1996.

Belavilas, Nikos. *Limania Ke Oikismoi Sto Archipelagos Tes Peiratias, 15os-19os Eones*, Athens: Ekdoseis Odysseas, 1997.

Bogdanou-Eliopoulou, Maria and Angeliki Fetokaki-Sarandidi. *Kalymnos.* Translated by Philip Ramp. Athens: "Melissa" Publishing House, 1984.

Bouras, Charalambos. "Architecture." In *Patmos: Treasures of the Monastery,* edited by Athanasios D. Kominis, 25-53. Athens: Ekdotike Athenon, 1988.

------------. "Architecture and Town-Planning in the Traditional Settlements of the Aegean." In *The Aegean: The Epicenter of Greek Civilization*, edited by Lambrini Papaioannou and Dora Comini-Dialeti, 201-41. Translated by Philip Ramp, Alexandra Doumas, and David Connolly. Athens: "Melissa" Publishing House, 1992.

-----------. "The Byzantine Tradition in the Church Architecture of the Balkans in the Sixteenth and Seventeenth Centuries." In *The Byzantine Tradition after the Fall of Constantinople,* edited by John J. Yiannias, 107-49. Charlottesville: University Press of Virginia, 1991.

Bradford, Ernle. *The Knights of the Order.* New York: Dorset Press, Marlboro Books, 1991. Published by agreement with Eton Court Publishers.

Braudel, Ferdinand. *The Mediterranean and the Mediterranean World in the Age of Philip II.* Translated by Sian Reynolds. 2nd ed. Vol. 1. New York: Harper and Row; London: William Collins Sons, 1972. Originally published as *La Méditerranée et le Monde Méditerranéan a l'Epoque de Philippe II* (Paris: Librarie Armand Colin, 1966).

Carrington, Richard. *The Mediterranean: Cradle of Western Culture.* New York: Viking Press, Studio Books, 1971.

Castagnoli, Ferdinando. *Orthogonal Town Planning in Antiquity.* Translated by Victor Caliandro. Cambridge: MIT Press, 1971. Originally published as *Ippodamo di Mileto e l'Urbanistica a Pianta Ortogonale* (Rome: De Luca Editore, for the Institute of Ancient Topography of the University of Rome, n.d.).

Cavafy, Constantine. *Collected Poems.* Edited by George Savidis. Translated by Edmund Keeley and Philip Sherrard. Rev. edition. Princeton Modern Greek Series. Princeton: Princeton University Press, 1975.

Cheetham, Nicolas. *Medieval Greece.* New Haven: Yale University Press, 1981.

Choiseul-Gouffier, Marie-Gabriel-Florent-Auguste, comte de. *Voyage pittoresque de la Grèce.* 2 vols. Paris: J. J. Blaise, 1782-1822.

Clogg, Richard. *A Concise History of Greece.* Cambridge: Cambridge University Press, 1992.

Curry-Lindahl, Kai. *Europe: A Natural History.* New York: Random House, 1964.

Dakin, Douglas. *The Unification of Greece, 1770-1923.* New York: St. Martin's Press, 1972.

Damianidis, K. A., ed. *Maritime Tradition in the Aegean: Boatyards and Wooden Vessels.* Athens: Ministry of the Aegean, 1997.

De la Croix, Horst. *Military Considerations in City Planning: Fortifications.* Planning and Cities series, ed. George R. Collins. New York: George Braziller, 1972.

De Nora, Emmanuela and Costas Vrettakos. *The Adoration of the Pigeon.* Athens: Tria Phylla, 1982.

----------- and Leonidas Ermilios. *Churches in the Islands of the Aegean. Athens*: Tria Phylla, 1989.

Doumas, Christos. *Santorini: A Guide to the Island and its Archaeological Treasures.* Ekdotike Athenon Travel Guides. Athens: Ekdotike Athenon, 1989.

Dountsi, Athena, ed. *Santorini: "And the Sea Gave Birth to the Land."* Athens: Publications Topio, n.d.

Doxiadis, Constantine A. *Architectural Space in Ancient Greece.* Translated by Jacqueline Tyrwhitt. Cambridge: MIT Press, 1972.

Durrell, Lawrence. *The Greek Islands.* New York: Viking Press, Studio Books, 1978.

-----------. *Reflections on a Marine Venus: A Companion to the Landscape of Rhodes.* Rev. ed. London: Faber and Faber, 1960.

Earle, Peter. *Corsairs of Malta and Barbary.* London: Sidgwick and Jackson, 1970.

Ethnikon Idryma. *Archontika tes kastorias.* Athens, 1948.

------------. *Spitia tes Zagoras.* Athens, 1949.

Etienne, Roland and Françoise Etienne. *The Search for Ancient Greece.* Translated by Anthony Zielonka. Discoveries series. New York: Harry N. Abrams, 1990.

Fleming, K. E. *The Muslim Bonaparte: Diplomacy and Orientalism in Ali Pasha's Greece.* Princeton: Princeton University Press, 1999.

Forbes-Boyd, Eric. *Aegean Quest: A Search for Venetian Greece.* London: J. M. Dent and Sons, 1970.

------------. *In Crusader Greece: A Tour of the Castles of the Morea.* London: Centaur Press, 1964.

Fox, Robert. *The Inner Sea: The Mediterranean and its People.* New York: Alfred A. Knopf, 1993.

Gage, Nicholas. *Hellas: A Portrait of Greece.* New York: Villard Books, 1986; originally published as *Portrait of Greece* (New York, American Heritage Press, McGraw Hill, 1971).

Galanopoulos, A.G. and Edward Bacon. *Atlantis: The Truth behind the Legend.* Indianapolis: Bobbs-Merrill, 1969.

Giedion, Sigfried. *Space, Time and Architecture: The Growth of a New Tradition.* 3rd edition. Enld. ed. Cambridge: Harvard University Press, 1954.

Glykatzi-Ahrweiler, Helen. "Historical Background." In *Patmos: Treasures of the Monastery*, ed. Athanasios D. Kominis, 11-14. Athens: Ekdotike Athenon, 1988.

Goldfinger, Myron. *Villages in the Sun: Mediterranean Community Architecture.* New York: Praeger, 1969.

Goulandris, Dolly and Tzeli Charitonidi. *Dovehouses in the Cycladic Islands of Tinos and Andros.* Athens: Alexandros Matsoukis Graphic Arts, 1979.

Grant, Michael. *The Ancient Mediterranean.* New York: NAL Penguin, Meridian Books, 1988.

Greece, Road Map, 1:500.000. With the cooperation of the Hellenic Army Geographical Service. Athens: Road Editions, n.d.

The Greek Islands. Eyewitness Travel Guides. London: Dorling Kindersley, 1997.

Greene, Molly. *A Shared World: Christians and Muslims in the Early Modern Mediterranean.* Princeton: Princeton University Press, 2000.

Hartley, John. *Researches in Greece and the Levant.* London: n.p., 1831.

Hata, Soichi. "The Cycladic Village." *Space Design: A Monthly Journal of Art and Architecture* 101 (February 1973): 32-79.

Hoepfner, Wolfram and Hartwig Schmidt."Mittelalterliche Städtegründungen auf den Kykladeninseln Antiparos und Kimolos." In *Jahrbuch des Deutchen Archäologischen Instituts* 91 (1976): 291-339.

Iakovides, Christos. *Chora Patmou: Pente Ktiriaka Syngrotimata Tou Oikismou.* Athens, 1978.

----------. *Patmos.* Translated by Philip Ramp. Athens: "Melissa" Publishing House, 1985.

Kallivretakis, Leonidas. *Questions on the Administrative History of the Aegean Islands (Thirteenth-Nineteenth Centuries).* Athens: National Hellenic Research Foundation, in press (in Greek).

Kefalleniades, N. A. *Peirateia: Koursaroi Sto Aigaio.* Athens: Ekdoseis Philippoti, 1984.

Kerestetzis, Manos. *Serifos: Kykladon Eliakos Lithos,* n.d.

Kharitonidou, Angeliki. *Andros.* Translated by David Hardy. Athens: "Melissa" Publishing House, 1984.

----------. *Tinos.* Translated by David Hardy. Athens: "Melissa" Publishing House, 1984.

Kollias, Elias. *The Knights of Rhodes: The Palace and the City.* Athens: Ekdotike Athenon, 1992.

Kostof, Spiro. *A History of Architecture: Settings and Rituals.* New York: Oxford University Press, 1985.

Kouroupakis, Katerina et al. *Naxos.* Translated by David Hardy. Athens: "Melissa" Publishing House, 1984.

Krantonelli, Alexandra. *Istoria Tes Peirateias, 1390-1538.* Athens: Estia, 1985.

------------. *Istoria Tes Peirateias, 1538-1699.* Athens: Estia, 1991.

Kriesis, Anthony. *Greek Town Building.* Athens: National Technical University, 1965.

Kultermann, Udo. *The History of Art History.* N.p.: Abaris Books, 1993

Lancaster, Osbert. *Classical Landscape with Figures.* 1947. Reprint, with an addition to the introduction, London: John Murray, 1975.

Lawrence, A. W. *Greek Architecture.* 4th ed. Revised with additions by R. A. Tomlinson. New Haven: Yale University Press, 1983.

Leontis, Artemis, ed. *Greece: A Traveler's Literary Companion.* San Francisco: Whereabouts Press, 1997.

------------. *Topographies of Hellenism: Mapping the Homeland.* Myth and Poetics series, ed. Gregory Nagy. Ithaca: Cornell University Press, 1995.

Liata, Eutychia. *E Serifos Kata Ten Tourkokratia.* Athens: Commercial Bank Foundation, 1987.

Luce, J. V. *Lost Atlantis: New Light on an Old Legend.* New York: McGraw-Hill; London: Thames and Hudson, 1969.

Mango, Cyril. *Byzantine Architecture.* Milan: Electa Editrice, 1978; New York: Rizzoli, 1985.

Marchand, Suzanne L. *Down from Olympus: Archaeology and Philhellenism in Germany, 1750-1970.* Princeton: Princeton University Press, 1996.

Marinatos, Spyridon. *Some Words about the Legend of Atlantis.* Athens: 1969.

Mathey, Kosta. "Peristeriones: An Architecture Not Made for People?" *Ekistics* 61, Nos. 368-69 (September-October, November-December 1994): 343-53.

Matvejevic, Predrag. *Mediterranean: A Cultural Landscape.* Translated by Michael Henry Heim. Berkeley: University of California Press, 1999. Originally published as *Mediteranski brevijar* (Zagreb: Graficki zavod Hrvatske, 1987).

McCoy, Floyd W. "Lab Fellow Explores Buried Landscape of Thera." *Newsletter of the American School of Classical Studies at Athens*, no. 44 (2000): 6.

McEvedy, Colin. *The Penguin Atlas of Medieval History.* Harmondsworth, England: Penguin Books, 1976.

----------. *The Penguin Atlas of Modern History (to 1815).* Harmondsworth, England: Penguin Books, 1972.

----------. *The Penguin Atlas of Recent History (Europe since 1815).* Harmondsworth, England: Penguin Books, 1982.

McNeill, William H. *The Metamorphosis of Greece since World War II.* Chicago: University of Chicago Press, 1978.

Michaelides, Constantine E. "Aegean Island Towns: A Current View." In *Shelter in Greece*, edited by Orestis B. Doumanis and Paul Oliver, 53-63. Athens: Architecture in Greece Press, 1972.

----------. *Hydra: A Greek Island Town – Its Growth and Form.* Chicago: University of Chicago Press, 1967; for Washington University.

----------. "Hydra: Tourist Economy and Traditional Architecture." In *Constructed Meaning: Form and Process in Greek Architecture,* edited by Eleftherios Pavlides and Susan Buck Sutton, 419-38. *Modern Greek Studies Yearbook,* Vol.10-11, University of Minnesota: Minneapolis, Minn. 1994-95.

----------. "Observations on Aegean Island Towns." In *Architects' Yearbook.* Vol. 13, *The Growth of Cities*, edited by David Lewis, 173-83. London: Elek Books, 1970.

----------. "Observations on Three Aegean Towns." *Architecture in Greece, Annual Review,* 1974: 136-44.

----------. "Site, Space, and Architectonic Form in the Aegean Island Towns." In *Islamic Architecture and Urbanism*, edited by Aydin Germen, 363-74. Dammam: King Faisal University, 1983.

Michelis, P. A. *An Aesthetic Approach to Byzantine Art.* London: B. T. Batsford, 1955.

------------. *E Architektoniki Os Techni.* Athens: Ekdoseis Tou Technikou Epimeleteriou Tes Ellados, 1951.

Miller, Helen Hill. *Greece Through the Ages, as Seen by Travelers from Herodotus to Byron.* New York: Funk and Wagnalls, 1972.

Miller, Henry. *The Colossus of Maroussi.* New York: New Directions, 1941; Harmondsworth, England: Penguin Books, in association with William Heinemann, 1950.

Miller, Nathan. *Broadsides: The Age of Fighting Sail, 1775-1815.* New York: John Wiley and Sons, 2000.

Miller, William. *Essays on the Latin Orient.* 1921. Reprint, Chicago: Argonaut Publishers, 1967.

------------. *The Latins in the Levant: A History of Frankish Greece, 1204-1566.* London: John Murray, 1908.

Ministry of the Aegean. *Sifnos.* Athens: Ministry of the Aegean, 1998.

Monioudi-Gavala, Dora. *Santorini: Society and Shelter, Fifteenth-Twentieth Centuries.* Translated by Christine Crystalli. Athens: Lukas and Evangelos Bellonias Foundation, 1997.

Morris, Jan. *The Venetian Empire: A Sea Voyage.* New York: Harcourt Brace Jovanovich, Helen and Kurt Wolff Book, 1980.

Moutsopoulou, Anastasia. *Rhodes.* Translated by Philip Ramp. Athens: "Melissa" Publishing House, 1985.

National Statistical Service of Greece. *Concise Statistical Yearbook of Greece, 1990-1991.* Athens: National Statistical Service of Greece, 1993.

Oliver, Paul, ed. *Encyclopedia of Vernacular Architecture.* New York: Cambridge University Press, 1997.

Orlandos, A. *Monasteriake Architektonike.* Athens, 1958.

Panousakis, Christos A. et al. *Astypalaia: Poleodomia Ke Architektoniki Tes Choras.* Athens, 1994.

Palmer, Alan. *The Decline and Fall of the Ottoman Empire.* New York: M. Evans and Company, 1993.

Papadiamantis, Alexandros. *Ftochos Ayios.* In *Alexandros Papadiamantis,* edited by Theodoros Xides. Athens: Aetos, 1955.

-----------. *Tales from a Greek Island.* Translated by Elizabeth Constantinides. Baltimore: Johns Hopkins University Press, 1987.

Papaioannou, Konstantinos Sp. *Ta Hellenika Monasteria San Architektonike Syntheseis.* Athens, 1977.

Papas, C. *L'urbanisme et l'architecture populaire dans les Cyclades.* Paris: Dunod, 1957.

Pellegrino, Charles. *Unearthing Atlantis: An Archaeological Odyssey.* New York: Random House, Vintage Books, 1993.

Pettifer, James. *The Greeks: The Land and People Since the War.* London: Viking, 1993.

Philippa-Apostolou, Maro. *To Kastro Tes Antiparou.* Athens, 1978.

-----------. *To Kastro Tes Sifnou.* Thessaloniki: Aristotle University of Thessaloniki, n.d.

-----------. *Mikroi Ochiromenoi Oikismoi Tou Aigaiou Sta Ichne tes Istorikes Tous Tautotetas.* Athens: Ekdoseis Erinne-Philippoti, 1999.

-----------. *Paros Andiparos.* Translated by David Hardy. Athens: "Melissa" Publishing House, 1984.

Philippides, Dimitri. "Historical Retrospect." In *Greek Traditional Architecture,* edited by Dimitri Philippides, 33-49. Vol. 1. Athens: "Melissa" Publishing House, 1983.

-----------. "Kanaves and Rakidia." In *Santorini,* edited by I. M. Danezis, 381-84. Athens, 2001.

———. "The Methodological Problem Today." In *Greek Traditional Architecture*, edited by Dimitri Philippides, 50-56. Vol. 1. Athens: "Melissa" Publishing House, 1983.

———. *Santorini.* Translated by Alexandra Doumas. Athens: "Melissa" Publishing House, 1980.

Raine, Pete et al. *Mediterranean Wildlife: The Rough Guide.* Rough Guides, ed. Mark Ellingham. London: Harrap-Columbus, 1990.

Rapaport, Amos. *House Form and Culture.* Foundations of Cultural Geography Series. Englewood Cliffs, N.J.: Prentice-Hall, 1969.

Riley-Smith, Jonathan, ed. *The Atlas of the Crusades.* New York: Facts on File, 1991.

Romanos, Aristeidis. *Mykonos.* Translated by Philip Ramp. Athens: "Melissa" Publishing House, 1992.

Roumani, Ioanna. *To Monasteri Tou Porou.* Poros, 1992.

Rudofsky, Bernard. *Architecture without Architects: A Short Introduction to Non-Pedigreed Architecture.* New York: Museum of Modern Art, 1965; distributed by Doubleday and Company.

———. *The Prodigious Builders: Notes toward a Natural History of Architecture with Special Regard to Those Species That Are Traditionally Neglected or Downright Ignored.* New York: Harcourt Brace Jovanovich, 1977.

Runciman, Steven. *The Great Church in Captivity: A Study of the Patriarchate of Constantinople from the Eve of the Turkish Conquest to the Greek War of Independence.* Cambridge: Cambridge University Press, 1968.

———. *A History of the Crusades.* Vol. 3, *The Kingdom of Acre and the Later Crusades.* Cambridge: Cambridge University Press, 1951.

Savvaris, E. and V. Tsamtsouris. *Astypalaia.* Translated by Philip Ramp. Athens: "Melissa" Publishing House, 1985.

Scott, Geoffrey. *The Architecture of Humanism: A Study in the History of Taste.* Garden City, N.Y.: Doubleday and Company, Doubleday Anchor Books, 1954.

Sifounakis, Nikos. *Mia Agnosti Architektoniki: E Mandres Ste Lemno.* Athens: Ekdoseis Kastaniote, 1993.

Simopoulos, Kyriakos. *Xenoi taxidiotes sten Ellada.* 3 vols. Athens, 1970-75.

Sire, H. J. A. *The Knights of Malta.* New Haven: Yale University Press, 1994.

Slesin, Suzanne et al. *Greek Style.* New York: Clarkson N. Potter, 1988.

Spencer, William. *Algiers in the Age of the Corsairs.* Norman: University of Oklahoma Press, 1976.

Stanford, W. B. and E. J. Finopoulos, eds. *The Travels of Lord Charlemont in Greece and Turkey, 1749.* London: Trigraph, 1984; for the A.G. Leventis Foundation.

Stoneman, Richard. *Land of Lost Gods: The Search for Classical Greece.* Norman: University of Oklahoma Press, 1987.

-----------, ed. *A Literary Companion to Travel in Greece.* Malibu, Calif.: J. Paul Getty Museum, 1994.

Thucydides. *History of the Peloponnesian War.* Translated by Rex Warner, with an introduction and notes by M. I. Finley. Rev. ed. Harmondsworth, England: Penguin Books, 1972.

Tolias, George. *The Greek Portolan Charts, Fifteenth-Seventeenth Centuries: A Contribution to the Mediterranean Cartography of the Modern Period.* Translated by Geoffrey Cox and John Solman. Athens: Olkos, 1999; for the Center for Neohellenic Research.

Toynbee, Arnold. *An Ekistical Study of the Hellenic City-State.* Athens: Athens Technological Organization, Athens Center of Ekistics, 1971.

Tsigakou, Fani-Maria. *British Images of Greece from the Benaki Museum Collections.* Athens: Benaki Museum, 1995.

------------. *Edward Lear's Greece from the Gennadeion Collections.* Thessaloniki: Cultural Centre of Thessaloniki-National Bank Cultural Foundation, 1997.

-----------. *The Rediscovery of Greece: Travellers and Painters of the Romantic Era.* New Rochelle, N.Y.: Caratzas Brothers, 1981.

-----------. *Thomas Hope (1769-1831): Pictures from Eighteenth-Century Greece.* Athens: "Melissa" Publishing House, 1985.

-----------. *Through Romantic Eyes: European Images of Nineteenth-Century Greece from the Benaki Museum, Athens.* Alexandria, Va.: Art Services International, 1991.

Tsirpanlis, Zacharias N. *Rhodes and the South-East Aegean Islands under the Knights of Saint John, Fourteenth to the Sixteenth Centuries: Collected Studies.* Rhodes, 1991.

Tzakou, Anastasia E. *Kentrikoi Oikismoi Tes Sifnou.* Athens, 1976.

-----------. *Sifnos.* Translated by David Hardy. Athens: "Melissa" Publishing House, 1984.

-----------. "Sifnos: The Evolution of a Traditional Unity." In *Ekistics* 61, Nos. 368-69 (September-October, November-December 1994). 321-42.

Vacalopoulos, Apostolos E. *The History of the Greek Nation.* Vol. 1, *Origins of the Greek Nation: The Byzantine Period, 1204-1461.* Translated by Ian Moles, revised by the author. New Brunswick, N.J.: Rutgers University Press, 1970.

-----------. *The History of the Greek Nation.* Vol. 2, *The Greek Nation, 1453-1669: The Cultural and Economic Background of Modern Greek Society.* Translated by Ian Moles and Phania Moles. New Brunswick, N.J.: Rutgers University Press, 1976.

Vaos, Zaphyris and Stephanos Nomikos. *Windmills of the Cycladic Islands.* Athens: Dodoni Editions, 1991.

Varming, Michael, *Elyseon.* N.p.: Nyt Nordisk Forlag, 1985.

Vassiliades, D. *To Acheiropoieto Symplegma Tes Paraportianes Mykonou.* Athens, 1961.

-----------. *Eisagoge Sten Aigaiopelagitike Laike Architektonike.* Athens, 1955.

----------. *A View of Aegean Architecture from a Restless Optical Angle*. Athens, 1971.

----------. *Wayfaring across the Forms and Countenances of Greek Space*. Athens, 1973.

Vougioukalakis, Georges. *Santorini: "The Volcano" – Palea and Nea Kameni, The Volcanic Activity in Historic Time*. Translated by Jannet Korniodos. Institute for the Study and Monitoring of the Santorini Volcano, 1995.

Vryonis, Speros Jr. "The Byzantine Legacy in the Formal Culture of the Balkan Peoples." In *The Byzantine Tradition after the Fall of Constantinople*, ed. John J. Yiannias, 17-44. Charlottesville: University Press of Virginia, 1991.

Watkin, David. *Thomas Hope, 1769-1831, and the Neo-Classical Idea*. London: John Murray, 1968.

Woodhouse, C. M. *Modern Greece: A Short History*. 3rd ed., rev. of *The Story of Modern Greece*. London: Faber and Faber, 1984.

Yiangakis, Yeorgios K. *Nesioloyio Ton Katoikoumenon Ellinikon Nesion, 1940-1991*. Athens, 1994.

Yiatromanolakis, Yiorgis, "The Aegean and Greek Literature." In *The Aegean: The Epicenter of Greek Civilization*, edited by Lambrini Papaioannou and Dora Comini-Dialeti. Translated by Philip Ramp, Alexandra Doumas, and David Connolly, 433-48. Athens: "Melissa" Publishing House, 1992.

Zakythinos, D. A. *The Making of Modern Greece: From Byzantium to Independence*. Translated by K. R. Johnstone. Totowa, N.J.: Rowman and Littlefield; London: Basil Blackwell, 1976.

ILLUSTRATION CREDITS

All color illustrations dated from 1960 to 2000 are from the author's collection. We gratefully express our thanks to the persons and institutions listed below who have supplied all other illustrations and drawings, or have given permission for copyright material to be used in this book. Every effort has been made to trace all copyright owners. If there is an instance where such efforts have not been successful we sincerely apologize and invite notification for correction in future editions of the book.

Benaki Museum, Fani-Maria Tsigakou Athens 3, 36(right), 43, 69, 71, 72, 73(left), 74, 75, 76, 81(left), 158, 160(lower left), 161(left), 162(left), 220, 221(upper left), 264, 267, 268, 307. National Geographic Society, Washington, DC 13, 15, 93. Musei Civici Veneziani, Venice 22 (Palazzo dei Camerlenghi). Museo Civico Correr, Venice 91(top). Swanston Publishing Limited, London 25, 32, 47, 48. Ekdotike Athenon/Elias Kollias, Athens 31, 33, 35, 37(right), 38, 167, 169(upper left), 181. Gennadius Library, American School of Classical Studies, Athens 40(right), 57, 60, 65, 67, 174(right). The Bodleian Library, University of Oxford (MS. Lat. Misc.d. 85, fols. 137v and 138r) 59. Bibliothèque Nationale de France, Paris 62. Royal Institute of British Architects, London 68. Melissa Publishing House, Athens 77, 144(upper left), 216(lower right), 224(middle). *The Burlington Magazine,* 83, 148(upper left). Ethnikon Idryma, Athens 85. Olkos Publishers, Athens 89, 91(lower half). Road Editions S.A., Athens 94, 119, 136(upper left), 144(lower left), 154, 164(upper left), 261, 310. Prof. Maro Philippa-Apostolou, Athens 121, 122, 123(top), 129, 130(left), 181, 182(lower half), 183(lower half), 323(middle right). Michael Varming, Architect, Denmark 132(lower half), 201(upper left), 237(lower left). Christos Panousakis, Architect, Athens 137, 139(upper half), 140(left), 141(lower half, middle), 142(left), 143(lower half), 181, 206(upper half). Prof. Wolfram Hoepfner, Berlin, and Prof. Hartwig Schmidt, Karlsruhe 149, 181, 189. Byzantine Museum, Athens 153. Saint John the Theologian Monastery, Library, Patmos 173. Prof. Anastasia Tzakou, Athens 193, 198, 204(lower left), 205(left), 208(upper half). Penguin Books, London 197, 293(right). D. Vassiliades, Architect, Athens 210(left), 211(left), 212(right). Drawing after Jewell-Hasluck 215(top). Stephanos Nomikos and Ilias Apostolides, Architects, Athens 221(lower half). Antonios-Aimilios Tahiaos, Thessaloniki 227. Prof. Konstantinos Papaioannou, Athens 230(lower half), 232, 233. Drawing after A.Orlandos 231(upper half). Anastasia Diamantopoulou, Architect, Athens 237(upper left). Drawing after H. Goldman 242(middle). University of Chicago Press and Washington University in St Louis 269(right), 270, 273, 275(upper half), 277(upper left), 279, 282, 283(right), 284(top), 287(top), 289(lower half), 290(upper half), 292, 294, 296(upper left), 298(upper left), 300(upper left). Cleveland Public Library 269(left). Drawing after Wiegand and Schrader 293(left). John Victor Luce, *Lost Atlantis: New Light on an Old Legend* 1969, with permission of The McGraw-Hill Companies, New York 312(left). Dr. Ioannis M. Danezis, Athens 321(lower half), 325, 327(lower half). C. Papas, Architect, Paris 324(left).

The quotation from William H. McNeill *The Metamorphosis of Greece since World War II* on pages 104-106 is by permission of the University of Chicago Press.

INDEX

A

Abdul Hamid II, Sultan, 80
Acre, 32–33
Acropolis, 2, 3, 4, 5, 6, 58–59
  Jacob Spon on, 62–63
  Morosini's bombardment of, 60,
  63, 174
  as tourist attraction, 80
  views of, 75
Adam, L'Isle, 39
Aegean Archipelago, 7
  climate of, 92, 96, 98–99, 104,
  191
  economy of, 101–5, 106–7
  geography of, 89, 92–96
  history and etymology of, 89–90,
  92
  isolation during *Tourkokratia*, 217
  population of, 96, 100–101
  topography of, 107–13
Aegean Sea, 6, 7, 14, 52, 90–95, 96
  maps of, 89, 91, 93
Aegina, 101, 110
Aeolian Islands, 15
Alamo, 238
Alexios I Comnenos, 164, 166
Algiers, 49–50, 51–52
Amorgos, 195, 218–19, 248, 333,
337
Anavatos, 252
Anderson, Rufus, 268

Andros, 93, 223, 251
Antiparos, 83, 119, 120, 145
  Kastro, 7, 118, 119–27, 128, 129,
  154, 181
    churches and chapels in, 139,
    140
    monochoro of, 190–91
antiquities, 6, 22, 41
  formal architecture and, 80–81
  preservation by Greek state, 80
  vernacular architecture and, 55
  Western European interest in,
  59–74, 76
archaeology, 65, 81–82, 313, 316
architecture
  Byzantine, 216
  development of profession of,
  55–56
  formal, 1–2, 41
    neoclassicism and, 80–81, 332
    relationship with vernacular
    architecture, 2–4, 42, 61, 63, 74,
    79, 216
  Greek Revival, 66, 74
  modern, 82–83, 87
  neoclassical, 6–7, 70, 77–79, 326,
  352
    formal architecture and, 80-81,
    332
    vernacular architecture and, 55,
    79, 194, 207, 248, 295, 328

vernacular, 1–2, 4, 329
  building types of, 8–9, 186, 206
  exhibitions of, 87
  Hope, Thomas and, 70–73
  neoclassicism and, 55, 79, 194,
  207, 248, 295, 328
  recent wider interest in, 87–88
  recycling used in, 61, 123, 125,
  194, 207, 333, 335, 336–38
  relationship with formal archi
  tecture, 2–4, 42, 61, 63, 74, 79,
  216
  Revolution of 1821 and, 75
  scale of, 186, 189, 201–2
  study of, 55–56, 82–83, 84–88
  use of outdoor space, 193–94
archontica, 275, 285–88
Arles, 2, 4, 5
Artemon, 193, 208
Aspronisi, 311–12
Astypalaia
  Chora, 135–36, 142, 143, 154
  churches and chapels of, 205–7,
  377
  Kastro, 7, 118, 137–43, 181, 189
  step-ramp-step, 143–44
  Venetians on, 136–37
Athens, 106–7
  Anafiotika, 61–62
  as cultural capital, 76–79
  expansion of, 101
  French descriptions of, 59–63, 64
  Jacob Spon on, 62–63
  Marquis de Nointel and, 63–64
  Parliament Building, 77
  Stuart and Revett on, 66–67
  superiority to Rome, 66
Atlantis, 314, 316
Augustinos, Olga, 60–61, 63–64
Austria, 265, 318
Ayion Oros, 229–30, 238

Ayios Konstantinos, 207–8
Ayios Menas, 157–58, 161–62
Ayios Spyridon, 205

B
Babin, Father Jacques Paul, 60–62
Balearic Islands, 15
Barbarossa, Kheireddin, 29, 30,
49–50, 125
Barozzi family, 154, 317
barrel vaults, 325, 326
Barsky, Vasily Gregorevich, 176,
227, 320
Bastion of Auvergne, 36–37
Belle, Henri, "Trois Années en
Gréce", 269
bell towers, 9, 102, 202, 203
  of Paros, 340
  of Patmos, 336
  of Sifnos, 131, 340–41
Belluschi, Pietro, 87
Benaki Museum, 155–56
Bent, Thomas J., 122–23
Black Sea, 12, 13, 92
Braudel, Fernand, *The Mediter-*
ranean and the Mediterranean World
in the Age of Phillip II , 47
Britain, 51, 76, 265–66
  taste for Greek Revival architec
  ture, 66, 74, 80–81
British Museum, 80
British School of Athens, 127
building
  analytical vs. monolithic
  approach to, 330
  materials for, 9, 240, 244, 248,
  258
    of Antiparos Kastro, 123–24
    of monochoro, 187
    on Santorini, 313, 324–26
  methods, 9

Bulletin of the German Archaeological Institute, 152
Buondelmonti, Cristoforo, 40, 59, 127, 137, 154, 220
Liber Insularum Archipelagi, 41, 56–58
Map of Santorini, 57–58
Burlington Magazine for Connoisseurs, 83
Byron, Lord George Gordon, 70
The Corsair, 53
Byzantine Museum, 152

C

caldera, 309, 312, 315
Candia, 63, 115
Caoursin, Guillaume, 37, 38
Carpaccio, Vittore, "The Lion of St. Mark", 22
Carreto, Fabrizio del, 36, 39
Carrey, Jacques, 64
Carrington, Richard, 18–19
Catherine the Great, 262
Catholic Church. *see* Roman Catholic Church
Cavafy, Constantine P., "Ithaka", 351
Central Archaeological Council, 307
Chapel of Christos, 126–27
Charles V of Spain, 29
Cheetham, Nicholas, 27
Chios, 63
Choiseul-Gouffier, Comte de, 67, 220
Voyage pittoresque de la Gréce, 68, 69–70, 71
churches and chapels, 113, 198–218, 239–40, 262. *see also* bell towers; monasteries
of Antiparos Kastro, 126, 139,
140
of Astypalaia, 139–42, 205–7, 377
of Crete, 238, 239
of Hydra, 233–34
of Mykonos, 199, 209–14, 328, 330
of Paros, 213–16, 217, 336–37
of Santorini, 325, 326
of Sifnos, 130–31, 205, 237-38
Church of St. George, 81
Clogg, Richard, 44
Cluny, Monastery of, 164
color, 342–46
Constantinides, Elizabeth, 163
Constantinople, 23–24, 52
Le Corbusier, 127
Journey to the East, 82–83
Corogna, Januli de, 128
Corogna family, 133
corsairs. *see* piracy
courtyard houses, 8, 187, 191–95, 196–97, 198
Crete, 13–14, 15, 26, 27, 42, 112, 316
Arkady Monastery, 238, 239
climate of, 99
geography of, 90, 93, 94
Crispi family, 115, 317–18
De la Croix, Horst, 36
Curry-Lindahl, Kai, 92
Cyclades Islands, 24–26, 100, 119–20
Cyprus, 13–14, 15, 33
Cyriacus of Ancona, 41, 58–59
Commentary upon Ancient Things, 58
drawing of the Parthenon, 60

D

Dalmatian Islands, 15
Dandolo, Doge Enrico, 23, 24, 39

42–43, 56
preservation of antiquities by, 80
"rediscovery" of, 41, 55–76, 71
Greek Archaeological Service, 82
Greek Archaeological Society, 313
Greek Orthodox Church, 4, 44,
126, 140, 164, 174
affinity with Russian Greek
Orthodox Church, 263
architecture, 199, 229-38. *see also*
churches and chapels; monasteries
during Duchy of the Archipelago
period, 27, 150-153, 227
Roman Catholic Church and, 39-
40, 56
Greek Revival, 71
Grigorios V, Patriarch, 44
Gropius, Walter, 87
Guggenheim Foundation, 87

H
Hadjikyriakos-Ghikas, Nikos,
"Grand Composition of Hydra",
268
d'Harnoncourt, René, 87
Hatzimihali, Angeliki, 84
Hecateus of Miletus, 12
Herodotus, 311
Hoepfner, W., 152
Homer, 316
Hope, Thomas, 155, 157
Anastasius, 70
Designs of Modern Costume, 72
"Downing Pamphlet", 71–72
"Drawing of Skaros", 8
"Town and Harbour of Hydra",
73–74, 220, 264, 307
vernacular architecture and,
70–73
"View of Skaros", 73–74, 155,
157-60, 161, 162

"View of the Town through the
Gate of the Archaic Temple", 74
houses. *see archontica*; dwelling
units; monochoro
houses, courtyard. *see* courtyard
houses
Houses of Zagora (*Spitia tes Zagoras)*, 85
Hydra, 9, 55, 78, 79, 87
autonomy of, 265–66
cisterns of, 251–52
descriptions of, 268–69
doors of, 284–85
economy of, 264, 266, 267, 268,
271, 275
houses of, 291–94
merchant marine, 264, 265–67
Monastery, 73–74, 271–72,
288--91
neoclassical elements in, 352
Panayia Monastery, 233–34
piracy and, 263
population of, 100, 101, 267, 268,
271, 272, 274, 275
portals of, 249
recent development in, 291–307
roofs of, 242, 272
settlement and history of,
261–68, 272–78
streets of, 280–83
Thomas Hope's drawing of, 220
topography of, 269–73
Tourkokratia and, 262, 263–64
town components of, 279–91
Twin Wells, 283–85
urban development of, 269–79
use of neoclassical elements on,
294–95, 307
walls of, 272
water on, 271, 283–85
windows of, 245–47, 284–85

wirescape of, 259–60, 295–304, 306

I

Ionian Islands, 15
Ios, 113, 219
Irakleion. *see* Candia

J

Janissary Corps, 44
Janissary Levy. see taxes
Jefferson, Thomas, 51, 66
Jerusalem, 30
John III, 115
Jones, John Paul, 52

K

Kalymnos, 241, 245, 341–46
Karpathos, 191
Kastro. *see also* individual names
  balance of, 351
  defined, 118–19
  as physical expression of *Koinotis*, 46
  relationship with monchoro, 194
Katholikon, 232–33, 234
Kheireddin. *see* Barbarossa, Kheireddin
Kimolos, 144–45, 195
  Kastro, 7, 118, 145–54, 180, 181
  piracy and, 53
King Henry, 31
King Ludwig of Bavaria, 77
King Otho, 76, 77, 80
Knights Hospitaller of Saint John, 6, 21, 30–34, 120
  on Malta, 49
  on Rhodes, 30–37, 39–42
  sieges of, 36–39
Koinobion, 228–29
Koinotis, 6, 45–46, 52, 185

Konstantinidis, Aris, 86
Krazeisen, Karl, "Greeks fighting Among Classical Ruins", 76
Kriezis, George D., 272
Kythnos, 112, 199, 321, 338

L

Laografia, 84
Laskaris, Theodore, 27
Latrobe, Benjamin H., 66
leisure time, 105, 106
Lepanto, Battle of, 47–48, 49
Linton, William, "The Scenery of Greece and its Islands", 269
Loredano, Giovanni, 119–20, 127
Louvre Museum, 80
Luce, J.V., *The End of Atlantis*, 316–17

M

Malta, 15, 30, 37, 39, 49, 50
Mansions of Kastoria (Archontika tes Kastorias), 85
Maybeck, Bernard, 10
McCoy, Floyd W., 314
McNeill, William H., 7
  The Metamorphosis of Greece since World War II, 102, 104–6
Mediterranean Sea, 6, 92
  climate, 16–17
  currents, 16
  basins of, 13–14
  etymology of name, 11
  geographical situation of, 12–13
  island chains in, 15
  size of, 13
Megas, George, 84
Mehmet II, Sultan, 37–38, 43
Melissa (publishing house), 86
Melos, 80, 113, 145, 220
Mesic Pasha, 37

P

Paestum, 65

Panayia Church, 139–42

Panayia Katapoliani Complex, 213–16, 217

Panayia Paraportiani Complex, 209–14, 330

Panayia Zoodochos-Pigi, 236-37

Papadiamantis, Alexandros, Poor Saint (Ftochos Ayios), 8, 155, 157, 160–62, 163, 319

Paros, 29, 110, 111, 119, 125, 145, 195, 196

  Ayios Konstantinos, 336–37

  bell towers of, 340

  Kastro, 335

  Naoussa, 264

  Panayia Katapoliani Complex, 213-16, 217

  Paroikia, 333, 334, 335, 336, 337

  population of, 100

  portals of, 333, 334

  streets of, 346, 349

  windmills of, 221

  wind turbines of, 225

Pars, William, 63

Parthenon, 3, 6, 56, 59, 174

  drawing by Cyriacus of Ancona, 60

  drawing by Marquis de Nointel, 65

Jacob Spon and, 63

paths, 143–44, 272–74

  of Santorini, 322, 328

Patmos, 8, 175–77, 181, 187

  Chora, 163–64, 165, 169, 170, 171–73, 178

  Monastery of Saint John the Theologian, 8, 118, 163–64, 165–70, 171–74, 175, 217, 231, 234, 336

  neoclassical elements in, 79

portals of, 249–50

  Skala, 163–64, 169, 172, 177–78

Philippa-Apostolou, Maro, 126–27

Philippides, Dimitri, 84, 87, 326, 328

Greek Traditional Architecture, 86

Pikionis, Dimitris, 84–85, 86

piracy, 6, 7, 29, 49, 52, 54

  centers of, 49–50

  by Christians, 49, 52–53, 54–55

  as distinctly Mediterranean institution, 47–48, 50–51

  end of, 76, 162

  France and, 51, 52, 63, 64

  Hydra and, 263

  Marquis de Nointel and, 63

  by Moslems, 49, 53, 54–55

  Serifos and, 117, 118

  on Skaros, 157, 161–62

  United States and, 51–52

Pisani family, 115, 317–18

Pitton de Tournefort, Joseph, 74–75

Poliegos, 95

Pompeii, 18, 65

Ponti, Gio, 87

Pope Innocent III, 23, 54

portals, 9, 248–49

  of Hydra, 249

  of Kythnos, 331

  of Paros, 333, 334

  of Patmos, 249–50

pozzolana, 313, 324–25

Priene, 194, 196–97, 293

privacy, 194

privateering, 49, 51

Profitis Elias Monastery, 113, 237-38

Pyrgos, 318, 322, 322–24

Q

Querini, Giovanni, 136–37
Querini family, 136

R

Rafos, Ioannis, 152–53
Rayas, G., *Traditional Architecture*, 86
religion. *see* Greek Orthodox Church; Roman Catholic Church
Renaissance, 56
Revett, Nicholas, 63, 66–67
Revett, Nicholas, The Antiquities of Athens, 66
Revolution of 1821, 42, 44, 53, 55, 175, 288
  vernacular architecture and, 75
  Western European sympathy for, 68, 69
Rhodes, 170
  Colossus of, 34
  Fortifications of, 33–37, 38
  illustrations of, 36, 37, 38
  Knights Hospitaller of Saint John on, 30–37, 39–42
  maps of, 33, 35, 40, 93
  population of, 100–101
  Siege of, 31–32, 37–39, 42
roads, 111, 258–59
Roman Catholic Church, 27, 40, 56, 152, 202
Rome, 60, 64, 66
roofs, 79, 133, 240, 241, 242, 272
Rudofsky, Bernard, 2, 87
Runciman, Steven, *The Great Church*, 227–28
Russia, 69, 70, 76, 140, 263–65, 266, 318
Russo-Turkish War, 263–64, 274, 275

S

sailors, 52, 262
Saint Basil, 228
Saint George Church, 139, 140
Saint John the Theologian, 164
  Monastery of, 8, 163–74, 175-77, 217, 231, 234, 336
Saladin, 23
Santorini, 9, 17, 18, 95, 99
  building materials used on, 313, 324–26
  Buondelmonti's map of, 57–58
  Caldera of, 309, 312, 315
  Choiseul-Gouffier drawing of, 71, 220
  churches and chapels of, 325, 326
  description and topography of, 309–13
  dwelling units of, 192, 313, 318, 325
  economy of, 318, 324–25, 326–28
  gates of, 196, 317
  Kastro, 318, 320
  merchant marine, 318
  paths of, 322, 328
  population of, 309–11
  stairs of, 191, 328
  windows of, 246–47
Sanudo, Marco, 24–25, 26–27, 28, 128, 317
Saronic Gulf Islands, 63
Schinckel, Karl Friedrich, 80
Schliemann, Heinrich, 82
Schmidt, H., 152
Scholarios, Georgios Gennadios, 43–44
Schranz, Joseph, "View of the Port of Corfu", 81
Scott, Geoffrey, *The Architecture of Humanism*, 239–40
Scuola, Basilio dalla, 36

Sea of Marmara, 92, 266
Sebastiani, Horace-François, 264
Selim II, Sultan, 29–30
Serifos, 7, 97, 116–17
  Chora, 186, 187, 241, 242
  City Hall, 332
  Kastro, 117–18
  neoclassical elements in, 79
  piracy and, 117, 118
  stairs of, 338–39
Sert, Jose Luis, 87
shipping, 106–7, 185, 264, 265-67
Sifnos, 97, 100–101, 107, 109, 116, 120, 135, 218–23
  Ayios Konstantinos, 207–8
  bell towers of, 102, 131, 340–41
  churches and chapels of, 130–31, 205, 237–38
  Kastro, 7, 26, 100, 127–35, 137, 180, 181, 182–83, 346
  monochoro of, 188
  neoclassical elements in, 78
  Vrissi Monastery, 234–36
Sifnos-Apollonia, 193, 198, 202, 203–4
Sikinos, 196
Skaros, 115, 118, 154–55, 158–60, 180
  Kastro, 318, 319–20
  piracy on, 161–62
  views of, 7-8, 73–74, 155, 157–60, 161, 162
Skiathos, 7–8, 118
  Kastro, 154–57, 158–62, 163, 180
Skyros, 242
Soane, Sir John, 72
Society of Dilettanti, 65, 66
Society of Greek Vernacular Art, 85
Sommaripa, Maria, 119
Spetses, 110
Spon, Jacob, 62–63, 64

stairs, 9, 189–90
  of Astypalaia, 191
  of Kythnos, 331
  of Mykonos, 190, 249
  of Santorini, 191, 328
  of Serifos, 338–39
Stoneman, Richard, 66
streets, 280–83, 346, 349
Stuart, James, 63, 66–67
Stuart, James, The Antiquities of Athens, 66
Suleyman the Magnificent, 29, 38, 39, 50, 170

T
Tadini da Martinengo, Gabriele, 39
Talos, 316
Tange, Kenzo, 87
taxes, 44–45, 46, 52, 262
Tenos, 8, 42, 102, 223, 224
Theologos Church, 131
Thera. see Santorini
Therasia, 311
Thucydides, 149–50
Timios Stavros, 202, 204
Tourkokratia, 6, 21, 24, 41, 42–46, 52
  Hydra and, 262, 263–64
  influence on neo-Hellenism, 82
  isolation of Aegean Archipelago under, 217
town, fortified. see Kastro
towns. see individual names
trade, 40–41, 51, 185, 264, 266
Treaty of Campo Formio, 265
Treaty of Kuchuk-Kainardji, 254, 266, 275
Tripoli, 51–52
Tsikagou, Maria, *Thomas Hope, Pictures from Eighteenth-Century Greece*, 155, 157

Turkish rule. *see Tourkokratia*
Turks, Ottoman, 29, 38, 39, 63, 64, 120
  attitudes toward foreigners, 65
  in Russo-Turkish war, 263–64

U
Uniates, 40
United States, 51–52, 66
University of Padua, 41

V
Valletta, 49
Vaos, Zaphyris, *Windmills of the Cycladic Islands*, 220
Vasari, Giorgio, "The Naval Battle of Lepanto", 48
Venetian Empire, 22–23, 24, 26–29
Venetians, 225–26, 265
  on Astypalaia, 136–37
  intermarriage with natives on Archipelago, 41–42, 119–20
Venus of Melos, 80
Verne, Jules, *The Archipelago in Flames*, 53–54
Vesuvius, Mount, 18
Villaret, Foulques de, 31, 32
Visscher, N., 89
volcanic activity, 17–18, 95, 154, 172, 309–10, 312–13, 314–17, 318–19
Voulgaris, Francesco, 286
Voulgaris family, 286–87
Voulgaris House, 285–88
Vrissi Monastery, 234-36
Vryonis, Speros, 217

W
Wace, A.J. B., "The Towns and Houses of the Archipelago", 83
walls, 9, 234, 240, 242

on Hydra, 272
of monochoro, 187–88
  stone, 250–51
Watkin, David, 70, 71–72
whitewash, 9, 205, 243–44, 252–58, 342–46
Williams, Hugh William, "View of the Propylaea", 3–4
Winckelmann, Johann Joachim, 65–66, 67
windmills, 8–9, 70, 108, 218–23
windows, 245–47, 284–85
wirescape, 259–60, 295–304, 306

X
Xanthos, Emmanouil, 175

Z
Zahos, Aristotelis, 84
Zakynthinos, D.A., 46
Ziani, Doge Pietro, 24